MARTIN LUTHER
AND THE
BIRTH OF PROTESTANTISM

JAMES ATKINSON

John Knox Press
ATLANTA

Library of Congress Cataloging in Publication Data

Atkinson, James, 1914-
    Martin Luther and the birth of Protestantism.

    Reprint. Originally published: Harmondsworth: Penguin, 1968.
(Pelican Books; A865). With new introd.
    Bibliography: p.
    Includes index.
    1. Luther, Martin, 1483-1546. I. Title.
BR325.A8 1981   284.1'092'4   [B]   81-82356
ISBN 0-8042-0941-3   AACR2

Copyright © James Atkinson, 1968

10 9 8 7 6 5 4 3 2 1
First published in Great Britain in 1968 by Pelican Books

Published in the United States of America in 1981
by John Knox Press
Atlanta, Georgia 30365

FOREWORD to This Edition

Why a reprint?

The present book was published in 1968, and the question presents itself: why a reprint in 1982? The reason is that the book went out of print within a few months of publication; since then there has been a steady and persistent demand for the book from university students and their teachers as well as from the general reader, and therefore the present publisher now seeks to meet that demand. Further, owing to certain restrictions, the book was never made available to the American market.

It was a Roman Catholic professor of church history, teaching the Reformation at one of the Catholic universities in America, who said to the author, 'I have put this book as number one on my book list for students of the Reformation for two reasons. First, it is the only *theological* account of Luther which I can put into the hands of the students, the others are essentially historical biographies. Secondly, it quotes so much of Luther's own words: it lets Luther talk.' Nothing could have been more complimentary, or more discerning for that matter. This is exactly what the book is. It is a theologian's account of Luther, allowing Luther to explain Luther.

The book seeks to make clear the theological issues which Luther worked out as the professor of biblical studies at the University of Wittenberg, issues which he was compelled to sharpen into what later became catch-phrases in bitter polemics, neither sought nor liked by Luther. His biblical theology brought him into conflict with Rome, not only on the basic principle of authority in the study of theology, but on the more important matter of true Catholicism. He criticised contemporary Catholicism in that it was based neither on biblical foundations nor patristic foundations: it was papist and medieval, riddled with modern accretions and ancient superstitions, and above all, as secularised as the court of any worldling prince. He found himself in conflict with the activists and their social gospel, confusing the Kingdom of Heaven with the kingdoms of this world. It is not commonly appreciated that Luther had much more sympathy with the Catholics than ever he had with the rebellious revolutionaries of the Protestant left wing. He found himself in conflict with the humanists, himself a highly competent Christian humanist with all the linguistic and historical critical faculties which distinguished them, yet too sensitive to the humanists' incapacity to understand the Christian doctrines of sin, grace and redemption. And, of course, he was always in open conflict with fallen and unredeemed mankind, whether peasant or prince, if he would not heed the Gospel. He groaned often that God demanded this role of him when all his preferences were for the quiet obscure life, but he would take heart when he reflected that the Prince of Peace was warred against for His message. Why should he be exempt? he asked himself. That is how I saw the story, that is how I told it, and I cannot change it.

Luther was at the death of the old medieval world, indeed he was at the death of the old world, and more than any other single person brought to birth the modern world. Because he sought to re-form Christianity nearer to the mind and intent of its Founder, he is continually significant for Christianity in any subsequent age for the simple reason that Christianity at any given time is always in need of re-formation. He is a constant challenge to Christianity as it is today, no matter whether it is the Catholic or Reformed version of it. In common with many doctors and fathers and saints of the Church, he restores our vision of what a true Christian is and what the true Church might be. He is also a powerful creative thinker on how a Christian is related to the body politic, what involvement in society means, and what criticism of society is. His thinking on the basic secular realities of work, marriage, civic and political activity, and all our common everyday life, challenges everybody to a true understanding of these things. He shows how clean and wholesome, good and worthwhile, these things are intrinsically, and at the same time reveals how secularised, how short-sightedly human so many Christians live out their lives. He was also involved in the care and education of the young, and did more for schools and universities perhaps than any other, saving perhaps Melanchthon, who lived to put Luther's ideas into practice. These are some of the grounds which make a theological account of Luther worth a reprint, especially since the book was directed to the thoughtful and intelligent layman and not to Luther researchers (who need no encouragement anyway).

The question then arises: what has happened in the world of scholarship and in the world of events since this book was written, which may demand that the book be brought up-to-date, perhaps modified in certain respects?

To answer this question the author suggests for consideration the following topics (after a brief glance at the world of events): Luther research in the last decade; the ecumenical movement, in particular, official conversations between the Church of Rome on the one hand and the Protestant churches on the other; contemporary liberal and liberation theology; the immensely significant Vatican Council both for theology and practice; the new leadership of Pope John Paul II.

Events

Before we turn to particular examination of these matters it is worth considering the total effect of them on the contemporary mind, recalling that these ideas are movements of men's minds and are not mere concepts handled in the cool analytical atmosphere of a study, but are ingredients in the world of events, which events not only influence them in turn, but often bring confusion to them. In the world at the moment we see the upsurge of Islam which, though a religious movement, is bringing, by the simple raising of oil prices, a grave economic threat, not only to the democratic Western powers, but more seriously to the developing Third World. Yet this is no simple economic matter, for it affects schools, universities, hospitals, even the work of the Churches. Iraq is now at war with Iran; Russia has invaded and occupied Afghanistan: the arms race accelerates, the peace and stability of life is threatened. The Church in South America, and elsewhere, is under threat of military and autocratic governments, and is more and more involved in the liberation of its peoples. Inflation, unemployment, recession threaten us all: they take on the nature of demonic forces, outside us, against us, beyond our control or understanding. These environments influence our thinking and we must address ourselves to them.

In the matter of Luther research many important books, articles and theses have been written, and of these we offer some account, not as a complete academic assessment of all this research, but rather as a survey of significant works known to us. Readers may not be aware of the interesting fact that more books have been written about Martin Luther than about any other single person who has ever lived (save Jesus Christ): last year, over one thousand books and learned articles known to me were written about him in some dozen languages. This happens every year: he is certainly one of the most significant men in history, and one of the great theologians of Christendom. The ecumenical movement pursues the quiet tenor of its way, and has produced not only some highly significant documents, pregnant with fresh thought, but has created a totally different atmosphere of brotherhood and understanding. Contemporary liberal theology is having a wasting effect on biblical theology which is based on a firm doctrine of revelation, but more dangerously, a corrosive effect on the doctrines of incarnation, redemption and grace: in fact, it seems determined to set Christ in the Pantheon, along with the other gods. Liberation theologians are having a life and death struggle with the state, and to some extent with their establishment churches. Pentecostal churches seek to bring the Holy Spirit as an ingredient of Church life.

At this point, two highly significant matters for this study must receive special and separate mention, and will be examined in context, viz. the ongoing significance of Vatican II, and the immense influence of Pope John Paul II. Vatican II has opened up all the resources of Roman Catholicism and taken it from the limbo of its ghetto theology, where it has sulked since the sixteenth century, into the marketplace of the world. Following this has come the remarkable charismatic leadership of the new Pope who has set out to bring to the whole world, and not just to Roman Catholicism, the certainty and joy of the traditional, classical Christian Faith. He shows to the world a faith firm and unflinching, and a moral standard pure and winning. All this is happening at a time when Protestant theologians have tended to criticise traditional Christian faith and relativize both traditional Christian morality and theology. It is a highly significant fact that those Roman Catholic theologians who are doing the most creative, even controversial work, at the moment, are those who in the implementing of Vatican II have taken full measure of Luther. Never was the debate between Luther and Rome more significant in that Luther's thinking is essentially Catholicism reformed.

Finally, apart from Christendom there is the spiritual and material upsurgence of the Arab world. World Islam is making an excoriating attack on the Christian West, or rather, its experience of the secularised Western world which, of course, is not Christian, but simply materialist. It should be remembered that true Christians have consistently and continuously throughout the centuries shown hostility to a so-called Christian civilisation which has been nothing else than one long and steady descent to a gross and crass materialist consumer civilisation, unaware of the purpose and meaning of life which Christ taught. The significance of this Islamic attack on what was once in principle a believing Christian society which has deteriorated into a materialised, secularised society hell-bent to consume itself to death, seems not to be perceived by the West, who see in this Arab upsurge a grave threat to oil supplies and to their standard of living. This is true enough as far as it goes. But the initiative in Western life has passed from the gentler hands of cultured men, from scholars and intellectuals, from Christian men and women who think and care, into the hands of self-seeking politicians, materially minded business men and equally materially minded trades unionists. Even the Church leaders have allowed themselves to be corrupted: all too often they choose the easier and more acceptable role of the concern for human rights than the sterner and more unacceptable ministry of the things of God. To read Luther on a Christian's relation to society is to give a perspective to these things that makes everything new.

Luther is so certain and sure-footed in his relationship to God and to man that he is the most penetrating and creative critic of Church, of government, and of man's role in the world. But it must be seen at once that this criticism is not that of a music or art critic who stands or falls by the penetration of his own judgement and the weight of his own knowledge. His criticism stems not from his acumen, sharp as that was, but from a man standing under the Word of God submitting man to the mind of God. His sensitivity into the frailty and failure of the Church, his awareness of the finitude and faithlessness of man, his faith that come what may neither man nor devil will defeat God, give him a relevance today as vibrant as in the sixteenth century. Of course, critics who recoil from his arguments tend to justify themselves by dismissing Luther as coarse, as vulgar, as seducer, as heretic–any stigma will do to beat a dogma–but such critics do not answer the arguments. We must stick by the arguments not by our preferences or prejudices. Only those critics who are unable to free themselves from centuries of propaganda and prejudice fail to see Luther for what he was, the Joshua who led the people of God into the new world of biblical theology. One recalls another Teacher whose preaching and teaching the pundits and theological experts would not heed, and who dismissed Him as a gluttonous man and a wine-bibber, a friend of publicans and sinners. But the whole world knows who was right and who was wrong. Truth cannot be worsted. *Il faut que Dieu gagne.*

Luther research since 1968

What have Luther scholars produced these last thirteen years? Certainly there has been no Luther renascence of the kind introduced by Karl Holl and his disciples in the 1920s. Nevertheless, there is a great deal of thinking and writing going on, as the wide range of publications demonstrates and the quinquennial International Luther Congresses show.

First, let us look at the work of English-speaking scholars. The most notable achievement must surely be the American Edition (Philadelphia) of a 56-volume translation of Luther's major works. Written in Latin (for the theologians) and in old High German (for the laity), these works were largely unknown to the general reader, save for a few odd translations of the Reformation Writings of 1520, and the commentary on Galatians and his book against Erasmus, *On the Bondaged Will.* Now they are available to all, historians, theologians and the general reader, in good translation with useful introductions and commentaries. To be mentioned in this context is the significant amount of bibliographical aids which are being built up by the Centre for Reformation Research in St. Louis, U.S.A.

Geoffrey Dickens continues to produce his invaluable researches and has produced some fine thinking on the social forces behind Luther's thinking. G.R. Elton has produced highly significant work on Thomas Cromwell (1972) and on Reform and Renewal (1973): nobody has written such penetrating assessments of men like More and Cromwell than Elton, work which casts a brilliant cross-light on Luther. Not to be mentioned in the same breath is the prejudiced biography of the religious sceptic Marius (1974). He understands neither Christ nor Luther, and in any case has not worked on the original source material but on translations: it is to be hoped he will stick to his novel-writing. Mark E. Edwards has published a significant and fresh study of Luther's polemics against his Protestant opponents (1975). I.D.K. Siggins has produced a fine book, small but of considerable importance, on Luther's doctrine of Christ (1970), where he draws widely from the total Luther, young and old: this is surely Luther's central concern. During this time considerable study has been made of the time and nature of Luther's evangelical breakthrough, without a consensus emerging: perhaps Luther simply grew. Not unlike one's own children, when one day by a chance remark the boy betrays the fact that he is no longer a boy but a young man, the girl that she must now be treated as a young woman. What day? What hour? No day! No hour! They just grew, like Topsey.

Two books on the trial of Luther were published in 1971, the 450th anniversary of the Diet of Worms 1521: the larger study by the present author is a documented book on the trial of Luther which also included studies of the examination before Cajetan (1518), the Leipzig Disputation with Eck (1519) and the bulls against Luther; the smaller, rather racy and popular, is an undocumented version of the same subject by Father Olivier, since translated into German and English.

In the area of the theology of Luther, Gerhard O. Forde has made an interesting study of Luther's understanding of the Gospel (1972), and Herman A. Preus has published his Luther Studies (1975), which is a significant though not an academic book. Harry J.

McSorley, a laicised Roman priest, produced a weighty study of *On the Bondaged Will*, which has maintained the interest of both Catholic and Protestant scholars (1967), English translation (1969).

Some work has been done on the social and political thinking of Luther, regrettably an area of wider appeal in the present climate of thinking than religious and theological studies. Of significance is John M. Tonkin on *The Church and the Secular Order* (1971), as well as James S. Preus on *Karlstadt* (1974), and Ronald J. Sider on the same subject (1974). The important (and nowadays popular) subject of the Peasants' War is handled by Robert N. Crossley (1974).

Ernest F. Klug produced a good and most readable study of Luther and Chemnitz (1971). Here one ought to note the valuable work on the post-Reformation period, a major contribution to Lutheran theology (Vol.1. 1970, Vol. 2. 1972) by Robert D. Preus. A fine study of the confessional statements appeared in 1972 made by Taito Azmar Kantonen. A very learned work on the doctrine of the Church appeared in 1974 by Scott H. Henrix, and a similar learned treatise on the rather neglected lectures by Luther on the Epistle to the Hebrews by Kenneth Hagen (1974). A related essay was that of Henry Heller on Lèfevre in *Studies in the Renaissance* 19 (1972).

In Germany there was a great burst of activity during the festive year of 1967, when the present author was actually writing his book. In the context of this introduction there is room only for a sketchy view of these works. Stephan Skalweit produced his book on Germany and the Reformation, a work which gave significant emphasis to the now fashionable consideration of political as well as theological matters (1967). In the authoritative *Catholic Handbuch der Kirchengeschichte* the significant volume four on the Reformation by the Muenster scholar Erwin Iserloh appeared in 1967, and in the same year Robert Stupperich's smaller though weighty and authoritative handbook on the Reformation was published. Equally reliable, and stemming from a long experience both of a close study of Luther and Luther in relation to the ecumenical movement, Peter Meinhold in his book *Luther Today* (1967) gives both a good account of Luther's theology, and further, discusses the new way Catholics are now looking at Luther, as well as Luther's significance for the ecumenical movement. Meinhold's book is not only intrinsically important, it is specially significant for the contemporary ecumenical debate. A large and colourful biography of Luther appeared in 1967 as a kind of Jubilee Edition to celebrate the event of the nailing up of the Ninety-five Theses. It was written by Richard Friedenthal, for laymen rather than scholars, but as interesting as it is, it is but the work of a journalist and is very weak on the heart of the matter, viz. Luther's theological struggle, and is weak also on the older Luther. A masterly study of the social and political background of Luther's Saxony by Karlheinz Blaschke (1970) will render much help to Luther research in the future. This will give encouragement to the work of Geoffrey Dickens and his school. There were several Marxist studies from East Germany. The late Hermann Doerries published his third volume of Luther Studies (1970), a sensitive study of central themes of Luther's theology.

There were a number of treatments of the young Luther in the 1960s, mainly researching into Luther's breakthrough into biblical and evangelical theology, but no consensus has emerged in this field yet and no certain judgements. Several good and highly significant articles have been written on this early period covering Luther's relation to Humanism (Junghans), to Thomism (Lief Grane), to Ockhamism (Junghans), and to his Catholic critics (Oberman). These papers are very much for specialists, but their conclusions are highly significant for a true understanding of Luther.

Of special significance is the research of Catholic scholars. Since Joseph Lortz delivered Catholic scholarship from the personal scurrility of the traditional Catholic abusive approach to Luther, which sought to destroy his person, in order to dismiss his theology, a new climate exists in Luther research. Catholic scholars (with freakish exception) study the texts as carefully and critically as Protestant historians and theologians, and a deep respect for Luther and his protest has been born. This movement is not only bringing new life into Catholic thinking, at least at the academic level, but is serving to transform the relations between Catholic and Protestant scholars. This may prove to be one of the most influential factors in the life of the universal Church this generation. Following the treatments of Jedin, Stauffer and Pesch of the changes in the Catholic approach to Luther, Werner Beyna has given a comprehensive survey of the modern Catholic approach (1969). A critical discussion of the central Protestant doctrine of justification by faith alone was conducted by August Hasler (968). The work of Pesch on Justification and of Jedin on Ecclesiology suggests a steady advance on Vatican II. Especially significant in the area of Catholic studies of Luther is the work of Peter Manns of the Joseph Lortz Institute, Mainz. A pupil of Lortz himself, he brings to bear his powerful critical faculty on the Reformation, and argues for a close organic relationship between Luther and Catholicism. He rejects many accepted opinions, and is highly critical of what Luther's successors did to Luther's message. He has a knowledge of the sources second to none, and offers a striking and original Catholic approach to Luther which demands both respect and attention.

Duchrow has produced a comprehensive study of that most distinctive Lutheran doctrine of the Two Kingdoms (1970), following the significant work on the same subject by Junghans and Jacobs that same year. At a time when so much talk is made of Christianity and politics, and to what extent, if any, Christianity should be embroiled in sociological and political activism, Luther's teaching on the secular kingdom and the authority of its officers, and the spiritual kingdom where there is no place for such authority, but where only forgiveness and love reign in faith, is going to be peculiarly apt. Nobody has been more clear-headed and realistic about the relationship between the secular and the spiritual than Luther. Not even Calvin, who erred on the side of theocentricity, and whose theology cannot meet the modern secularised world at this point. This whole area needs fresh appraisal. Related to this theme is Kunst's book on Luther and war (1968), but the net result is to show that Luther has no teaching on war.

Reference must be made to the important books and articles on Ecclesiology: Maurer (1966), Beintke (1967), Kantzenbach (1968), as well as to the earlier article of John on Luther and the Council (1966). Rudolf Mau has produced a detailed discussion of the meaning of salvation, and makes the right emphasis that it must be seen as emanating from God and not arising from man (1969).

The sacraments have been handled by A. Peters (1969): baptism by Groenvick (1968) and by M. Ferel (1969); the Lord's Supper by C.F. Wisloeff (1969). Luther's views on the Virgin Mary are given exhaustive treatment by H. Duefel (1968). A significant work on Luther's dealings with the Catholics, in the form of his discussions with von Miltitz in 1520, has been written by Hans-Guenther Leder (1969). K. Petzold has researched into Luther as educator (1969). A scholarly yet highly interesting study of the biblical prefaces, where he compares the work of Jerome and the medieval translators with that of Luther, was made by Maurice E. Schild, (1970), where he shows how Luther's prefaces were the first to bring the reader into the Bible itself. Following McSorley's treatment of the bondage of the will (1967), Schwarzwaeller produced a book on Luther's doctrine of predestination as found in the same book (1970).

A continuing enquiry in Luther studies has been to probe into the real concern of Luther. Not a little of this appears in articles and booklets (Georg Gloege, Ferdinand Ebner, Robert Scholl). What appears to be emerging in all this enquiry is the view that Luther's concern was less with doctrine and ideas, and more with the experience that was vouchsafed to Luther by grace under the power of the Holy Spirit. The essays of Wilhelm Maurer, published in 1970, argue that the root of the matter is what God has done in Christ, which is expressed in scripture and witnessed to by the creeds and fathers. It is out of this root that the doctrine of justification by faith alone grows as a fruit. Maurer is reminding us of a truth that writers such as Schwarzwaeller and Muehlen tend to overlook. The present writer attaches considerable weight to Maurer's views. Maurer has immense Patristic and historical learning, and looks at religious questions in religious terms: he always shows discernment and judgement.

The emphasis of Maurer and of Gloege have produced further results in the younger scholar Marc Lienhard in his important book, *Luther, témoin de Jésus Christ* (1973), since translated into English, and in Dorothea Vorlaender, *Deus incarnatus* (1974). This is a happy emphasis on Luther's Christology, an emphasis the present writer has sought to make and which he believes primary to Luther's thinking. The four hundred and fiftieth anniversary of the September Bible 1522 brought out studies on Luther as Bible translator and expositor by Soenke Hahn, Winfried Kolb and Erwin Muelhaupt. Wolfgang Stein in his book on the role of the Church (1974) offers a most timely treatment of the doctrine of the Two Kingdoms, the kingdom of this world and the kingdom of heaven. It is being increasingly appreciated that Luther's emphasis was on God's personal revelation in scripture, and that it is the Christ living in the Word which forwards His unique mission.

Much more work has been done on the theological stance of Erasmus in recent years, a convenient summary of which may be found in Manfred Hoffmann: *Erkenntnis und Verwirklichung der Wahren Theologie nach Erasmus von Rotterdam* (1972) as well as in the two volumes of research papers of the Erasmus Jubilee held at Tours, entitled Colloquia Erasmiana (1972). It is now being argued that Erasmus had a much more clearly defined theology than Lutherans have appreciated, yet the question is still there, why then did the two men engage in such sharp polemic, for they would understand one another better than we can now. Be that as it may, all this research sharpens the issues on which Luther was engaged, issues which are perennial, for the Erasmus-Luther debate is the fundamental theological debate. Indubitably, the difference between the theological approaches of the two men are striking. Luther was a theological man through and through, but it is doubtful whether the fine, cultured humanist had any theology at all, though he certainly believed in Christianity as a way to be lived. Erasmus is a sceptic, Luther a believer; Erasmus sees no certain or compelling revelation in the Bible, Luther sees everything essential decisively revealed there; Erasmus knew only an active faith, a faith he possessed and worked at, Luther knew only that passive faith which was the direct gift of God. It may be argued that Erasmus has triumphed over Luther in the course of the centuries, in that modern man (even many theologians) prefer to look at Christianity through the tolerant, ethical eyes of Erasmus, than through the falcon theological eyes of Luther. A strong case could be argued that *mutatis mutandis* it was the same debate between Augustine and Pelagius, that the debate is still active today and still to be sustained, even if modern scholarship seems heavily Erasmian rather than Lutheran. The Luther argument that the will is enslaved to itself and can only be freed by deliverance in Christ is the essence of Christianity, the very Gospel, a truth Erasmus could no more perceive than can his modern counterpart. Nobody makes Luther clearer than does Erasmus. As Luther expressed it, Erasmus was the only person to grab him by the throat, and not play about with paltry abuses.

In this vital debate we are concerned with the truth of Christianity, as was Luther. The discussion affects other areas, almost all areas of Luther research and of Luther understanding. For example, using the New Hermeneutics as a tool, Erasmus believed that he could understand an author better than the author understood himself, just as later Christians could understand Christianity better than the contemporaries of Christ (Paraclesis, 1516). Does not almost every modern commentator adopt this position? They are baffled by John and Paul, whom they explain away but cannot explain. This means that Erasmus has prevailed over Luther in the New Hermeneutics. Yet Luther's protest and position stand unanswerable. Whereas Erasmus stood above scripture and judged it, Luther sat under scripture and was judged by it. Luther argued that scripture is its own interpreter and is not to be interpreted as the modern mind seeks to interpret, nor even as the modern mind seeks to make it relevant to its own needs, but only in and from itself. Scripture always confronts the natural man, and this includes the scholar and the priest, no matter how good or wise he may be.

A further area of confusion is the network of presuppositions people bring to bear in their understanding of Christianity, and derivatively of Luther. Erasmus held the presuppositions of Philosophy as prerequisite for Theology, as did Origen, Augustine and Thomas before him. Luther rejected Philosophy outright as a means of explaining the Bible, a rejection he made even before his nailing up of the Ninety-five Theses against indulgences in his disputation against scholastic theology. Protestantism has followed Erasmus, a process begun by Melanchthon, to permit philosophical presuppositions to build up a synthesis of Theology and Philosophy, e.g. Schleiermacher, Dilthey and Ebeling. To the sixteenth century area of philosophical presuppositions modern man has added the scientific, even the sociological. Consequently, not only the contemporary commentators, but the historians, have to undergo a severe critical discipline to tread their way back to understand Luther's real concern, and what he did and said, and meant to do and say.

Another very important field of study is Luther's teaching on the two kingdoms, the one the secular, where law rules and has the sanction of force, the other the spiritual, which is the Kingdom of Heaven, where only love and forgiveness reign. Here again the differences between Erasmus and Luther are unbridgeable. Erasmus thought of these spheres of influence as in two concentric circles, Luther of two kingdoms, not of some academic system of thought but the way things are, viz. God's revelation in the Bible against which the Devil rages and fights. Luther taught, wrote and preached incessantly against any and all efforts to rule the world with the Gospel, as the older theologians, e.g. Franz Lau, insisted. Recent work has not seen this as perceptively, and (probably under the influence of Barth) treats the subject largely from modern presuppositions of social, ethical and political thinking, and does not handle Luther's clear biblical account of the doctrine (e.g. Ahti Hakamies [1971], Rudolf Ohlig [1974] and Ulrich Duchron [1970].). It is understandable for men to think like this having experienced the Church struggle under the Nazis and the post-war period, but again, the most important thing to hold fast to, is not to interpret Luther through four centuries of tradition, but to sit with Luther in his study, sit under him in the pulpit, and learn at first hand what he wrote and said, and meant to write and say. This is not to say that Luther is an authority slavishly to be followed today. He spoke against such servile thinking in his own day. It is to see exactly, by fine research and scholarship, Luther's real concern. From that perception the Bible and tradition will be seen with new eyes, as will the situation in which we stand today.

The best way to understand Christ is by a receptive study of the New Testament, not by an approach of modern writers who seek to "apply" Christianity to our present day situation. The only way to understand Luther is by the same technique. The student has to cut his way through many thickets before he reaches the pastures where Christ would have him live and feed, thickets which too often the Church and scholars have ignorantly cultivated. In this field of the Two Kingdoms we have to hack our way through the thickets of presupposition and tradition before we win through, but as Luther said as early as his *Commentary on Romans* (1515-16), Truth emerges still more sublime when attacked; it becomes still more triumphant when oppressed (WA.56. 213. 19f.).

Bernd Moeller's book on Germany at the time of the Reformation appeared in 1977. It is not a large book but it represents an important emphasis of contemporary Luther research: he gives his characteristic emphases on the importance of the socio-historical factors, a stress which opens him up to the criticism of giving a lesser place to the theological issues. Following the publication of the massive correspondence (850 pages) of von Pflug (1977), there appeared in the same year the correspondence of Johannes Gropper (500 pages), both Catholic theologians of some import for relations between Luther and Catholicism, and whose letters comprise a substantial bulk of significant source material. Heiko Oberman continues his massive contribution to the origins of the Reformation and its essential relation to medievalism (1977). He emphasises (rightly) the vital organic relationship of the Reformation to its late medieval background, a fact too often overlooked and which could hardly be overemphasised.

Let us now turn to Luther research in Scandinavia. Following his earlier classical study of Luther's debate with Biel (1962), Leif Grane of Copenhagen has written an epoc-making work, again on the early Luther, which is a study of how Luther worked out his theology not in relation to the controversies but rather from himself. Grane seeks to show how Luther worked out his theology in and from the situation in which he found himself, and establishes new ground. His work is detailed and only for the specialist, but it is original and highly significant (1975). Herbert Olsson (Uppsala) produced posthumously a learned work on Luther's teaching on creation, a theme which often appears in Scandinavian theology (1971). In the area of sacramental theology Lorenz Gronvik produced in Abo, Finland in 1968 a work on Luther's teaching on baptism, which, heavy though it was, added nothing to previous studies, while Frederic Cleve produced at the same time and in the same place a volume on Luther's eucharistic teaching. T.G.A. Hardt followed with a rather idiosyncratic study on the same subject (Uppsala 1971). In the previous year (1970) Ingemar Öberg defended a thesis on absolution and confession, also in Uppsala. The Catholic theologian Jan Aarts defended a dissertation at Helsinki in 1972 on Luther's teaching on ministry. Another dissertation, this time on prayer, was defended by Gunnar Wertelius at Lund, 1970, and a further dissertation on Luther's two-government theory was defended by Ahti Hakamies in Helsinki, 1971. Arvid Wikerstal produced a study of Luther on his Christological exposition of Genesis in Lund in 1969, and Aarne Siirala his *Divine Humanness*, which appeared in Philadelphia in 1970. Inge Lønning examined Luther's study of the canon within the canon, Oslo 1972. Frederick Brosché of Uppsala has written a balanced study of Luther on predestination (1978), wherein he reconciles Luther's often misunderstood teaching on the Wrath and the Love of God. Ninna Jørgensen pursues an examination of the Reformation in the light of the Marxist revolution (1978).

The famous Lund school has now passed into history, sad to say: Aulen and Nygren are both dead; Ragnar Bruïg is too old to produce more. The younger member of the school, Gustav Wingren, even though he long ago retired, is alone left of the famous theologians, but he no longer writes his fine, critical studies of Luther's theology, for he seems to have lost his former theological interests and to have strayed into the field of sociological-ethical questions. Nevertheless, he is working to set Luther free of confessional Lutheranism, and that has a not unimportant theological significance. Bengt Hägglund continues to write significant learned articles in journals, in addition to his history of theology (1973). His last major work was on Belief (1974). We may expect little more Luther research from that fine Luther scholar from Aakhus, Regin Prenter, who has retired from his chair at Aarhus and taken up a country living in Denmark.

The Latin countries, traditionally Catholic, have not been in the forefront of Luther research. It would hardly be within the purview of this book to look at works done in these countries other than in French, though it is worth recalling that significant work has been done and is being done in all the European languages, even a little in Japan. First is a series of translations into French of Luther's main works, writings, commentaries, letters and table talk, editor Rene J. Lovy, begun in 1957 and still being published. A significant book, already referred to, has been written by the young French scholar Marc Lienhard: *Luther, témoin de Jésus Christ* (1973). The work of Father Olivier on the trial of Luther has already been mentioned. At present he is working on a book on Luther's doctrine of Christ. Roland Dalbiez approaches Luther from a Freudian point of view, and in his *L'angoisse de Luther* (1974) takes up the position that Luther's psychological concerns drove him into heresy, and that he was not responsible for his religious and theological aberrations: this impossible position makes any discussion with Luther's theology impossible. Like so many impercipient Roman Catholics over the centuries they seek to discredit the person of Luther, and think thereby they have dismissed his theology. The truth of Luther's theological position must be analysed and criticised by critical, historical, rational analysis of his actual theological and intellectual position. Dalbiez is not alone in this game, and it certainly serves to lead the popular mind astray, who tend to pick up their views of historic figures (More, Henry VIII, Luther, Galileo spring to mind), from films and television plays. It is a variant of the earlier attacks of Cochlaeus and Emser, and of the more recent ones of Dénifle and Grisar. No responsible Catholic theologian known to the present writer takes up this kind of position any longer: now only the psychologists and sociologists adopt such positions, aided occasionally by the journalist or playwright in his predatory hunt for a theme to catch an audience or a reader. The work of such men is irrelevant to the serious study of Luther the theologian, yet they always receive considerable publicity in the media, when a first-class study receives no notice at all, save in the learned journals.

The Ecumenical Movement

A further factor which lends contemporary significance to Luther's theological concerns is the firm development of the ecumenical movement of this century. In the first instance it was Luther's theology which really divided Christendom. True, Christendom had already divided into East and West in 1054, but the theology and worship of the Eastern Orthodox Church on the one hand and the Western Roman Catholic Church on the other hand remained similar in essentials: it had been the arrogant claims of Rome which by now had virtually identified itself with the secular culture of the West that made the East withdraw into the independence of its own very attractive spirituality and into a Catholicism more traditional, even more Catholic, than that of Rome. Both East and West were essentially Catholic, and remain so to this day: the East was undisturbed by the theological controversies which divided the West in the sixteenth century. Luther sought to establish within Christendom (i.e. the Latin Western half and not the Greek Eastern half), the authority of the Word of God as it had once addressed the Church and was again addressing the Church. Such theology established the priesthood of all believers, and at the same time compelled a priest not to be a sacrificing priest calling down the very Presence of God, but a minister of God's Word, serving the people as Christ ministered to the people. The mysterious authority of the priest was lost, the tyranny of the people vanished: Christ was the centre, not the mass, nor the pope. The Church was envisioned as it once was, the called and elect people of God, an organism rather than an organisation. Luther's theology knocked the bottom out of the popular Catholic cultus, which of course many litterateurs, scholars and theologians laughed to scorn, but more guardedly, lest they lost their place and favours. Indulgences, purgatory, pilgrimages, good works, transubstantiation, the place of the Blessed Virgin Mary, to mention a few, were all called into question. Luther was never answered, simply condemned and excommunicated. There was at that time no reconciliation of Luther's biblical theology with the then Catholic cultus.

Today it is all different. Distinguished Catholic scholars such as Hubert Jedin, have said that Pope Leo X made a ghastly mistake, and that he misunderstood and mismanaged Luther's protest. Catholic scholars, with Protestant scholars, largely regret the ruptures of the sixteenth century, and now openly and sincerely seek both understanding and reconciliation, but, and this is the difference, not on the basis of the Catholic cultus hitherto assumed to be the only true basis, but much more on a mutual respect for the Bible with a critical regard for Patristic tradition rather than on ecclesiastical tradition. This is exactly what Luther begged for, and what many Catholic scholars and churchmen of his day wished to grant, but which the Papal Curia refused even to consider. Owing to its individualistic approach, and having to work out its theology in polemical situations, Protestantism developed fissiparous tendencies and spawned further denominations, yet all the successors of these divisive tendencies, now largely the so-called Free Churches, are anxious to discuss within an ecumenical framework all the issues which divide all the Churches.

Not the least value of the present book is that it examines all these theological differences as they emerged in Luther, and all Christian men, Catholic and Protestant alike, need to see them in these terms before they can understand the contemporary situation. This is not to say that we need to fight the old sixteenth century battles all over again. God forbid! Nor is it to say that Roman Catholic scholars must listen to Protestant scholars and thereby reform themselves. On the contrary, the biblical theology of Luther addresses itself to all Churches. It is the view of the present writer that, in the areas of spirituality and in Christian ethics, the Roman Church has remained more faithful to Christianity than have many of the Protestant Churches. The reformed Churches have tended to go liberal, even political, and in the process their theology, spirituality and ethics have become secularised, often indistinguishable from contemporary society, de-Christianised, almost humanised, if one could be allowed the term. Such Churches have nothing whatever to say to the world which the world does not already know and think, little to offer to a world uncertain of right and wrong, a world satiated already with materialism, yearning for spiritual values. Were Protestant and Catholic men to think together again on these theological, spiritual and moral matters, and under God to respond to God in the way Luther called the Church to do, the entire Church would experience a fresh birth of the Spirit, and thereby be given a fresh spiritual and moral power to inspire a lost and jaded world.

Perhaps the greatest single factor in the new and universally welcomed theological climate is the leadership emanating from Rome. The aged, and universally loved, Pope John XXIII called the Second Vatican Council, and this provided, and is still providing, not merely the bringing up-to-date of Catholicism which he called for, but virtually its re-birth. A study of the Vatican II documents is a most invigorating and enheartening experience. Gone is the old language of anathema and condemnation, and in its place the plain, vital and dynamic language of the Bible, unchallengeable in its authority, creative in its testimony. In these documents one reads the words of serenity and faith, expressed in love, couched in hope. With this kind of language, and with this kind of theology, Catholics and Protestants may move forward together in amity and unity.

In the context of this introduction it is of considerable interest to note that (apart from the strictly contemporary matters such as radio and television, modern communications and computer technology, mission in the modern world, education and pastoral and priestly training and the like), the main theological and religious matters such as the doctrines of God, Christ and the holy spirit; revelation, scripture, tradition; the Gospel; the Church and its message to the world; word and sacrament; eternal life; Christian morals; the relation to society, government and the state, were all raised by Luther and handled in a fresh compelling way, i.e. not offering what the Church was teaching at the time, but asking whether what the Church was teaching had the authority of the Bible. The striking feature about the Vatican II documents is the simple, historical, biblical way in which these great themes are expressed. Still more striking is the way in which the Vatican fathers stubbornly returned for re-thinking and re-submission those draft documents which did not comply with the new thinking but had been couched in terms of yester-year. The Spirit would not be blocked. It is perhaps here and in this way that Vatican II may yet issue in the movement which Luther inaugurated. It is not a case of back to Luther but forward to Luther. Certainly, Luther will never be the same again to any Catholic who has read the documents of Vatican II: he is the harbinger of Vatican II. It would be true to say that in informed circles the debate is not between Catholic and Protestant any longer, now that scurrilous and personal attacks on Luther are no longer acceptable. In fact, the discussion is not at a denominational level at all, nor is it even inter-confessional: it is biblical and theological. The debate is not between Catholic and Protestant theologians, but between theocentric and anthropocentric theologians.

Vatican II and the Papacy

A factor, the importance of which we cannot yet rightly assess, is that of the new leadership emerging from Rome in the person of Pope John Paul II. His ministry is having an impact on the Roman Catholic Church and the world such as has never before been seen or experienced. There is more to his influence than his warm, spiritual, charismatic personality, gracious as this is. He is obviously seeking to re-present to the entire world the sure and certain foundations of the Roman Catholic faith, and with that the traditional morality.

The Faith has been suffering a great deal of erosion owing to the advance of education which causes the educated person to ask questions and construct a faith for himself in the light of his own needs and experiences, rather than to receive without question all that is offered him. Further damage has been done under the influence of fascist, communist and other totalitarian ideologies, whereby the total allegiance has been weaned from the Church. Moreover, the influence of a permissive society, so specious in its arguments for freedom and self-expression, threatens the "traditional" moral values in those basic areas of marriage, work and material possessions.

The net result of these movements is that the educated Roman Catholic of the Western democracies is growing away from the traditional Catholic position. Educated Catholics by and large no longer hold the doctrine of transubstantiation, no longer believe the immaculate conception nor the assumption of the Blessed Virgin Mary, no longer go to regular confession, and certainly do not follow the line on birth control and sexual ethics. Admittedly, the uneducated Catholics of Latin America and the Third World, to some extent most of the Catholics of those traditionally Catholic countries of Europe who have hardly met Protestantism as a spiritual and intellectual movement, receive uncritically the Catholic view, including those on birth control and sexual ethics. Consequently, a polarisation is emerging in the Roman Catholic world between a sceptical intelligentsia and a superstitious underworld.

The whole world admires the Pope's stand for fundamental theology and his witness for true Christian morals and values, done as it is with such Christian grace and such pure human love. He is surely right to do so. Yet, the ultimate effect of re-asserting the old truths, no matter how sincerely believed, genuinely practised and effectively proclaimed, may serve to strengthen this polarisation. It is precisely in such a situation that a concerned look at one of the great Catholic scholars and preachers, Martin Luther, whose sole aim was to restore his deeply loved Catholic Church to its biblical basis and its rightful mission and message, could effect the

greatest *aggiornamento* known to the Roman Catholic Church. If
at the same time Protestantism could bestir itself and terminate its
suffocating liaison with liberalism, deliver itself from its crippling
intellectual and moral permissiveness, and free itself from the se-
ductions of secularisation and politicisation, in order to see again
and hear again what the Reformation was calling men back to say,
to be and to do, all of us, together, may yet hear what the Spirit is
saying to the Churches, and in hearing, obey. Doctor Luther is a
doctor of the Church: he has more to teach us than any other teacher,
save Christ.

The Reviewers

Finally, about the reviewers. As I recall they were generally
favourable: most of them saw that I was seeking to give a theological
account of Luther for the English reader. Catholic reviewers were
more sensitive than Protestant reviewers, for they understood the
deep spiritual battles and theological struggles of the sixteenth
century. Protestant reviewers tended to argue about Luther and
the peasants, Luther and the princes, Luther and the Jews, rarely
about the real matters, justification by faith, the role of the Church,
eternal life. The evangelical and biblical men saw in a flash the
central issues, for they have not been de-theologised as liberal protestants have been. Certain readers found the book difficult, but on
questioning further of their difficulties, I discovered that they found
the book demanded too much of them in the way of historical and
theological knowledge. This criticism I accept. I would only plead
that there is no understanding Luther unless one grasps the spiritual
and intellectual outlook of the late Middle Ages against which and
for which he wrote. He did this to liberate men from that prison
into the glorious freedom of the sons of God: we have to understand the nature of that bondage and the power of that liberation.
Simplification is always falsification in one way or another. The late
medieval scholastic position was formidable and highly respected,
and is not easy for modern man to understand. Nevertheless, when
that is said, it is the nature of his liberation I sought to express, and
this liberation all men can experience.

Some reviewers found the book partisan, biassed in favour of Luther. They are entitled to their opinion. I can understand why they think so. The book is certainly sympathetic to Luther, an earthy and simple human being with the faith of a St. Paul, the love of a St. John, and the courage of a St. George: the man above all others who declared the truth of Christianity to a faithless and perverse generation. One penetrates to the heart of a man's life further by love and warmth, than by cold, critical analysis. Is not the object of the exercise to understand Luther better?

FOREWORD

THERE is a story that on the eve of battle, 17 June 1815, during the ball at Brussels, the Duke of Wellington, withdrawing from the festivities, took out his map and laid his thumb on a little, insignificant village, called Waterloo and said, 'That is where I shall meet Napoleon.' But who, before 1517, could have taken a map of Christendom and picked out the small university town of Wittenberg amid the forests and hills of Saxony and said that here would be the end of one era and the beginning of another in Christian history? The number of books in English on Luther is happily mounting apace, and studies begin to accumulate which in sympathy and objectivity resemble a spring after a long, hard winter; but it is still important, still salutarily shocking to the mind, to have a thorough treatment of the life of Luther which centres on the conviction that 'Luther's main concern was to preach Christ'.

This is a great merit of Dr Atkinson's study. It has been said of Luther's enemy Thomas Müntzer that any attempt to explain him fails which does not take account of the fact that he was 'altogether a preacher, altogether a theologian'. How much more is this true of Martin Luther! To make sense of the Reformation, of the Reformers, and above all of Luther, a theological equipment is indispensable. That is why students will turn to Dr Atkinson's pages for a long time to come, since he has the gift of imaginative simplicity and is able to clarify these intricate issues without dangerous over-simplification. No doubt there is an important distinction between Luther's religion and Luther's theology, but certainly one cannot be understood without the other, and here, close-packed within one volume, is a biography in which the great and grave ideological and theological issues are lucidly explained.

G. R.

Abbreviations

References are made to the definitive Weimar edition by volume, page and line.

W.A.: *D. Martin Luthers Werke, Kritische Gesamtausgabe*, Weimar, 1883– . (Books, commentaries, sermons etc.)

W.A.Br.: *D. Martin Luthers Werke, Briefwechsel* Weimar, 1930– . (Correspondence)

W.A.D.B.: *D. Martin Luthers Werke, Deutsche Bibel*, Weimar, 1906–61. (Luther's Bible translation)

W.A.Ti.: *D. Martin Luthers Werke, Tischreden* Weimar, 1912–21. (*Table Talk*)

CONTENTS

INTRODUCTION

Two things are necessary in order to understand Luther. The
first is to grasp the turmoil of thought and development, social,
political, cultural and intellectual, in which Luther lived and to
which he addressed himself. The second is to understand what he
was about. He was not the great champion of individual liberty
and private judgement, the rugged peasant who challenged
Pope and Emperor, the Germanic Hercules, or the great social
emancipator. To believe that he was would be to introduce alien
presuppositions imported from the nineteenth and twentieth
centuries. His sole concern was to tell a sinful world of his own
experience of the great God who had shown His Hand in Christ,
so that man might know God's pardon and God's peace in the
living Christ, and so to live in this Kingdom of God within a
corrupt, sinful, hostile but temporal world as to be received in
death into God's everlasting Kingdom. He was simply a man
with a Gospel. He had a message to offer to the world because in
the long, painful, single-minded search for God which followed
his disillusionment with the medieval techniques of penance and
good works, suddenly, in the depths of his despair, he felt God
tapping him on the shoulder. All his polemics against the
secularized corrupt Church of his day, against the unreal and
remote disputations of scholasticism, against Erasmus and the
humanists, against the radicals and enthusiasts, against the
peasants and socialists, against the political careerists, are ultimately reducible to this one issue, that his opponents all rejected or modified the sole sufficiency of Christ in the interests
of tradition, learning, inspiration, social justice and similar
considerations, not least for reasons of brutal self-interest.
Luther was thrust into the tumult of the Reformation and never
sought it.

More than four centuries have passed since Luther lived, and
it demands effort to understand him not from the heights of
modern technical and scientific advances but as a medieval man

among medieval men. To the general reader it may be a little
irksome, even embarrassing, to discover that Luther's main concern was to preach Christ. If the reader finds it too much to
concede that Luther's sole purpose was to preach and to teach
Christ, he may read this book with little profit, and Luther's
books too for that matter. But it is worth granting Luther this
as a working premise, and then seeing how the whole picture
fits together, and how the supposed tensions and uncertainties
resolve themselves into clear principles. Certainly no one will
understand Luther who does not see him as a theologian of the
sixteenth century, educated in the dying world of scholasticism,
caught up in an upsurge of humanist excitement and profound
social and political change, as a man with the single and simple
religious motivation of preaching and teaching Christ.

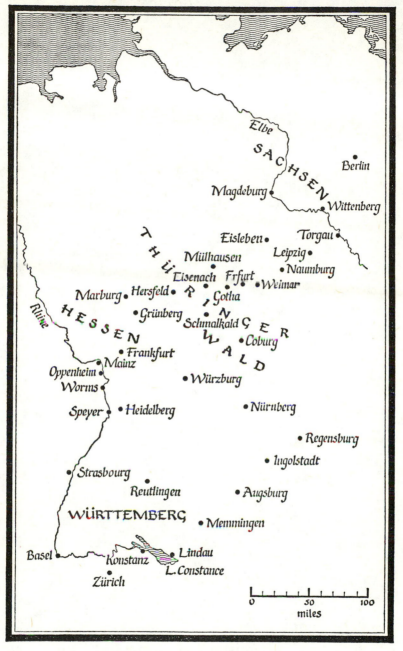

Principal Places Mentioned

PART ONE
CHILDHOOD AND YOUTH
1483–1505

CHAPTER I

LUTHER'S HOME

TOWARDS midnight on 10 November 1483 Martin Luther was born in the village of Eisleben in Saxony on the edge of the Thuringian Forest. When her son was famous his mother recollected the hour clearly but the year vaguely. Early the next morning the parents presented their first-born to the parish priest for baptism, when he was named Martin after the saint of that day. His parents, Hans and Margaret Luder, as the family was then called, if not refugees, were little more than pilgrims. Hans was the eldest son of a large family facing poverty and starvation on a barren and fruitless land, and with his young bride he was seeking a fresh chance to earn a new living in the more lucrative and hopeful world of industry and mining. His position was not unlike that of countless Scots today who have crossed the border to earn a better living in industrial and urban England.

Martin's boyhood was normal. Two favourable circumstances only did he enjoy as a child. First, his parents were upright people. Secondly, his father had to fight for and earn everything that he later enjoyed. All his life Martin was to be aware of what it meant to be brought up as a growing boy in the dignity of godly poverty and the nobility of hard labour. Hans had voluntarily left his own father's land, which he knew was too barren to support the whole family. Later, when Martin was but a babe in arms, he went on from Eisleben, where he found a crowded labour market, to Mansfeld, where the prospects looked more promising. In the short space of seven years he became a town councillor (1491). By 1511 he was part-owner of six shafts and two foundries, and when he died he was to leave at least 1,250 gulden. With such a father and such a background Martin was bound to take life seriously and seize every opportunity for advancement.

In these democratic days it is fashionable to make much of Luther's humble origin as a miner's son. But the real parallel is not the rough, ignorant miner of our own Industrial Revolution, cloth-capped, squatting at the end of the colliery row, without status, without rights, without schooling, without even a Church to care, whose children were mercilessly exposed to the scouring and embittering winds of unemployment, poverty and bad housing, whose horizon was enclosed by the pit heap and whose relaxation was a whippet, a brass band, a quoit to throw. The parallel is on another plane. Hans Luther was a man known personally to the counts who owned the land he mined, and was much esteemed by them and other landowners. He had a large house in the main street, where his coat of arms still adorns the front door. He went to his son's ordination with fifty horse and left a substantial gift, and when Luther grew famous, he and his wife moved among the Wittenberg scholars with quiet dignity and enjoyed much esteem. If a more recent parallel to Luther's parentage were sought it could more properly be found among those nineteenth-century independent mill-owners of Lancashire and Yorkshire, or perhaps those 'little maisters' or master-cutlers of Sheffield appearing in the parish church on Sunday morning with a top hat and a cutler's apron, newly laundered. In America he would have been in the fore of those long wagon-trains 'just moving west'. Had he been living today he would have been on the Coal Board, and mentioned in the Birthday Honours. There was character in Luther's parentage: uprightness, determination, integrity, ability and independence. When all the monks at the monastery sought fruitlessly to persuade old father Hans how right his son was to choose the monastic life, he bluntly silenced them, 'Haven't you read the Fifth Commandment?'[1] Luther was always proud of the sturdy folk from whom he stemmed, as any man might be, and knew himself to be a chip off the old block.

It is worth considering for a moment the religious atmosphere in which Luther was brought up and against which he was to make such effective protest.

With all his family he would go to mass on Sundays and

1. 'Honour thy father and thy mother.'

feast days. He would believe in the real presence of Christ in the elements at mass. He would go to confession, pray to the Virgin and the saints, recite the rosary, reverence the relics, seek to gain indulgences and say his prayers at home, just like any other good Christian at the time. There is contemporary evidence of a heavy emphasis on the fear of eternal damnation in hell for wrongdoing, or at least long and painful retribution in purgatory, as well as the hope of eternal bliss in heaven for the good. There is still clearer evidence, however, of a very natural gaiety in Church life as well as real Christian joy in the family, of devoted prayer leading to works of genuine goodness and charity. We know very little of this from Luther's own writing, for the little he said about his childhood amounts only to the reminiscences of an older man at table.[1] Nevertheless, from contemporary evidence and from certain remarks made by Luther, the position described is reasonably accurate.

The worst feature of his religious upbringing must have been the atmosphere of superstition. Luther's contemporaries still believed that the world was dominated by a world of spirits, many of which were malevolent. The educated were beginning to comprehend a rational cosmology of cause and effect, but this liberating movement hardly gained hold in Europe until the eighteenth century. It is important to be sympathetic with medieval man at this point. It was but a small step to seek the cooperation and favour of the good spirits against the bad, and therefore the cult of holy water, exorcism and the invocation of the Virgin and the saints who had attained glory were accepted as normal. The Devil, witches, bogies and malevolent evil spirits were as real a part of Luther's life as were the Blessed Virgin and the saints in glory. Therefore equally as real were all the counter-attacks Mother Church had devised against the depredations of these subtle and dark powers. We must seek to understand this spiritual otherness of medieval thought: the spirits who caused the milk to go sour or brought about the still-birth were as real as the mercy of Christ and the spiritual ministry of the godly priest. To be wrong on one does not necessarily mean to be wrong on both.

1. See p. 323 for reference to the *Table Talk*.

The prevailing atmosphere of superstition had a more disastrous effect on the practice of the mass. The true Catholic doctrine of the mass, which demands a real spiritual experience and a genuine theological education of the layman, seemed to have lapsed into the performance of an act which gave a man the right to heaven. There was too little of the meeting of God with His creature in mercy and the re-creation of the believing man, too much of the performance of a required ritual. The payment of money to a priest to say masses for a particular purpose set the mass in the context not of God's work for man's salvation but of man's works. With this there developed the gross scandal of indulgences, and their association with relics. All these were but pagan accretions to Christian theology, or perhaps we should say, lapses from a theocentric religion to an anthropocentric religion.

We need to understand sensitively the world in which Luther was brought up before we can understand the Reformation he initiated. This does not mean the suspension of our critical faculty, yet we must transport ourselves into the sixteenth century before we can allow this faculty its full play. The total picture is one of a deeply pious peasant culture of practising Christian men and women, where every child was a living part of it. The centre of their life, apart from their heavy daily work, was the parish church, often beautiful in itself, where a noble liturgy was performed and from whose tower the bells rang out daily. All this was supported by an immense weight of intellect and learning stretching back nearly fifteen hundred years.

To understand this old-world life, to transport ourselves to the days when the Church stood powerful, unchallenged and erect, when she penetrated into the whole of a man's life from the cradle to the grave, is not easy. The Church had almost cast a spell over society. The English historian, Froude, expressed in his inimitable nineteenth-century prose the transition of the thought world of our forefathers and the inability of his contemporaries to enter it:

... we have lost the key which would interpret the characters of our fathers and the great men even of our own English history before the

Reformation seem to us almost like the fossil skeletons of another order of beings. . . .[1]

Writing of the decay of the old system and the change wrought by the Reformation he said:

For, indeed, a change was coming upon the world, the meaning and direction of which even still is hidden from us, a change from era to era. The paths trodden by the footsteps of ages were broken up; old things were passing away, and the faith and life of ten centuries were dissolving like a dream. Chivalry was dying; the abbey and the castle were soon together to crumble into ruins; and all the forms, desires, beliefs, convictions of the old world were passing away, never to return. A new continent had risen up beyond the western sea. The floor of heaven, inlaid with stars, had sunk back into an infinite abyss of immeasurable space; and the firm earth itself, unfixed from its foundations, was seen to be but a small atom in the awful vastness of the universe. In the fabric of habit in which they had so laboriously built for themselves, mankind were to remain no longer.

And now it is all gone – like an unsubstantial pageant faded; and between us and the old English there lies a gulf of mystery which the prose of the historian will never adequately bridge. They cannot come to us, and our imagination can but feebly penetrate to them. Only among the aisles of the cathedral, only as we gaze upon their silent figures sleeping on their tombs, some faint conceptions float before us of what these men were when they were alive; and perhaps in the sound of church-bells, that particular creation of mediaeval age, which falls upon the ear like the echo of a vanished world.[1]

A century later than Froude we now stand on ground far less certain, where the old landmarks are down and the signposts no longer upright: a world whose thinkers in the literary, philosophical, psychological, theological, social and scientific disciplines have opened up ways of interpreting history and life wholly different from those of our forefathers. As we reconsider that old world of the fifteenth and sixteenth centuries and its cataclysmic transition into our own era we should seek to avoid any simple mono-causal explanation of its complex phenomena as well as to import into it our own twentieth-century criteria (valuable though these are in themselves). The medieval world

1. *History of England*, James Anthony Froude, Parker, London, 1862, Vol. I, pp. 3 and 61 f.

is a kingdom wherein only those as humble as children may enter.

Into this world in transition Luther was born, and more than any other man he was responsible for its collapse and reconstruction. It is important to discern what collapsed and what was reconstructed. The Reformation was not a bolt from the blue: it was rather a re-formation, a re-orientation of some thousand years of Christian living and thinking.

CHAPTER 2

SCHOOL LIFE

AT the age of five little Martin is seen plodding his way to school on his stout legs, sometimes being carried on the shoulders of an older boy. There he went every day for eight years; there were no holidays in those days. At school he learned reading, writing, singing and Latin: Latin, because competence in this tongue was required for entrance into the professions; music, because a student could later earn his education by singing at the church services. The education was little more than mechanical cramming, a training of memory prompted by the birch; but what else could one man do with all his classes from five years old to university entrance in one room all day every day of the year! Nevertheless Luther gained an uncommon mastery of the Latin language and developed into a highly competent musician. Yet he always thought of school as a hell on earth and the master as a tyrant and executioner.

There was an official at the mine whose son went to school at Magdeburg, and at the age of fourteen (1497) Luther joined this boy. The school belonged to a brotherhood of pious clergymen and laymen who had combined to practise a godly life as well as to serve society by preaching, teaching and social service. Here Luther had to eke out his father's allowance by singing in the church as many another boy did and still does in our cathedral choir schools. The sentimental stories about poor little Luther singing in the streets like some urchin in Dickens do not belong to the sober facts. He was a privileged boy and he sat at his desk alongside others whose fathers were of highly professional standing. His father paid for his education through school and university, and like most students, except those of the welfare state today, Luther had to make a very little go a long way. His was not the grim poverty which was a feature of the nineteenth-century industrial slum towns, but a noble, dignified and respectable state of a very different kind where men endured penury without feeling stigmatized or degraded.

At Easter 1498 Luther was brought back to Mansfeld and sent off to Eisenach. He did well at school during these four years at Eisenach and always looked back on them with gladness. As at Magdeburg, he eked out his allowance as a 'crumb seeker' by singing at church. Here his earnestness in prayer and singing in church were noticed by a kind lady who took him into her home, in return for which he took her little son to school and helped him with his home-work. One can readily picture the young teenage Luther with his large head and black locks sitting alongside the little boy in that Christian home, coaching him and teaching him his home-work. Here he came into contact with a devout circle of Christian people at a very impressionable age. All who came to the house, clergy and laity alike, were characterized by a deep piety and simple godliness. This atmosphere influenced the boy profoundly and profitably. He was once struck by some remarkable words casually spoken in conversation about the wonder and beauty of a godly marriage, and the words burned in his mind, for he had always assumed that celibacy was the noblest and purest form of living. In later years he always referred to this beautiful Thuringian town as 'my Eisenach'.[1]

1. The places referred to in this chapter still stand today, most of them in the unspoiled simplicity of their original character. In Eisleben, the beautiful house where he was born, with its quaint balcony overlooking the garden entered by a fine old gate, is indicative of the quality and dignity of Luther's parents. The church where he was baptized is hard by along the cobbled lane. The massive patrician house where he died stands up the hill from the market-place, opposite the church where he preached his last sermon. With incongruous abandonment the Communists have recently erected a very fine statue of Lenin in the midst of all this Lutherana! In Eisenach, his home, his school, his church, the town gate, through which he often walked, still stand, though the home and school were damaged during the final stages of the last war. All roads out of Eisenach lead through the wonderful Thuringian Wald, beloved of Luther, and dominating the countryside towers the impressive Wartburg, where he was later to be imprisoned.

CHAPTER 3

THE SECULAR CLIMATE

WHEN Luther was eighteen (1501) his father sent him to the ancient and famous university of Erfurt. It must have been a great moment to have been eighteen at the beginning of the sixteenth century and matriculating at one of Germany's most famous universities. Contemporary man is sometimes tempted to think that his own age is *the* era of change and development with its technical and scientific advances in nuclear physics, but history may record our days as essentially 'the end of an era', an era ushered in by the men and ideas which are the subject of this book, but one which since Luther's time has markedly lost direction and purpose. Luther's world had an intellectual excitement all its own. It was the day of the great sailors and discoverers and voyagers, when Columbus and Cabot were bringing back evidence of a new world, of flora and fauna formerly unknown; when Copernicus was still young and proving to the world that the sun was the centre of the universe; when the Renascence scholars were stimulating thought in Europe with their rediscovery of Hellenism. These were great and exciting days, when Colet preached the Gospel and the Pauline theology in St Paul's; when men of the stature of Erasmus, Melanchthon, Bucer, Zwingli and Calvin occupied our chairs of theology and marked students' essays. The world was intellectually agog; the new wine could but burst the old wineskins.

THE RENASCENCE

The influence of the Renascence on the German Reformation needs careful assessment. To explain Luther in terms of the Renascence would be to produce a gross distortion. In one sense he was solidly opposed to the this-worldly materialism which the Renascence tended to produce as well as to its non-theological religion. But it must be remembered that he was born in an atmosphere affected by this movement which was both older and more universal than the Reformation. Zwingli was essentially a Renascence man, as was Erasmus. Calvin was strongly shaped by its scholarship, as was Melanchthon. Luther's tracts were published and read in those German cities strongly influenced by Renascence learning, Augsburg, Nürnberg, Strassburg and Basel. At the same time he reacted against the humanist theology of his day in favour of a stubborn Hebraic and biblical theology. He took advantage of some aspects of the humanist movement, using for instance its linguistic tools to great profit, but he remained outside its powerful stream, shut up in a monastery in his tiny corner of Saxony, and when he stepped out into the world to teach he stood simply as a teaching monk under the vow of obedience. True, the movement had extraordinary influence on the development of natural science and historic and literary studies, but it had singularly little effect on the real concern of Luther. There was a sensuousness about the Renascence, a throbbing power generated by and for man in his own interests. As a movement it believed in man rather than God. At its most religious, in Erasmus for example or in the Florentines, it was little more than a 'Jesus-religion', a new ethic, a new law, but no Gospel. True, it rediscovered the grandeur and natural dignity of man, body and mind; it reviled and reduced scholasticism to ridicule and broke its chains; it gave man a new sense of liberation. But it struck fatal blows at man's sense of dependence on God, at the other-worldliness of his interpretation of life, at the spiritual reality of death followed by judgement. Looking back on four hundred years of the process, as we now can, we realize that every subsequent advance in man's thought has removed God from that field of inquiry as an unnecessary hypothesis. Copernicus and Newton removed Him from the cosmos, Darwin from life, Marx from history, Freud from the last citadel of the mind and soul. Luther could not foresee all this, but by 1524 before he was forty he was engaged in a great death struggle for the Gospel with the good Erasmus (see pages 228–35). It is interesting to see the visible influences of the Renascence in those lovely South-German cities as one walks their streets again, and to think of the Renascence splendour of the courts of the German ecclesiastics and princes of Luther's day, and then to consider the pure biblical pressure Luther put on society. He seemed to turn away from the Renascence like an old horse turning its hindquarters to an inclement wind, yet breathing the very air against which he had turned.

THE POLITICAL SCENE

On the political scene, too, it was a time of violent, almost cataclysmic, upsurge. When everybody stopped in 1517 and looked at this quiet monk of Wittenberg who had taken Christianity off its hinges and rehung it, Europe was preparing for the election of a new Emperor and was about to enter a long series of world wars. By the time of Luther's death, some thirty years later, the long military struggle between Germany and France had just ended and his foe, Charles V, was in a position to 'settle' the German question. Luther spent his days against a background of political tension, intrigue and war. The great Sultan, Suleiman II, had made a critical advance and was knocking ominously at the gates of Europe. When Luther was engaged in his great contest with Erasmus, Hungary was wiped out. When Luther and Zwingli argued at Marburg in 1529 and before the Confession of Augsburg could be agreed on in 1530, the Turk stood before the gates of Vienna. Luther was always deeply conscious that the Turk could strike at any moment and subjugate Christendom. This made Luther intensely eschatological in that he feared the end of the world was at hand, and that human history was in its final throes. This kind of belief is more often associated nowadays with cranks and freaks, but Luther in common with many of his contemporaries held it in the New Testament sense – that history had fulfilled itself and was about to be brought to its final end and its final judgement, in the line of certain prophecies of Jesus (Mark xiii, for example).

Further, there was a deep disturbance within Christendom at a time when the single-minded Turk towered over a disunited Europe. The Hapsburgs controlled the lands of south-west Germany, Austria, Burgundy and Sicily–Naples, and, when the young Charles V succeeded Maximilian in 1519, the New Spain and the New World were added to all this. Over Italy, the Pyrenees and the France–Netherlands border, a bitter struggle raged between Charles V and Francis I, whose desire it was to wreck the power and influence of the Hapsburgs and establish the sovereignty of France. Francis showed himself ready to pay any price for success and played a deceitful hand. He was prepared to make alliances with the Protestant princes, even with the Turk, to gain his ends. Though its theology was of the Bible and its inspiration of God, Protestantism took its rise within and spoke its message to a Europe in political, social, economic and military travail.

But within Germany itself there was a still deeper complex of political eddies, for Charles V was engaged not only in a desperate contest with Francis but in a great power struggle with the German estates. The shift from centralized power to territorial power in the German empire, long before Luther's time, had led to a reform movement within the estates. These estates consisted of local princes, high ecclesiastics and the free cities. They wanted a greater influence in the affairs of the empire and were seeking from the Emperor some form of independent civil government (*Reichsregiment*), and from the Pope relief from papal taxation. But even between these estates there were strong disagreements, and many of them (particularly in Eastern Germany) had enlarged their borders and built up sound administrative units. The estates suddenly became aware of their power and solidarity in a rapidly changing situation.

Another lively progressive group was made up of the towns and cities, insufficiently represented in the Diet owing to their recent origins but nevertheless embodying very largely the intellectual vigour, economic energy and culture of the new Germany. The lesser nobility, now the flotsam and jetsam of the flowing economic tide, were being cast up on the shore to rot and waste. The Emperor sought to regain control of his vast empire. The estates sought to escape being enmeshed in his plans and to preserve their integrity and individuality. The princes saw this as their great moment when Francis and Charles (with Ferdinand) were embroiled in their conflict, and when Luther preached evangelical liberty (easily camouflaged by secular men as social freedom, and not altogether unconnected with it). The princes sought to assert themselves against central authority and to enhance their own power. They were now able to take any ecclesiastical reformation into their own hands, and proved to be ready to do so, not all of them with the pureness of motive of a John Frederick.

There were eddies within eddies. The estates were much troubled by revolutionary movements both among the poor peasants in the country as well as among the downtrodden artisans in the towns, who were violently and desperately trying to attain some kind of influence in government. Luther's religious movement penetrated deeply into both the peasantry and the left-wing urbanized proletariat, to find there a very deep echo, though tragically for them as well as for Luther's religious cause, it was a false echo, as we shall learn later (see page 236).

To make matters worse, the papacy itself was embroiled in sordid political intrigue and power politics. The Pope and his curia seemed to regard themselves primarily as the rulers of the Church's states and when the test came were more concerned for their secular interests than for the theological issues Luther raised. The Pope showed himself prepared to let the problem of Luther bide until the tension between Charles and Francis resolved itself. By his scandalous delay he played into Luther's hands. Germany was restive at her shocking treatment at the hands of Rome as well as of her despoliation by the all too secular prince bishops. She was aware that she had to wrest her rights not only from the Emperor but from the Pope. It is important to have a firm grasp of these matters in order to understand and evaluate Luther. Franz Lau, the Leipzig historian, points out the importance of this long 'twenty-five years' war' when Luther broke up the monolithic intellectual and spiritual totalitarianism of the great medieval Church, a war in which Luther read only the hand of God and saw himself as a tool in His Hand.[1]

1. Franz Lau, *Luther*, tr. Robert H. Fischer, London, 1963, pp. 21 f.

THE SOCIAL SCENE

In the matter of social reform, feudalism was marching with a Marxist inevitability into capitalism. Currency, rather than goods, was now taking pre-eminence in trade. The great banking houses had arisen, as well as trading companies, monopolies and all the machinery of capitalism. To walk through the streets of Augsburg today is to enter that old world, even to the gold-adorned bones still displayed as relics in the church. For the first time 'money talked'. A new monied class had come to the top in the early sixteenth century, and social divisions began to be marked less often by family or human worth and more often simply by wealth. The old leading classes were being ousted by merchants and manufacturers. At the same time a mysterious and inexplicable rise in prices was taking place all over Europe, aggravating the situation. No one could understand this problem and everybody tended to put the blame on everybody else. The lot of the peasant (and others) was desperate. Luther's involvement in this social revolution was twofold. In the first instance during his boyhood and youth his father was fighting his way out of it to relative affluence by leaving the land and taking to metal mining. In the second instance as a man Luther had to take a stand against involving the Reformation in social revolution, a stand which lost him the support of the peasants (see page 236). The consequences of all these social changes are still being experienced today. The people who suffered most were the knights and farmers, and the peasants and artisans, and the new reforms aggravated their grievances more and more. They thought of Luther, the great reformer, as on their side, but this was one of the tragic misunderstandings of history. He was on their side but opposed to their cause. Luther's concern was religious and theological, while their interest was in the main materialist and socialist. The peasants were justified in their grievances. They were right in assuming that Luther understood them and was sympathetic. Where they were fatally wrong was in assuming that Luther would bless their rebellion and support them in it. He had no prime interest in political, social or national reforms as such. To him, society had always been corrupt and always would be, while God suffered it to last. Society could never save a man, neither would a better society make better men. A man must be saved from society. He had no illusions about man's building the Kingdom of God on earth. Nevertheless, he had the clearest and strongest views on what constituted a just society, what God intended society to be, and on the various responsibilities of prince, magistrate and layman.

CHAPTER 4

UNIVERSITY LIFE

LUTHER, the pride and joy of his father, matriculated at the ancient university of Erfurt[1] at the age of nearly eighteen, in the year 1501, to take his seat among the favoured few. The entry reads today *Martinus Ludher de Mansfeld.* He was known as a cheerful lad, witty and full of fun, a hard worker, musical and deeply religious – a candidate any university admissions officer would at once grant 'unconditional offer'.

The ancient universities were not the free institutions they are today. Luther lived a hard, controlled, disciplined life in one of the colleges of the university, a life not unlike that of the students in a theological seminary today. The university of Erfurt was then the most famous in Germany. Though closely allied to the Church, it had been founded by the burghers of the town in 1392 and had always enjoyed, as do some of our provincial universities now, a close relation with its city (with occasional estrangements). What did Martin learn there? Who were his teachers? What did he think of his education?

For his first degree of Bachelor of Arts he read the *trivium* – grammar, rhetoric and dialectic. This developed in him the ability to use words exactly, and the capacity to argue and to think rationally and logically, as well as teaching him to write effectively. Those virtues were considered of far more importance then than now, when men may sometimes pursue a university course without them. The teachers under whom Luther studied the *quadrivium,* the remaining four of the seven liberal arts, music, arithmetic, geometry and astronomy together with Aristotelian philosophy, were Trutvetter and Arnold. The completion of these studies earned the degree of Master of Arts. Luther thought highly of his teachers but was severely critical

1. The great portal of the university received a direct hit from aerial bombardment in 1945 and is still unrestored.

of the restricted content of their instruction, bound as they were to Aristotelianism.

The dominant theological tradition at Erfurt was that of the Nominalists, sometimes called the '*Via Moderna*' – though in the half century before the Reformation there is what Joseph Lortz, the Catholic historian, calls 'confusion' (*Unklarheit*), an overlapping of theological schools and a melting of labels. The Nominalist pioneer had been the English Franciscan William of Ockham, and the great fifteenth-century Nominalist Gabriel Biel (d. 1495) had held a chair at Erfurt. According to medieval exegesis, there could be many interpretations of scripture, according to two, three or four levels of interpretation, though a dominant figure in this field was Nicholas of Lyra who, while teaching four levels (literal, allegorical, moral and anagogical), emphasized the importance of the literal interpretation. Humanism had won an early entrance there, and in Luther's day the circle of 'Poets' was already famous, though Luther, concerned no doubt with far more serious issues, seems never to have been a member. Wessel Gansfort, a theologian whose independence has made him seem to many a precursor of the Reformation, had taught in Erfurt in 1445–60.

CHAPTER 5

THE SPIRITUAL CLIMATE

THE SCHOLASTIC TRADITION – AUGUSTINE TO OCKHAM

IN the study of Luther it is a mistake simply to begin with his biography. In order to understand his real significance, all that he wrote, said and did must be seen both as following from the spiritual climate in which he was born, and as a criticism of it. This involved him at two levels, first, that of the nominalist scholasticism of his university and monastery, and secondly, that of the everyday spiritual pastoral practice of the Church, in which, it should be remembered, he was monk and prior, priest and doctor, and town preacher. Luther was not a remote academic, but a deeply committed churchman. He inherited and wholly accepted the scholastic tradition as well as the Church tradition, but was to reject both for a theology that was biblical and patristic and a practice that was evangelical and pastoral.

Neither Roman Catholic nor Protestant scholars have yet arrived at settled judgements on the nature of late medieval thought, and are therefore reluctant to hazard opinions on the exact relation of the immense corpus of rich and varied material to Reformation theology. However, in the current ecumenical debate certain agreed findings are emerging. For our purpose all that is required is a few explanatory pages on scholasticism to relate Luther's reaction to it.

There is a certain harshness of judgement in some modern historical and philosophical schools, almost an impatience with scholasticism. This is due in some measure to the dullness of scholastic writing as well as to the great liberation from authority the scientific movement brought in its train. It is easy to see medieval scholasticism as a system of thought tightly bound in the chains of traditional religious belief to the dogmas of the Church and to the authority of the Church Fathers; it is easy to caricature it as wasting the understanding and intellect in dry formalism and subtle but barren controversies. This harshness is also due to our looking at it when, in the hour of its decay, rendered ineffective by foolish party strife between the schools, it fell before the twin thrusts of the Renascence and the Reformation. These caricatures have enough truth in them to pass as currency.

Nevertheless, scholasticism was a wholly creditable attempt to understand Christianity and to integrate it with current thought. It was a method of philosophical and theological speculation rigorously controlled by fine logical analysis. Scholasticism sought to penetrate the meaning of revealed Christian truth by definition, analogy, logic and dialectic, and by means of these tools to systematize that knowledge.

The Influence of Augustine

The best place to begin the study of the medieval mind is with Augustine of Hippo (354–430). Though he stands within the ancient *imperium romanum*, he is nevertheless the theological father of scholasticism, even if Boethius (d. 525) and Cassiodorus (c.485–c.580) were the mediators between the classical world and monasticism and medievalism. The Catholic Church has never accepted the Augustinian theology in its entirety, yet Augustine's massive intellect and profound Pauline theology, effectualized by powerful spiritual perception and deep religious experience, virtually shaped Western theology. Over and above his deep insight into man's nature and the work and power of God for man's redemption, authenticated in his own experience, Augustine left a further abiding influence in Europe with his Platonic realism and his general approach to philosophical and theological matters. He was mainly responsible for urging the need of dialectic in the study of Christian doctrine. To 'believe' to Augustine meant to 'ponder with assent', and he coined the maxim, 'Understand so that you may believe. Believe so that you may understand.'

He gave the schoolmen the basis of a metaphysic by opposing the views of the Manichees on the problem of evil. The Manichees posited an evil agency eternally opposed to God, and Augustine countered by arguing that God is the sole creator and sustainer, and that evil is essentially a negative idea, being rather the privation of good. In the case of physical evil this results from the imperfect character of creatures; in the case of moral evil, it springs from free will.

Against the Donatists (the Puritans of his day), Augustine fought a fine battle for a sounder doctrine of the Church and for a better doctrine of grace, an achievement which still influences the whole of Christendom. He reminded the world that the Church was a divine institution, whose nature was derived not from the quality of its individual members but from God. It could never fail in the long purposes of God; the gates of hell could not prevail against it. Grace to Augustine was the irresistible operation of God. Man was a fallen creature, mankind a mass of sin. Man could only expect damnation from the hands of a good God, but God in His mercy had chosen to save a few elect souls. Without the operation of divine grace man could but sin, and could do no good works.

Against Pelagianism, which exalted man's nature and saw man as essentially good and free to do good, Augustine intensified his teaching on the fall, original sin and predestination. Every man he understood as fallen in Adam; from which state only the grace of God might deliver him. He championed the absolute supremacy of God who gives all grace, originates man's desire to do God's will, accompanies all his efforts and makes them efficacious, and preconditions any bringing of man to perfection. Though controversy led him to stress God's grace at the cost of man's free will, and though his personal religious experience of conversion made him heavily predestinarian, Augustine did not underestimate man's responsibility before God. More than any other single factor it was the rediscovery of the Augustinian theology by Luther that spelt out the spiritual inadequacy of later speculative scholasticism.[1]

1. The rediscovery of the Augustinian theology in recent years owing to the thinking of Karl Barth and Reinhold Niebuhr had the same effect on liberal theology.

The Influence of Scholasticism

In the times of Augustine the centres of intellectual life in Christendom were Athens, Alexandria, Antioch and Carthage. In medieval Christendom the centres moved northwards to the courts of Theodoric and Charlemagne, to Canterbury, Paris, Oxford and Cologne. This shift meant that medieval Christendom had to acquire a language, a culture, a philosophy, a theology quite new to its traditions, and in addition master the patristic corpus of the East. That whole scholarly activity was what we now call scholasticism. In essence it was a long process of *learning*: it was an ordering and an assimilation by the Frankish-Nordic mind of that immense and alien corpus. The tragedy of scholasticism was that at the end of a thousand years of this remarkable process the new developing world of science demanded a learning attitude that would not merely conserve old knowledge but face fresh empirical evidence. When the learning attitude which had been the strength of the schools for a thousand years ceased to be its vital concern, scholasticism failed. Grabmann argues an internal decay; Gilson sees it as a matter of intellectual confusion and disorder; de Wulf as a lack of minds not of ideas. Whatever the causes, it was a failure. And this failure was one factor which made men's minds the more ready to hear the reformers.

The inherent strength of scholasticism, a titanic strength that eventually became its own undoing, was its rationalism. All the medieval thinkers sought some kind of conjunction of faith and reason in order to preserve for rational man a religion based on revelation and lived by faith. The corrective to an uninhibited rationalism came at an early stage not from an anti-rationalist movement as such but from the works of Pseudo-Dionysius, mediated through the philosopher–mystic John Scotus Erigena (c.810–c.877), who introduced this eastern mystical strain to the West. Pseudo-Dionysius thought of God in terms of mystery and mystical experience, and argued effectively the limitations of rational thinking in expressing the reality of God. This valuable corrective to medieval rationalism influenced Luther some seven centuries later.

Diametrically opposed to this kind of approach was Anselm of Canterbury (c.1033–c.1109), whose rationalism courageously construed an imposing defence of Christianity on the sole basis of reason without necessary recourse to scripture or tradition. He related faith to reason in certain striking expressions which made faith the beginning of understanding: *credo ut intelligam* (I believe so that I may understand); *fides quaerens intellectum* (faith questing for understanding). At this time there developed in the schools the technique of disputation (the system under which Luther was trained). For this technique, as well as for the development of the dialectical method, Abailard (1079–1142) was mainly responsible. His rationalist, logical techniques opened up the controversy of realism and nominalism,[1] a philosophical debate which lasted until Luther's day and beyond.

The introduction of the works of Aristotle into Western Europe in the thirteenth century shattered the Platonic-Augustinian world view and caused the rise of three movements in the schools: first, those who remained determinedly Augustinian; second, those who turned Aristotelian (Averroists, followers of Averroës); and third, those who under Thomas Aquinas (1226–74) made a synthesis of Aristotle and Augustine.

The method of Thomas Aquinas was to present argument, counter-argument and solution, and to seek a harmony between reason and revelation. Philosophically he was an Aristotelian realist, theologically an Augustinian, especially in regard to his theology of God, sin, predestination and grace. Thomas was undoubtedly the greatest of the scholastics, not only for his massive contributions in his *Summae* but also for his *Quaestiones Disputatae*, questions examined in debate. He achieved an exemplary system of conjoining faith and reason. Reason was not the capacity to out-debate an opponent but rather to 'listen to

1. The realist thought of reality in terms of ideas and universals. The nominalist denied that ultimate reality lay there. Ideas (for example, 'power') or universals (for example, 'rose') do not in fact have any real existence; all we know are particular examples of these ideas or universals. The words are simply names (*nomina*, whence nominalism) useful for logical purposes but nevertheless unreal. This controversy had the effect of liberating medieval thought from its Platonism (which was good for theology) to a new Aristotelianism (essential for developing empirical, scientific thought).

everything one encounters', as Dieper expresses it. The kind of conjunction Thomas sought released natural reason to inquire into all the facts of experience. The Thomist approach was later attacked, but has not been invalidated.

Thomas sought to vindicate the Christian faith at the bar of reason, and to answer any and every objection to it. He knew that in this mortal life man could never attain truth, an experience only to be realized in the beatific vision, but he strove to approximate to it. He argued that man had two sources of information about God – God's creation and God's revelation. Creation could be explored and examined: revelation could only be accepted, shown to be reasonable, and, finally, related to other knowledge by analogy. He was essentially rationalist, distrustful of mysticism.

He took the two decisive steps which were responsible for the substitution of Augustinianism by Christian Aristotelianism. The first was to separate faith from reason, though he conjoined them rather than alienated them: the second was to make the senses the sources of all human knowledge. Starting from the senses, he argued the necessity of a first cause, the necessity of the Universal Mind from the unity and order of the world. He saw man as under the authority of a natural law which he must obey for his own well-being, and also under a supernatural law whose demands he could meet only by the grace of God. In this respect his doctrine of sin leaned to concupiscence (as Augustine's) rather than to rebellious self-will (as the Bible). He made room in his thinking for merit, though not in the later sense of merit earned. In the matter of ethics he taught first the theological virtues of faith, hope and charity, possible only through an infusion of grace. The cardinal virtues of prudence, justice, temperance and fortitude he taught as belonging to natural law, but it is fair to say that he often supplements and corrects Aristotle's ethical teaching. He held a high doctrine of the sacraments as the instruments of God's grace.

Roman scholars are inclined to maintain that Luther was not adequately informed on Thomist theology, though it cannot be denied that he attacked the developed form of that theology with unerring certainty. He found himself opposed to the

Thomist school on its loss of the Augustinian doctrine of sin and grace, on its admission of merit, on its 'pagan' ethical teaching (Luther's word), on its idea of the freedom of the will, on its later 'semi-Pelagianism', on its teaching of the doctrine of transubstantiation based not on biblical categories but on a heathen philosophy of substance and accidents, and also on its papalism. Certainly by 1516 Luther was uncompromisingly anti-Thomist. There is no reconciling Luther's biblical evangelicalism with Thomas's philosophical Catholicism.

Duns Scotus (*Doctor Subtilis*), the Scottish Franciscan monk (*c.*1264–*c.*1308), was Thomas's most vigorous critic. He thought of God in terms of will and purpose and act, not in terms of mind and concepts. 'There is no rational argument for those things that belong to faith,' he categorically laid down. Gilson argues that Thomas and Scotus are not so far apart as Scotus believed, though it cannot be denied that Scotus wreaked irreparable damage on the Thomist synthesis. Whatever the eventual assessment of Scotus may be, he certainly prepared the way for the impending dissolution of scholasticism.

This movement was developed further by another English Franciscan, William of Ockham (1300–49), the ablest pupil of Scotus. At an early age he entered into controversy with the Pope on the meaning of apostolic poverty. Excommunicated and expelled from his order, he was sentenced to life imprisonment but escaped from prison and fled to Bavaria, where he continued his feud with the Pope. He resumed his denunciation of the wealth and temporal power of the papacy, arguing that the plenitude of power belonged to the Emperor; it was spiritual not temporal power that Christ gave to Peter.

Ockham found the fatal flaw in Scotism. This was the hypostatization, for the purposes of logical argument, of abstract terms and the consequent multiplication of entities. Ockham pared these down with his celebrated 'razor'; he wanted known realities. This spelt the death of Scotism (and at the same time made Ockham the first prophet of modern science). Ockham argued that man could know nothing of God apart from revelation, and at once the ordered world of Thomas seemed ready to dissolve. This iconoclastic intellectualism of Ockham served to intensify that strange mood of agnostic and pessimistic melancholy that began to creep over Europe at this time. Though stiffly embattled against the Thomistic synthesis, he nevertheless firmly held to the validity of revelation, even its infallibility. His influence on scholasticism, apart from the solvent and destructive tendencies in his theology, lay in separating faith from reason so markedly, setting the being and attributes of God in the realm of faith not reason.

The Influence of Mysticism

German mysticism is accorded an influence on Luther's development by some historians. The evidence they give for this lies in some early enthusiastic remarks by Luther on Tauler (c.1300–61) and other mystics. Naturally a monk would read the devotional writings of the period, Dionysius, Bernard of Clairvaux, Bonaventure and Gerson. Luther certainly did sing their praises early in his life, but closer investigation of the matter shows that his theological views were virtually shaped before he had any real experience of the mystical writings, and further, when he did read them and began to use their vocabulary in his lectures on Romans, the vocabulary will be seen to have been utterly transformed in meaning under the influence of his new Christology and evangelical experience. This will be argued in the next chapter when we study Luther's lectures at the time.

Meanwhile, it is sufficient to say that probably during 1516 he came across a collection of Tauler's sermons, and in 1518 he came across the text of a mystical work (which he believed to be Tauler's) and published it under the title *A German Theology*. Marginal notes of these texts show that the reason for Luther's praise lay in that the mystics' treatment of the anguish of the soul seemed to speak to Luther's travail of soul. But the mystics and Luther meant two utterly different experiences. To the mystics the travail of the soul meant the birth of God in the soul, but to Luther it was related to his *Anfechtungen* (temptations).[1] Luther's travail was owing to the anguish before God of a

1. See pp. 42, 123.

terrified conscience together with his uncertainty of his election. When the mystic spoke of resignation in this context he spoke of a state of mind inculcated within himself as an act of voluntary humility. Luther, on the contrary, understood his plight as a condition in which God had put him. It was in essence an *attack* (*Anfechtung*) on the sinner by God in His holiness and righteousness. Religion to Luther had nothing to do with the cult of peace and blessedness by an individual, but with the elective work of a holy God upon an unholy creature. He was in a different world from the mystics.

This is very closely related to his doctrine of justification, as will be developed in the next chapter. The mystics were thinking of a vigorous preparation of the soul to make it worthy of God's indwelling, Luther of the mercy of God who redeemed Him in Christ while and because he was a sinner. This again found further expression in all that Luther said of the 'sham humility' of the monks, the 'monkey business', when they 'aped' a self-generated humility. True humility to Luther was something a man as man could never seek for himself in this way. True humility was that unconditional self-condemnation which came to a man against his own will when the judgement of God overcame him in the hour of his moral collapse.

Boehmer argued that it was only because Luther misunderstood his antecedents (theological and spiritual) that he was able to use them at all in the clarification of his own religious position. It is important to see that Luther was much more than his antecedents, for all were transmuted under his influence. He was like a plant which takes in only what it needs from its environment and transforms that in the process.

The importance of mysticism in Luther's life lies in the general sensitizing of his spiritual development rather than in any particular influence. The longing to experience God became a consuming passion of his soul, but the God the mystics sought tended to be less the New Testament God and Father of our Lord Jesus Christ whom Luther sought and who found Luther, and more the universal Divine Being, ineffable, sublime. Similarly, the mystics encouraged him in his quest for purity of heart, but Luther far outstripped them in earnestness, and therefore found a different answer, in that there was no answer in a human pursuit after purity, for the farther he journeyed along this road the more he realized his own failing.

Another point on which Luther was helped by the mystics, but again journeyed so much farther as to find a different answer, was suffering. The mystics invented sufferings, tormenting themselves after the manner of an oriental penitent. Luther revolted against such pathological eccentricities. The cross had not to be sought after in this way. The cross was not a device to train the soul. The cross was inflicted upon a man *against* his own thinking and choosing, and this divine activity served to break the natural man and make the spiritual man. So important was this for Luther that he called his theology a 'Theology of the Cross'. The cross was a gift from God and was a proof of membership of the Kingdom. The cross was God's blessing on man.

When Luther met the mystics he had already begun to work out his biblical theology. During the critical years 1516–18 he found congenial and helpful stresses in the late German mystical tradition which strongly marks the theology of his teacher and friend, John Staupitz. In the sermons of Tauler and the little tract *Theologia Germanica* Luther found a 'Theology of the Cross' which had deep affinities with his own teaching – the solidarity of Christians with Christ in suffering, the mortification of the Old Adam in lifelong penitence, the conformity of Christians with Christ. Here was a debt which he never renounced, though he gave these ideas his own accent and bound them into his wider biblical view. He was later to dismiss mysticism as a technique to know God. He described it, with rationalism and moralism, as one of the ladders men erect to reach heaven, contrasting these 'heavenly ladders' with the ladder God had lowered in Christ.

LUTHER'S REACTION TO SCHOLASTICISM

In the above summary of scholasticism from Augustine to Ockham, attention was drawn to the stamp the Augustinian theology imprinted on the Middle Ages. The rise of the medieval school was traced and with it the development of the scholastic method. We saw the synthesis of Aristotle and Augustine, the harmony between faith and reason, and the discord arising from the realist–nominalist controversy. We witnessed the critical power of Scotus disintegrate medieval theology in arguing that scholasticism had failed to resolve the antinomy between faith and reason. The solvents of Ockham were still more effective (or destructive). He dissolved the ordered universe of Thomas and transferred the articles of religion to the province of faith. This mighty intellectual movement had corresponding concomitants in the world of religious practice and belief. The important thing for us now to investigate is Luther's reaction to scholasticism, for it was with the scholastic theology his grave disquiet first grew, not with the scandal of indulgences.

It is an interesting phenomenon that all religious revivals have been Augustinian, deriving from a Pauline theology. The Reformation was no exception. It was the Augustinian theology that spoke to Luther's condition, and his first achievement as a young professor of theology was to root out scholastic theology from the syllabus and establish a new curriculum on the basis of the Bible and Augustine. It was Augustine's stark realism of the stranglehold of sin and its consequences of eternal death, of the total bondage of the will to self, of the overpowering grace of God in His elective mercy seizing and redeeming man, that spoke directly to Luther's condition. Luther built on the theological basis of the Middle Ages.

His relations to the later schoolmen were much less sympathetic, more often hostile. Roman Catholic scholars tend nowadays to suggest that Luther (and most of his contemporaries) had little first-hand acquaintance with Aquinas and that he was more familiar with the Scotist–Ockhamist theology of his day. Nevertheless, in his writings Luther was later to criticize Aquinas and his influence on several important issues and on these occasions he clearly argued from knowledge. First, Luther argued that traditional Catholic theology had undergone a disastrous transmutation under Aristotelian influence and had utterly lost its dynamic, biblical nature. One of the first academic tasks he set himself was to expose this baleful influence ('devilish' was Luther's word) and to banish Aristotle from the theological syllabus. (The violence of his reaction was not unlike that of Tertullian to Greek philosophy thirteen hundred years earlier.) Secondly, Luther rebelled at the intellectualizing and conceptualizing of Christian theology and experience, and sought to restore them to their simple New Testament pattern. He judged the Aristotelian metaphysics of Thomas as irreconcilable with the tenets of the Gospel and rejected his close coordination of grace with merit. Luther traced the doctrine of papal infallibility to the Thomist theology. He also argued that it was Thomas who had provided the philosophical foundation of substance and accidents which had given the doctrine of transubstantiation intellectual currency and respectability, to the injury of a New Testament doctrine of the mass. Luther found here the fundamental cause of the development of the mediatorial priesthood and the loss of the New Testament doctrine of the priesthood of all believers.

It is with Scotus, or at least the Scotist reaction to Aquinas, that we enter the theological climate of the schools in which Luther was educated. Luther had come under the influence of the logic of Scotus, which had split wide open the Thomist synthesis of natural and revealed theology. He granted that the natural man might know that there was a God, that God was moral, and that God punished wickedness, but any saving knowledge of God was given in Christ only to the believing man. This was Scotist if not Scotism.

Luther disapproved intensely of the logic chopping of Scotism which had served to make theology an exercise in reasoning and to divorce its content from the everyday experience of man. He sought to restore theology to the biblical dimension of the confrontation of man by God in normal life as a personal experience, and thereby rescue theology from its limitation to the schools and restore it to the secular life.

The Scotist emphasis on the 'freedom' of God had turned men's thinking away from the idea of God as He is to that of God in action. This influenced Luther strikingly. He was always afraid of God as He is, the *deus nudus* or the *deus purus* as he described Him. Luther always emphasized that we could never know this God; the only God we could know was the *deus reve-latus*, the God revealed in Christ. Luther railed against any and every kind of speculation on the nature of God as He is, and always pointed to the God revealed in Christ for us, crucified and risen. This kind of emphasis could only come where the ground had been prepared by Scotism. There was, however, one serious effect of the Scotist stress on the 'freedom' of God. By analogy it was argued that freedom was the true nature of spiritual man too, and there is little doubt that this Scotist emphasis served not a little to prepare the way for that Pelagian doctrine of merit Luther sought to extirpate.

Scotus denied, or came very near to denying, the medieval doctrine of the sacrifice of the mass in his distinction between Christ's sacrifice on the cross and the Church's offering of the mass. This prepared the way for much Protestant criticism of the mass and allowed Luther to distinguish the once-for-all-ness of Christ's sacrifice. A less beneficial consequence of the same teaching was that by making a distinction between Christ's activity and the Church's Scotus contributed to the vast multi-plication of masses that dominated late medieval practice and the shocking abuses of 'satisfactory' masses. This traffic in paid masses proved to be one of the bitterest contentions between Luther's evangelical theology and late medieval practice.

The brilliant critical faculty of Scotus had served to disinte-grate the medieval synthesis. The paradoxical effect of this was to create what was virtually a blind reliance on the Church as authority, even as ultimate intellectual arbiter. It was as if to say: the synthesis so brilliantly built by Thomas has collapsed, therefore let us no longer put our confidence in man but in the Church. Exactly at this point, Luther sought to correct the Church by setting it under the Gospel. At Leipzig in 1519, in disputation with John Eck, his views were made available to the world. There, he argued that both councils and the Church may err, and that authority lay in scripture, to which councils, fathers and Church must all submit. This was a direct challenge to Scotism.[1]

1. See pp. 176–81.

The real step out of the Middle Ages was taken by Ockham. There are many assessments of Ockham and many views of his possible influence on Luther, but all scholars are unanimous in believing that the divorce of *fides* and *ratio* which Christendom had patiently kept together for one thousand years was now in process. When Ockham denied that human reason can achieve any knowledge of God he generated in Christendom not a mood of inquiry but one of anxiety and uncertainty. This uncertainty had the unexpected effect of driving men not to further questioning (as in the case of Luther), but rather to a general unquestioning obedience to the authority of the Church as the sole and certain possessor of infallible truth.

Luther, too, mistrusted reason as a guide in the realms of divine truth but not for Ockham's reasons. Certainly he never drew Ockham's conclusion of unquestioning obedience to the Church. Rather than throw men unquestioningly into the arms of Mother Church, he pointed them to Christ after opening their eyes. Luther knew perfectly well that the faculty of reason could in itself lead a man to a knowledge of God, but not to a *saving* knowledge of God, which only Christ gives. To Luther, human reason was capable of discerning that there was a God, that he created the world, and that he punished rebellious man. It was capable, too, of arguing logically and profitably. Where it was inadequate was in its attempt to judge the 'foolishness of God' by means of 'the wisdom of man'. Man's reason was to be distrusted only in the matter of his salvation. Luther meant here that when the good, normal, rational man thinks about God he always thinks he can find him by using his intellect; by growing more worthy by means of his goodness and decency, his ethics and morality; and by drawing near to him by means of a sensitized spirituality or religious practices. These ladders he erects to 'approach' or 'draw near' to God. But that is exactly what he cannot do. What this man is doing is devising for himself a god out of his own intellect, his own morals, his own spirituality; good as these things are intrinsically, this god is not the God and Father of our Lord Jesus Christ. Such thinking is idolatrous, and therefore deceives a man, and when Luther dismissed reason as the 'Devil's whore' he meant that it was man's most disastrous

deceiver, though attractive and seductive as all whores must be
if they are in business. In the matter of salvation a man's reason
is a false guide, but in other respects it is the only guide he has,
and God-given.

To put this whole paradox in other words – Christianity runs
counter to pure reason. Its whole *Heilsgeschichte* culminating in
the Incarnation, the Crucifixion, the Resurrection, are scandalous to fallen human reason. But when they are viewed as the
power of God unto salvation, man begins to find *in the practicalities of everyday ordinary life* a remedy for his sin and self-centredness, the healing of a bruised conscience, the certainty of a
constant series of new starts in the forgiving mercy of God, a
fresh dimension to time and eternity, a new way of looking at life,
fresh springs to drink. Here is faith in its quest for understanding. It is at this practical and verifiable beginning that the un-
reasonableness of Christianity begins to make a man's existence
into a life that is reasonable, whole, purposeful. Luther knew
that the Christian Gospel might appear unreasonable. Christ
taught, for instance, in the parable of the labourers in the vineyard, how, rightly, they were grieved at the unreasonable and
preposterous conduct of their employer. A man should get what
he earns, they argued. This is common justice. Yes, says Christ,
in man's dealings with man. But in God's dealings with man, can
any man seek justice, either now or at the gate of eternity? So
then is the mercy of God 'unreasonable', so is the Gospel 'foolishness to the wise'. How Luther resolved this problem will be
seen in our next chapter.

Ockham reacted sharply against the abstractions of the
Scotists and carried Luther with him in his insistence that
theology was a matter not of speculation but of experience.
Ockham's reliance on empirical investigation served to prepare
the way for Luther's empirical analysis of sources and authorities,
biblical and historical. This was to be of supreme importance,
for the battle of the Reformation was fought not on the field of
logic and speculation, but of fact and evidence. It was at this
moment that the modern university came into being and critical
scholarship was born.

Ockham's teaching that man could know nothing of God apart

from revelation, and his emphasis on the infallible authority of revelation, found a profound echo in Luther's mind. (Readers of Barth will know that this is a living issue today.) It further increased the importance of scripture in formulating theology, and of seeing the councils and fathers as testimony to that revelation. It should be recalled that the Bible was not studied in those days and the only knowledge of the fathers was that found in various *catenae*. Wittenberg's senior professor, Carlstadt, admitted that he was a doctor of theology and had never seen a Bible. Luther staggered Christendom when he emerged in 1519 as a master of the biblical text, an authoritative Church historian and a patristic scholar. In these studies he was a pioneer and stamped his influence on Church and university for all time.

When Ockham supported a doctrine of merit Luther was utterly alienated from the contemporary climate. It was precisely at this point that he broke through to his cathartic New Testament experience. He did all he could by standards of supererogation, standards that disturbed his father confessor by their sincerity and purity, as well as making his more easy-going brother monks a little uncomfortable. They disliked Luther's intensity. Their remedy was to push him out begging 'saccum per naccum' to stop his wrestling so much with God. 'Sack on back, brother,' they said, pushing him on to the streets. But no man can escape God or flee Him down the years in cell or street. Luther knew that hard as he tried, and that devotedly and greedily as he fastened on the forgiveness and counsel of Mother Church in perfect belief of their efficacy, the more he was left with a broken and bruised conscience gnawing at his balance of mind. It was as he held on to his aching certainty, and also to his unresolved problem, that God led him to question this entire scheme of salvation. It failed in the acid test of experience, the only test there is. His questions led him to the New Testament and there he found the hand that raised him, the touch that gave him sight. Luther's greatness is that he asked the right questions and was given, therefore, right answers.

Ockham's stress on the freedom of God, and derivatively, the freedom of spiritual man, exercised Luther's mind enormously.

Luther utterly rejected Ockham here and turned to Augustine and Paul for his teaching on the bondage of the will. He was always aware that his doctrine on this matter was his greatest theological contribution to the sixteenth-century debate, and Erasmus realized that it was here that Luther reached his point of no return.[1] Certainly his teaching on the will was basic to his theology and fundamentally opposed to that of Ockham.

Further, Ockham's political views played an important part in the development of the Conciliar Movement[2] of the fourteenth and fifteenth centuries, and influenced Luther as well as the rest of Christendom. He advocated a radical separation of the Church from the world and denied the Pope the totality of temporal power that he claimed. He believed all authority rested in the godly prince and conceded large powers to the layman. He seemed to incline towards the possibility of national Churches under a modified papal monarchy. In all these respects Luther was a disciple of Ockham.

There may be a further Ockhamist influence on Luther. Ockham taught the Real Presence in terms that may be described as consubstantiationist rather than transubstantiationist. This is not to imply that Luther's view was consubstantiationist (a word he never used), but that there certainly was a similarity of opinion. This is noteworthy when one comes to consider Luther's trenchant criticisms of the medieval mass and the mediatorial priesthood.

Because the great schoolmen had been too successful in the thirteenth century they dominated their successors and the later schoolmen were in intellectual servitude to their distinguished predecessors. In the end, with no freedom of thought, they wrangled among themselves until nobody listened to them. The Dominicans followed Thomas to a man. Those who did not were not allowed to teach, and so they ceased doing original work. The Franciscans, on the other hand, were loyal to Scotus or to

1. See p. 228.
2. The Conciliar Movement was an unsuccessful attempt to compel the Curia to govern the Church by general council rather than papal fiat. It originated with French canonists in the twelfth century and reached its peak in the fifteenth.

Ockham his pupil: Oxford was divided between Scotus and Ockham; Clement VI persuaded Paris to condemn Ockham and they burned his books there; but in Germany Ockham reigned supreme. In 1425 the Elector sought to persuade Cologne to study less of the 'old-fashioned Thomas and Albertus' and to direct their studies towards Ockham. This kind of sectarianism proved disastrous. Men were more loyal to their master than to truth. When they got into a tight intellectual corner they wriggled out of it by multiplying verbal distinctions. By the fifteenth century, scholasticism had reached a state of senility, but she was jostled to her grave by her squabbling sons as a result of the sectarianism of her dissident adherents. These later schoolmen lived in secluded retirement, speculating on abstruse problems, not caring whether the laity were interested at all. They gave brilliant answers to clever questions which none but they ever dreamed of asking. Given over to barren logic, they loved arguing – even the absurd. The kind and sympathetic Thomas More said that to read the schoolmen was like milking a billy-goat into a sieve. Every schoolboy knows of the debate on how many angels might dance on a needle point, and of the argument between a father and son at supper time as to how many eggs were on the table. Six eggs were in a bowl before them. The son declared that there were twelve, and challenged the less educated father to find a flaw in his argument. The father admitted wryly he could not fault his son's logic, but, with shattering realism, said rather charmingly that he would eat the six eggs on the table before them and leave his son to eat the six eggs he had so cleverly created by his logic.

Scholasticism was now a spent force unable to meet the demands of the hour. The fear of heresy, the encroachments of civil powers, the now highly lucrative study of law, the poverty of scholars, all contributed to the decline of theology. But no factor weighed more heavily than the unreal theology taught. Like bad currency in its effect on good currency, bad theology drove out the good. By the sixteenth century men were thrilling to the classics. They found the philosophy of Cicero better and fresher than all the subtleties of a Scotus. They found the deductive reasoning of the schoolmen unacceptable because they felt themselves unable to accept the premises with which the school-men started. The schoolmen were utterly unable to meet the intellectual demands of their own day and generation. Natural science was born and metaphysics died, and the old learning was flouted, ridiculed and overthrown by humanism. The age of logic and speculation was past. The battles and controversies of the Reformation were to be fought out over questions of fact and truth, whether a passage of scripture or a point of doctrine. Theology could no longer be a vast corpus of dogma deduced from elementary data. What was meant by elementary data? What could a reasonable man make of them? Were they true? Did they meet the acid test of experience? These were the questions the reformers asked in their studies, their pulpits, their lecture rooms – and answered. The scholastic theologians were no match for the reformers and could put up no fight. They were pedants who had lost the ear of the people, and, like Aunt Sallies at the fair before the lusty village youth, they went down before the energy of the equally lusty and irreverent scholars of the Renascence. Under the onslaught of reformer and humanist, scholasticism lay down and died. No attack was more effective than Luther's. Luther not only laid bare its inadequacies but at the same time restored a biblical theology.

More and more, research is showing how intricate is the theological and spiritual jungle of the late fifteenth century, the importance of theologians who cannot be tied within earlier theological categories, such as Nicholas of Cusa and John Gerson. It is a time of melting categories and we need more monographs to bring out the characteristics of the later scholastics, and not least of those with whom Luther had direct contact. Although Augustine is a main ingredient in all medieval theology, it does seem as though there was an important revival of Augustinianism in the fourteenth century, and a number of theologians – Wyclif but also Bradwardine, Holcot, Gregory of Rimini – are now emerging as contributors to the return to Augustine in the later Middle Ages. Luther's own personal discovery of the importance of Augustine has now to be seen against this general revival and influence.

Just as it took a Paul, scholar and rabbi, to tell the world exactly and fully the relationship of the New Testament to the Old, so it took a Luther, who had been through both scholasticism and monasticism, to know exactly where both were wrong and how under God they might be redeemed. Luther was the most catholic and conservative of men. When he discovered that in his case the whole scheme of salvation did not work (the only test of its truth, validity or claims), and wrestled with it until it was given him where it was wrong and where the truth lay, he imagined that the Church would thank him and that she would promptly set about putting things to rights. He found instead that the Church attacked him! He fought the Roman Church in the interests of the Church, and sought to establish her authority (1) on the basis of the Bible understood and studied, (2) in the light of an inspired patristic tradition and (3) with the help of reason and common sense. It is important to see that what Luther did was to provide thinking, reasonable men with better answers than the patently false ones of his day. Some of his work is polemical, not simply because he was attacked and fought back, but because a large part of it was the removal, even the demolition, of accretions and innovations that had served to blind men to the reality of the Gospel, for example, meritorious works, saint worship, Mariology, paid masses for the dead, indulgences and Purgatory. Half the Church resisted (or was persuaded to resist) Luther's theology, and consequently polemical writings and disputations arose. In these battles the great catchwords of the Reformation were sparked off, for example, 'the authority of the Word of God', 'grace alone', 'faith alone', 'the sole mediatorship of Christ', 'the bondage of the will', 'the priesthood of all believers'. They arose in a situation where the authority of the Church was assuming pretentions to be infallible and above scripture, Catholic tradition and sound reason. This supreme authority was denied and resisted by Luther, and in the great argument which ensued these phrases summarized the truths denied or modified by the papist protagonists. The catchwords of the argument should not be regarded as having intrinsic value, nor should they be employed in current ecumenical debate as summarizing the Protestant position. They arose as terse and effective expressions of that larger truth of

God's redemptive work in Christ in the hour of its betrayal. They express no new Protestant truth but safeguard common Catholic truth.

*

It was in such a world of secular and spiritual change and uncertainty that the young graduate of twenty-two came to believe that the only way open to him to find the meaning of life and to give himself to God was to become a monk. Against his father's advice, and after much inner conflict, Luther turned his back on the world and on a promising university career to offer himself wholly and unreservedly to God. Some biographers make much of Luther's experience of a terrible thunderstorm, or of his accidentally falling in the country far from medical help when his dagger severed an artery in his thigh, and of a sudden dedication to take vows if his life were spared. It is not very clear from the reminiscences available what really happened. A careful study of all the evidence, late and early, rather gives the impression of a long struggle by a religious young man to find God, and of his quiet resolution to offer himself wholly to God in the only way known to him at the time.

PART TWO

MONK AND PROFESSOR
1505–17

CHAPTER 6

THE RELIGIOUS BECOMES PROFESSOR

ON 17 July 1505 Luther applied for admission to the Order of the Augustinian Eremites in Erfurt,[1] one of five monasteries in the town. This monastery enjoyed much prestige. It was peopled mainly by scholars and clergy, and the hard work (except for token disciplinary chores) was done by illiterate lay brothers. Luther was kept in the hostel to observe the state of his soul, to test his vocation and to see whether he would be able to endure the harshness of the discipline. When his father learned of his son's irrevocable step he was filled with a furious anger at the utter futility and waste of it all, and cut him off 'from all paternal grace and favour' for his rank disobedience. The poor father received a far more terrible blow at this time when two of his sons died of the plague. In the hour of his grief some Job's comforter told him that Martin in like manner was taken dangerously ill and was at the point of death, and pointedly went on to persuade him that the hand of God's disapproval could only be restrained if Hans were to 'offer something holy to God'. The grief-stricken man relented, and as a solace 'offered' Martin to God, or at least accepted his son's decision as a *fait accompli*. It is hard to imagine how a sensible man such as Hans Luther could be harried and humbugged by such superstition: how men could allow themselves to be suffocated by such primitive theology. But this same Martin was to sweep all that out of a large area of Christendom within a few short years, as well as emptying the monastic strongholds of reaction.

In September 1505 he received the tonsure and took the cowl. As a clerical novice he was taught all the prescribed acts of reverence: how, when and before whom to bend the knee or

1. In 1945 the monastery received a direct hit during aerial bombardment. Part of the cloister was destroyed, including Luther's cell, but it is all now restored.

throw himself prostrate on the ground; to go about with eyes downcast; never to eat or speak except at times prescribed; never to laugh; how to speak with signs; to do the various nominal chores, for example, scrubbing floors, helping in the kitchen; to keep up a happy pretence of humility; even to go through the (quite unnecessary) motions of begging bread in the street.

His whole life was ordered strictly and completely by his preceptor. Great stress was laid on confession and on the reading and study of the Bible. He enjoyed a single cell, nine feet by six, in which were one chair, one table, one candlestick and a straw bed. He had no heating in his cell, a very severe discipline in a German winter. He ate twice a day only, once a day on fast days (of which there were some hundred in the year).

A complete authoritarian filling-in of every moment of life tends to resolve questions and personal difficulties by removing any opportunity of preoccupation with the self. As Luther later said, the devil leaves a monk alone during his first year. Yet, paradoxically, a monk is in far greater danger of falling into sin and guilt than a man of the world. Luther had entered the monastery because he was in anxiety about his soul, but the monastery served to sharpen these anxieties. He could never feel sure that he had actually confessed all his sins, that he had done all that was required of him. His preceptor was a kind old man of much experience. He silenced Luther by refusing to listen to his continual confessions, whilst assuring him always of God's mercy and forgiveness, pointing out that it was not the case that God was angry with Luther but that Luther was angry with God. Helpful and true as all these assurances were, they failed to cure him, because they failed in their diagnosis of his real trouble. Luther was right in believing that he could never know all his sin. Consequently he could never enjoy that blessed state of forgiveness, because some of his sins remained unconfessed and therefore unforgiven, and for all his best endeavour he could only earn the wrath of a pure and righteous God meeting his sin. He was right in believing that he could never know that he had done all that in him lay, and right in believing that he could therefore earn God's condemnation only. All this was pure Augustinian teaching. It was not that he was a bad or faithless

Catholic; he was simply too good and too faithful and too conscientious a Catholic. He believed it all. As long as Luther remained within the lines of current Catholic practice, which he was later to regard as essentially a form of Judaism, a salvation by works and ethics, his spiritual disorder (which is Everyman's, intensified) remained largely undiagnosed and was only alleviated, never cured. He broke through this neither at the confessional box nor at the altar but in his study. He had, however, much farther to go yet. His preceptor helped him with books, such as the legends of the fathers, and discussed with him other 'difficult' cases he had had. He even spoke sympathetically of John Huss on one occasion, obviously seeing some affinity with Luther's evangelical theology, and condemned the execution of Huss, assuring Luther that many others in the Order felt as he did. All our information shows an earnest and zealous young monk, guided by a kindly and godly father, and wholly approved by vigilant and competent monastic authorities.

In September 1506, one year after taking the cowl, Luther professed the vows of poverty, chastity and obedience, and proceeded through the orders of sub-deacon, deacon and priest. When, on 2 May of the following year, he was ordained priest in the Cathedral at Erfurt, his father was invited to the ceremony, and though he appeared with a fine company of some fifty horse and gave a handsome gift to the monastery, even at that late stage he openly showed his disapproval of his son's self-chosen career.

After his ordination Luther was not to work in silence for the perfection of his soul, but was to resume studies in the school connected with the monastery. This proved to be the pattern of his life. He was born to preach and teach. Fortunately his spiritual mentors saw this and gave him the opportunity to study and work. This will always stand to their credit. That God set his seal to their judgement is plain for all to read and see. He attended lectures on Lombard's[1] *Sentences*, given by John

1. Peter Lombard (c. 1100–1160), the Paris theologian, known mainly for his four books on the *Sentences*. They cover (1) the Trinity, (2) Creation and Sin, (3) Incarnation and the Virtues, (4) the Sacraments and Last Things, and contain a wealth of patristic learning. Four-fifths of the book consists of

Nathin, a pupil of the famous Tübingen Ockhamist, Gabriel Biel. He studied the *Glossa Ordinaria*,[1] the *Collectarium* of Biel,[2] the *Quaestiones* of d'Ailly[3] and Ockham, with other of Ockham's writings. This is all very difficult material but Luther read it eagerly. The interest of these books lay in that they discussed the very problems which were besetting Luther's mind. Much theology a modern student may have to study strikes him as raising issues which are dead, or at least remote and academic, such as the complex systems of the Gnostics or the disputations of the scholastics, but in Luther's case his studies spoke to his condition. To give instances, they dealt with questions such as whether a man can achieve the perfect love of God and earn the grace of God; whether sins are actually done away with in absolution; whether the will is really free to do what is right; whether a soul is elected and predestined to salvation. Luther found no compelling answer to these problems in Ockhamism,

---

quotations from Augustine. It became the standard textbook of the Middle Ages and almost every theologian of repute was expected to comment on it. It was later superseded as a textbook only by the *Summa* of Aquinas.

1. The standard glosses of the biblical text which were universally studied.

2. Gabriel Biel (1420–95), the founder of the university of Tübingen, was one of the last great scholastic philosophers and theologians. Luther's marginal notes to Biel's commentary on Lombard's *Sentences*, *Luthers Randbemerkungen zu Gabriel Biels Collectarium*, were published in a facsimile edition as a supplement to the Weimar Ausgabe, Weimar, Hermann Böhlaus, 1933.

3. Pierre d'Ailly (1350–1420), a Paris theologian and Ockhamist, who devoted his life at much personal cost to the movement of conciliar reform. Towards the end of his life he wrote *A Tract on the Reformation of the Church*, a work which had much influence in England and Germany. He took the Ockhamist view that the existence of God was not rationally demonstrable and that God should be understood in terms of will rather than intellect. Sin he interpreted as activity against the will of God. It could be maintained that in his view the authority of clergy derived from Christ and not the Pope, and also that in his conciliarist outlook generally, as well as in his Ockhamist slant on God's arguability and the nature of sin, he exercised some influence on Luther. There was another fascinating side to d'Ailly. He was a geographer and astrologer, and propounded the view (later studied by Columbus) that India could be reached by sailing west instead of east. *Quaestiones* refers to the medieval way of raising questions for disputation and discussing them by the method of dialectic before arriving at an answer.

nor even the beginning of an answer. It was his glory that he steadfastly refused to accept a theology of salvation which did not fit the facts of his own historical experience. It was precisely because he held on to his doubts long enough, and persisted to set the right sort of questions to orthodoxy long enough, that God broke through his questions with answers, his perplexity with certainty. At this moment, the autumn of 1508, Luther was suddenly called to the chair of moral philosophy at the new university of Wittenberg, but his spiritual and intellectual frame of mind was still no clearer. His doubts were more informed, and therefore sharper, but his darkness was more profound.

Wittenberg was the capital of the Electorate, but a tiny and unpropitious site for a new university. It is today still a backward town of two streets. In 1513 the town register showed a population of about 2,000: there were 172 burghers entitled to brew beer, 210 small householders, 26 of them in the suburbs, and 56 cottagers (non-taxable), making only 382 tax-paying persons. There were two monasteries, together with the famous Castle Church, renowned for its unique collection of 5,005 relics. Among these, appropriately advertised and published, were pieces of the burning bush of Moses, 9 thorns from the crown of thorns, 35 fragments of the cross, some hay and straw from Christ's manger. There were remnants of the manger, the cradle and the swaddling clothes of Christ; hair from the Blessed Virgin, phials of her milk, fragments of her petticoat and other garments; 204 pieces of the bodies of the innocent babes of Bethlehem, including one body intact. Any tourist organization nowadays would make much of such a venue, but it was not the singularity of the relics that was important, but their spiritual potency. 127,709 years and 116 days remission of time in purgatory could be secured by adoring them, saying the formula of prayers – and making the appropriate payment. This indulgence also carried with it the Portiuncula Indulgence of 1398 which promised 'remission of punishment and guilt for all repented sins'. Closely connected with the chapter of this church was the new university, founded (not unlike the university of Durham) as far as possible on ecclesiastical benefices for purposes of economy. The Augustinians provided two professors:

Staupitz (very much an absentee professor) occupied the chair of the Bible, and Luther that of moral philosophy in the faculty of arts. Luther had to lecture on Aristotelian ethics for four periods a week, and had responsibility for the disputations. After obtaining his *baccalareus biblicus* in March 1509 he had in addition to lecture on the Bible. He finished his own theological study by passing his examination on the *Sentences*, but before he was to read his inaugural lecture, he was suddenly recalled to Erfurt. He returned in the same spiritual and intellectual frame of mind in which he had left a year earlier.

Luther received rather a cool welcome on his return to his Alma Mater (1509), his former brethren refusing to recognize his degree of *sententarius*[1] from this obscure upstart of an institution calling itself the university of Wittenberg. (Only Oxbridge men here!) His former teacher, Nathin, unlike the others, was having none of this nonsense. He knew what was in the man. And so we find Luther reading lectures on the *Sentences* to a small group of monks. We still possess the book he used as well as his volume of Augustine. It was his practice (general at the time) to write in the margin his own lecture material, and from these notes we may discern the growth of his critical faculty, which enabled him to establish, incidentally to his main studies, the spuriousness of two works formerly believed to have been written by Augustine. Nevertheless his position was not unlike that of many another Ockhamist, and, except for starting to learn Hebrew (later to bear important consequences), he still breathed the same old air of Erfurt.

A grave tragedy overtook Erfurt this year (1510), a warning skirmish in the great battle that was to end in the lamentable Peasants' War of 1525. In January 1510 craftsmen and apprentices rebelled in open conflict against the misrule of the Town Council. Their grievances were legitimate, and force was the only weapon to hand that might effect some change in their plight. In the course of the revolt they executed the chairman of the Council and later burned down and totally destroyed the magnificent great hall of the university with its fine library.

1. *Sententarius* meant the qualification to lecture on the *Sentences*, which in effect meant a licence to lecture in the university.

Luther never forgave these outrages, and dated the decline and fall of the fine old university from this moment. Erfurt was later to suffer again from rebellion. The episode shows an important and determinative aspect of Luther's attitude to social reform, a side of his character wrongly assessed by many historians, social historians in particular. He hated violence and mob law. His sympathy was with the peasant and the new type of working man arising in the towns, but he never agreed that the justness of their cause gave them the right to self-determination at the price of law and order as well as of human lives. In Luther's view, to destroy law and order, or even to jeopardize its ability to function, was the most complete social disaster, even if the law seemed harsh or unfair. The remedy lay in working together for a better and more just society, not in destroying it.[1] Nobody hated and feared 'Lord Everybody'[2] more than Luther. Nobody would be more opposed to the so-called People's Courts of the Communist world today than he, were he alive, yet nobody would be more sympathetic to lawful and just claims. The answer was not as simple as transferring power from the prince to the peasant, for both were capable of abusing it. It was a matter of submitting both to the authority of the law, and law to Luther was a divine dispensation.

Reform was in the air at this time, but with the exception of Spain, where some progress was made, the papal curia would appear effectively to have stifled it everywhere. It was not reform which interested the papacy, but politics and war, music and hunting, comedy and carnival. The failure of the papal office at this decisive hour was lamentable. Among attempts at reform was one to bring the 'lax' houses and the 'strict' houses of the Augustinian orders into line. Several houses resisted, chief among them those at Nürnberg and Erfurt, on the grounds that they had already reformed their practice and did not want the general levelling up of all houses. After local efforts failed, Luther was instructed to accompany an older brother to Rome to take the appeal there. He gladly accepted the task with the prospect of a pilgrimage to Rome.

1. See pp. 236–45 for a fuller treatment of this important point.
2. 'Herr Omnes.'

Luther had a month in Rome, four weeks of steady disillusionment. The simple, devout, learned monk sought anxiously to unburden his soul in confession and to seek pastoral advice and enlightenment, but all he found were miserable, ignorant, unlettered men unable properly to hear or handle any confession, much less his own. When he celebrated the mass he was pushed around by priests anxious to grab their quota and gabble through their stint. 'Get a move on, you,' they thundered at him, wanting his altar when he had but reached the Gospel. His normality created a bottleneck in the production line of masses. He once saw seven masses performed in one hour; *opera operata* indeed! He dutifully faced his due pilgrimages to the seven main churches of the city along abominable roads and through vile conditions, fasting all the way, and ending with holy communion, all in the prescribed single day. He crawled on his knees up the twenty-eight steps of the *Scala Sancta*, the staircase Christ was supposed to have ascended to Pilate, saying a Pater Noster on each step and kissing each piously. This drill was reckoned to free a soul from purgatory at one fell deliverance, and the young man was occasioned some concern that the only soul he knew dwelling in that miserable place was his old grandfather. There is a story, not well authenticated though it accords with the general picture, of how when he reached the top of the steps he asked himself the corroding question, 'How do I know all this is true?' Luther's son Paul attested most carefully in 1544 that his father told him that it was while he was ascending these steps that the text from Habakkuk struck him, 'The righteous shall live by his faith', the text which led him back to St Paul and which he finally resolved in Wittenberg.[1] Every step Luther took was punctuated by devastating questions, a sure proof that the hand of the Lord was laid upon him for good. He ran, to quote him, 'like a mad saint through all the churches and catacombs', and dutifully went through all that was expected of a northern bumpkin visiting Rome for the first time. He was horrified to learn of the goings-on of Pope Alexander VI and of his illegitimate children. He was distressed by the frivolous unbelief of

1. Otto Scheel, *Dokumente zu Luthers Entwicklung*, Tübingen, 1911, 2nd edn 1929, No. 2.

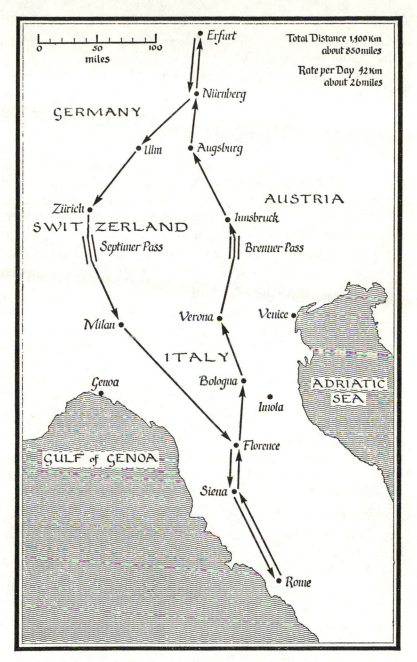

Luther's Journey to Rome

the Roman priests and the scandalous conduct of the cardinals. What he heard and saw of the common people seemed equally low, even dissolute. He was aghast to see people performing their natural functions at the street corner with no more privacy than a stray dog. He was shocked and horrified, distressed and disillusioned, by all he saw and heard.

It is interesting to consider the things Luther never noticed at all. He seems to have made no comment on the art or architecture of Renascence Rome or on the historic sites of classical Rome. He was greatly impressed by hospitals he visited in Florence, not only for their godly and pastoral care of the sick, but for their standards of cleanliness and nursing. One is inclined to think that hygiene and nursing originated with Florence Nightingale but the following words speak for themselves:

The hospitals of the Italians are built like the palaces, supplied with the best food and drink, and tended by diligent servants and skilful physicians. The painted bedsteads are covered with clean linen. When a patient is brought in, his clothes are taken off and given to a notary to keep honestly. Then they put a white bed-gown on him and lay him between the clean sheets of the beautifully painted bed, and two physicians are brought at once. Servants fetch food and drink in clean glass vessels, and do not touch the food even with a finger, but offer it to the patient on a tray. Honorable matrons, veiled, serve the poor all day long without making their names known, and at evening return home. ... They also have foundling asylums, where children are well sheltered, and nourished and taught; they are all dressed in uniform and most paternally provided for.[1]

About the end of January 1511 the two brothers began their long, silent walk back home, when Luther enjoyed the plains of Lombardy and the countryside of southern Europe in the spring. At Nürnberg they reported the outcome of their visit and reached Erfurt in April. Here Luther counselled peace with Staupitz, now at Wittenberg, but the brothers were not so easily mollified. Staupitz, true to his gentle self, wavered and was reluctant to pursue the controversy by allowing himself the freedom of action Rome had granted. It is generally believed that Staupitz

1. Quoted by Preserved Smith, *The Life and Letters of Martin Luther*, Boston, 1911, pp. 17–18.

arranged for Luther (with Lang, the monk who had accompanied him to Rome) to be transferred to Wittenberg. The matter died down without leaving any bitterness.

Luther learned two things from this controversy and its associated visit to Rome. First, even all that Catholicism could offer (including a visit to the eternal city itself) had been unable to still his disquiet. This was momentous, for in his search for peace he now realized the brute fact that the Church had lost the key to the Kingdom. He said later, 'Like a fool I took onions to Rome and brought back garlic.' It was because he could sum up his disillusionment in these words and refused to talk himself into making garlic other than what it was, that he would one day be charged with the precious truth from God. Secondly, he learned in his exile from Erfurt what the compact majority can do to a man bold enough to disagree. This stand was to foreshadow that greater stand he was to make against Pope and Emperor some ten years later. We do not know much about his feelings when he was transferred again to Wittenberg in the summer of 1511, but his resistance to the majority and his loyalty to Staupitz set him on that higher inward plane of the authority of a great integrity. Be that as it may, close contact with the good Staupitz gave him much-needed spiritual help. He lived to turn the despised Nazareth of Wittenberg into the spot where Christendom would ever remember that it was here on that 'miserable heap of sand' that Martin Luther initiated the reform of Christendom and almost succeeded.

At Wittenberg, Staupitz informed Luther that he intended him to become a doctor and a preacher. Under the famous pear tree in the garden (Wittenberg was too poor to have cloisters) he persuaded the reluctant Luther to assume the office of preacher and to acquire the degree of doctor of theology, remarking darkly that this would provide him with the opportunity of saying what he wanted to say. Staupitz had no means of paying the required academic fees (nor of course had Luther) and appealed to the prince successfully. But Frederick laid down the condition that Luther, who was now twenty-eight years old, should occupy the chair for the duration of his life. Eventually, in June 1512, Luther assumed his new office in Wittenberg. He was allocated the room of his predecessor, Staupitz, a room in the tower which remained his study till his death, the room from which he stormed the papacy, guided the Reformation and prepared his lectures for the university and his sermons for the Church.

All the formalities were not yet over. In October, he received his licence to become a candidate for a doctorate, swore allegiance to the Church and walked to Leipzig to receive the necessary promotion fees of fifty gulden. On 19 October at 7 a.m. the promotion ceremony was observed in the aula of the university, where he swore on oath not to teach strange doctrines. Here he received a closed Bible and an open Bible, the symbols of his work, as well as the academic hat and silver ring, symbols of his academic authority. Three days later he was admitted to Senate, and on the following Monday at 7 a.m. began his lectures on Genesis. His appointment to such high honour and office at so early an age caused a stir, but that was nothing compared with the stir going on under that academic hat. He still 'did not know the light', to use his own words. He had gone through dark doubt in the last seven years. The next seven were to be far worse, except that they were to produce the sweet reward of doubt resolved in faith, and fear swallowed up in hope.

CHAPTER 7

THE DAWN OF LUTHER'S REFORMATION CONSCIOUSNESS

THOUSANDS of men and women before Luther had entered the cloisters to put themselves right with God and to avert the final condemnation on the day of judgement. The occasion, as in Luther's case, was as often as not some emotional experience, sometimes gross sin, which had suddenly brought them face to face with death and judgement. Just as the reasons for Luther's entering were the same as those of most of the others, so were his experiences in the monastery. As countless thousands before him, he had doubts and scruples. In Luther's case, none of the prescribed, accepted and proved methods ever resolved his, but rather intensified them. He found it difficult to accept on authority teaching which he did not find true to the facts of his own experience. What evidence was there, he asked himself, for God and His activity in the world? What was wrong in a world of war and want, and sin and selfishness? What was man here for? Was there any purpose to it all? He stood a simple empiricist and experimentalist. He knew he was half-blind, he knew he was a sinner; this he knew to be as true of all men. Did God care? How did God handle men? Was the Church right in her theology and in the handling of souls? Has she lost her original commission and the truth of her mission? By his sheer honesty in facing up to these painful questions, by his refusal to be satisfied with half-truths, or to be intimidated by authority, Luther was to arrive at his evangelical theology.

The most important means of bringing peace to the troubled heart was the confessional. Luther had been taught that the moment the priest whispered *deinde te absolvo* (I now absolve you) all sins were driven from the soul, except, of course, what was described as the *fomes* or 'tinder' of original sin. This remained and could always be sparked off, but being only tinder for sin it was not actual sin. Luther's heart-ache was that he knew all this better than anybody else, but he knew equally well that he never felt certain of its reality. Therefore for him, in his condition of mind, it was not true. He did not conclude that the doctrines were false, but rather that there must be something wrong with him, or that his confession was inadequate – at any rate that the fault lay somewhere in him or with him, and not in the teaching of the Church. And so he continued struggling.

He turned to the other well-tried means – private chastisement, fastings, vigils, prayers. As Loyola, he wanted not only to propitiate God by doing extra works, but to compel God to remove from his soul the consciousness of guilt. He failed. But it was himself he blamed, not the methods. He tried harder and succeeded only in ruining his health. The bones stood out of him like those of the overworked enhungered old nags one meets in Mediterranean countries. He found that the more earnestly he tried to make God gracious towards him, the more real did the day of judgement loom in his thoughts, the more intensely did the fear of hell sear his soul.

Luther often attributed the chief cause of his distress of soul to the notion that man can do everything he wills to do, and that he is able to earn the reward of eternal blessedness by his own works and efforts. He believed, with the Ockhamists, that the absolute fulfilment of the Ten Commandments was possible, even the further command to love God with the whole heart. This he imbibed in his monastery. A further consequence of the Ockhamist theology was that God was conceived in terms of arbitrary will. Good was not good *in eo ipso* but because God had willed it. Man's salvation was simply the arbitrary choice of God, but God had enabled man to earn His favour by meritorious acts, setting His seal to man's acceptance in the sacraments. Luther rejected this idea of God. He felt an overpowering fear of Him, a trembling awareness of Him as the terrifying destructive power the sinner senses before his Holy God. He was like the moth longing for the flame, yet being scorched to death by its proximity. Was God going to scorch him to death? So terrifying was his confrontation with God that he once likened it to seeing the Devil: 'When I looked for Christ it seemed to me I saw the Devil.'

A Christian will ask, but did he not learn of grace? We have to remember that spiritual and academic teachers alike all taught that a man had first to earn grace by doing everything that was in him; 'all that in him lay' was the technical phrase. This only sharpened Luther's anguish. How could he or any man ever know he had done 'all that in him lay'? Was it a quantitative matter at all, or a qualitative one? How could a man ever know that he had done enough to merit grace? Anyone who knows the force of these questions knows that he is harder on his own achievements and failings than any friend would be, harder even than God is! All this only shows that in the matter of God's handling of man, the wrong questions were being put.

Luther could have snatched at the straw of 'gallows repentance'. The Church was aware that if the fear of eternal punishment was always kept alive, this very fear would impel men into some kind of repentance, even if half-hearted. The theologians and father confessors knew that confession wrested out of a human soul under pressure was no pure confession at all – in fact, they had a word for it. It was *attritio* not *contritio*, attrition not contrition. Contrition they taught, and quite properly, was only the fruit of a pure love of God and a hatred of all evil and sin. But this was rare. So they taught a method of upgrading attrition into contrition by means of a systemized sacramentalism through the confessional. Confession trained the soul to attain the pure love of God and to know genuine contrition. Luther knew all about this. But he stood like a man with a lame horse; he could not ride him, he could not carry him.

He also knew Biel's 'hangman's doctrine', a desperate theology which taught that a man could procure the love of God if he devoted himself to St Bernard's prescribed method to the death. But Luther questioned whether God had ever meant to put a human soul on the rack to stretch and torture it to the size required. All the theorizing that went with these practices broke down before the acid test of experience. Luther knew nothing at all from his own experience of the transition in the confessional from the fear of hell and judgement to the rapturous emotion of the love of God. Although he could never have used the word, such a doctrine of redemption was 'neurotic'; it was wish fulfilment improperly related to reality. He doggedly struggled on, surrendering nothing. Few realize the long years of anguish he paid for his freedom; we simply live on his achievement.

It would appear from contemporary evidence, as well as from what he said in later years, that in these dark days Luther began to invest his hope in the Bible. True, he read the Bible differently then from the way he was to read it later. He seems at this stage never to have realized that the problems which tormented him were problems that were posed not by the Bible but by Christian practice. He saw only a demanding, angry God, and not a gracious, merciful Father. This influenced his picture of Christ, whom he envisaged as the judge rather than 'the Lamb that taketh away the sins of the world'. He was later to hold these twin concepts of the wrath of God and the love of God in an equilibrium which was to intensify both realities: God as holy judge, God as merciful deliverer.[1] Even Moses, in the old dispensation, though he had an experience of the burning, consuming presence of God, the God consuming yet never consumed, was given in those experiences the saving redemptive word of mercy and deliverance for his people. Luther had not yet grasped this paradox of love and wrath. He had not understood that the Light that blinded Moses was to prove the Light of the World.

There were other ways of finding peace with God. He could climb the mystic's ladder and gaze rapturously at the naked majesty. And to climb it he tried. But he found nothing hovering there, and, assuming that he was much too impure to attain the dizzy heights others claimed to reach, returned to his starting point, not unlike Noah's dove, who 'found no place for the sole of her foot'. He was later to become a staunch opponent of the mystical path as a way to God. None of the traditional soulcures helped – not even the sacrament of the mass.

The reader might pause for a moment and reflect. Lesser men toned down the demands of their consciences in varying degrees;

1. See pp. 105–8, 265.

lesser men also accepted what they were told. Had Luther been content merely to do his best and to resolve his conflict by submission to authority, the emancipation of Christianity from intellectual bondage and spiritual tutelage, with academic freedom to interpret her history and theology, would most certainly have been delayed for years, would even have been considerably modified when it made its final appearance. The capacity to want to know the truth even when it hurt was what distinguished Luther. This disquietude with the theology and practice of Christianity, this refusal to be subdued, this following the argument wheresoever it leads, is the permanent pattern for progress. At the present time Christian theology and practice are undergoing heavy criticism at the hands of the philosophers, the humanists and the moralists. The real answer is not to reassert the traditional fundamentals, no matter how cleverly or more vociferously than before, for these are the very statements which are not weathering the years. We need to allow the criticisms full play, and out of that new dialogue we shall all emerge into a larger grasp of the issues. It may be unnerving for a man to discover how right the critics are, but the very facing of their arguments full front may serve to convince him that the armour wherein he trusted is worthless in the day of battle, and like David realize that his very nakedness turns out to be his strength.

There was in Luther's character a saving strain of conservatism. He would let no dogma go, not even a scholastic opinion, merely because it was not true to his own experience, or even because it was false to his own experience. He blamed himself and clung tenaciously to his authorities. This was what made him not a prototype of liberal Free Churchmanship but of Catholicism reformed. (If Roman Catholicism as a whole, instead of a few of its theologians, were to concede that Luther was a reforming Catholic, a wholly fresh atmosphere would be created in Christendom.) It was Luther's conservative loyalty to his authorities that eventually broke the impasse. It was the authority of the Bible that modified the authority of the Church and her tradition.

Luther was in deep spiritual agitation at this time. He was drawn to the Augustinian idea of predestination as a view which best explained his own experiences as well as the biblical teaching. Biel he found inconsistent and wavering, making sometimes the divine and at other times the human element the determining factor in man's salvation. To Augustine any reason for the divine choice was a mystery beyond accessibility to the human mind, but it was a choice made in perfect justice. The choice was made not only to grace but to eternal glory. It depended not on human acceptance but on the eternal decree of God, and was therefore infallible, without thereby violating man's free will. This doctrine was later to be of great comfort to Luther but now it was one of exquisite torture. He had always believed as a spiritual axiom that a good God is bound to accept a good man doing all he can. But it began to dawn upon him that this was not the teaching of the Bible, nor was there much support for it even in the Fathers. God became for him a Being not only incomprehensible in His nature but also in His activity. At this hour he became almost fatalist, determinist, a state of mind he was to outgrow. He knew that he was impotent to change the fate determined for him from all eternity, and what was far worse, could never *know* whether he belonged to the elect or the reprobate.

Thus Luther felt he stood accused by God, and accused by life, yet was certain that he could escape neither. This was particularly painful for a man of exuberant spirit, joyous wit and high-hearted happiness. At times wild hatred welled up in his heart against God. Yet he knew perfectly well that as a creature he had no claims on God, no claims against God. He knew and never doubted that God lived and was holy. He knew that he himself was a sinner. He knew that man as a sinner could never, under any circumstances, be acceptable as he is to a righteous God as He is. As long as he analysed the problem on such moral principles, there was no answer; there never could be, for the relationship was not reducible to moral principles. His anger against God sometimes ebbed out to the lowest tide of despair, and when the ebb-tide flowed it pounded unavailingly in anger against the eternal cliffs of God's immutability and inaccessibility, to ebb once more. This inner turmoil wrecked his health; he paid a high and painful price for his devoted monkery.

Staupitz helped Luther at this time in the summer of 1511 at Wittenberg. His views enabled Luther to work out his own. Staupitz believed that no man could ever will, know or do good by his own reason or strength. He believed that if a man belonged to the elect and received the heavenly medicine of grace poured in through the sacraments, then ability to will, know and do good was granted him. Not that a man could ever be certain of his election, rather the sacramental signs were appointed to nourish that hope continuously and drive out despair. A diligent and faithful use of the sacraments could overcome anxiety as to predestination.

Staupitz was not only a master in scholastic philosophy, he was also deeply read in the Bible. He sought to steer Luther clear of his torments into seeking peace with God not on his own good resolutions (which he would never have had the strength to carry out) nor by his own good deeds (which could never have satisfied the Law of God) but in God's forgiving mercy only. He turned Luther's mind away from the system of penance to the reality of repentance, to an inward change and conversion. He taught him to see God in the perspective of Christ, whom God sent not as a condemning judge but as a living and redeeming saviour. This truth a man could no more learn from others than he could learn to see from others. But when all is said that can be said of Staupitz, of his sheer goodness and pure Catholic piety, it is now obvious that the pupil had long outstripped his teacher. It was true that Staupitz relied on the merits of Christ, but he relied also on the merits of the Virgin Mary and the saints. He had always believed that a man had to earn and deserve his salvation, and years after this held it as a temptation of the Devil to believe that a man was saved only by divine mercy and not also by his own works. In fact, Staupitz was never able to grasp Luther's inward battle. He comforted Luther greatly in his problem of predestination by holding up to him the thought of Christ actually wounded and actually suffering for us men and our salvation. The contemplation of Christ and his death on the cross, so earnestly taught by Staupitz, helped Luther enormously in combating the scholastic doctrine of completing Christ's merit by one's own. Yet Staupitz never fully understood Luther's mind, and this compelled Luther to solve his problems for himself on the basis of scripture, without regard to theological tradition. As a theologian Luther now began to 'go it alone'.

It was his work on the Bible that saved him. He was preparing his summer lectures on the Psalms (April–May 1513) when the familiar phrase 'deliver me in thy righteousness' (Psalm 31) began to take on a new and disturbing air. He had hitherto thought of the phrase 'the righteousness of God' in the passive meaning which theologians had always given it, namely, the righteousness of the holy and pure God. This idea had always given him disquiet, because any meeting of his sinful self with God, any approach to God could be met only by His annihilating reaction on righteousness confronting unrighteousness. The 'lying lips' of the psalmist 'are those which establish their own righteousness, deny the righteousness of God and make Him a liar'. Their wickedness lies 'in that they speak against God, for they are against the righteous Christ and His righteousness, as though it were not necessary or useful, as though their own was sufficient for them'. 'God judges us and makes us liars . . . when we want to be thought true and without sin, and think we have no need of Christ, who yet died on account of our sins.'[1] He questioned whether the biblical term 'righteousness' meant the same thing as the schoolmen's term 'righteousness'. He searched for Bible texts of the word and studied them. He turned up Romans i, 17:

For therein is the righteousness of God revealed from faith to faith: as it is written, The just shall live by faith.

He read this with scholastic eyes, and thought that the righteousness of God that was revealed in the Gospel meant what he had always understood the term to mean, that punitive righteousness with which He meets sin, only a little keener now in the light of a fuller revelation. In agony he wrestled with the text. It grew into his mind that what Paul was expounding was precisely that insight which he lacked, that a man was justified by faith not by works. Therefore, the New Testament idea of righteousness was not the punitive righteousness of God, valid

1. W. A. 3, 170, 30 ff.

as this was and is in so far as the natural unredeemed man is 'in Adam'. It was a wholly new idea of righteousness. It was the forgiving righteousness of God which set a man in a new relationship by setting him 'in Christ'. This righteousness was manifested not because of man's moral worth and deserts, but simply because it was of God's nature to have mercy and to forgive. He saw this righteousness as the righteousness of a God reconciling sinful man to Himself while he was yet a sinner. His righteousness was of a kind no human mind could conceive; it was a righteousness of love and mercy reaching out for a lost soul who could never on his own find God or even know forgiveness. It was while man was in that state, *because* that was his condition, that God acted in Christ to reconcile man to Him. Not because man was good and worthy, nor even because he worked to become good and worthy, but, because he was a sinner and could never bridge the gap, God drew nearer. Luther described this experience in these words:

When I had realized this I felt myself absolutely born again. The gates of paradise had been flung open and I had entered. There and then the whole of scripture took on another look to me. . . .[1]

This is a more exact description than we might at first realize. For over a thousand years the Church had been growing farther and farther away from the Gospel that had occasioned her birth. In allowing accretions and the growth of corruptions, she had virtually ceased to understand the Gospel, and had bartered her birthright for the pottage of a powerful institution, a semi-pagan philosophy and a semi-pelagian theology. It was this anomalous position of the Church that occasioned Luther's difficulty, and it goes a long way to explain the rancour with which the establishment met his simple gospel. He was indeed reborn, and the gates of paradise were flung open, for he was no longer a prisoner in the aeon of Adam but a pilgrim in the aeon of Christ. The whole Bible began to take on a simple forthright meaning and purpose, and at the same time he forged clear links and patterns in the patristic tradition. All that Luther did was to restore the Gospel again to men after eradicating corruptions and accretions.

1. Introduction to the Latin edition, Wittenberg 1545 (W. A., 54, 186).

He innovated nothing but renovated everything. When the name 'reformer' was coined for him it was an exact description of the role history forced on him.

Luther never made the error of trying to foist on to the Church some idealized external primitive pattern of life from the early Church, as the Independents and Radicals were to do later. Nor did he seek to force on her a literal application of primitive doctrines, as did the Puritans. He rediscovered and revived evangelical faith in God, and in the world and place in which God had set him accepted all that God had done in 1,500 years, seeking in a changed and changing world the true Gospel rather than human ideas. Unlike many other great personalities in religion he had no use for petty miracles, dreams and visions to lend a dubious support to his message. Luther's soul was saved in his study by hard, costly work on the text of the Bible. He had found the theology offered by the Church true neither to the Bible, experience nor common sense. He wanted every man to look again with fresh eyes at God's work for man as recorded in the Bible; to see the facts for himself in the light of plain common sense; to verify for himself whether these did not accord with his own experience, as well as beginning to give a meaning to his own life in that raw secular condition in which and out of which God called him. Luther's pilgrimage was an invitation to a like pilgrimage to Everyman. When his enemies came later to answer him, they thought in terms of repression, to silence the man or limit his influence. As Amaziah could only answer Amos by questioning the authority of his commission but not the authority of his words, Luther was told that his authority was limited to the parish of Wittenberg and that he had no right to teach the whole world (as Wesley was told later, and many others). Luther's reply was interesting. He said that he was a 'Doktor der Theologie'; it was his responsibility to preach and teach the scriptures to all the world; to that commission he had been duly called and publicly instituted and it was his responsibility to raise disputations. There was a further measure of justification, he added, in that he had prepared himself for this great office against his own will and inclinations, having been commanded and encouraged by his father in God, Staupitz.

Before we move on to the next four years of Luther's life there is an important point to be made on the relation of Luther to Lutheranism on the one hand and to the rest of Catholic Christendom on the other. Catholic Christendom rejected Luther's reformation, and thereafter the movement known as the Reformation pursued its independent way in Germany, Holland, France, Switzerland, Norway, Sweden and the British Isles, supported and encouraged by the great reformers Calvin, Zwingli, Bucer as well as by the lesser known national reformers.

In Germany and the Scandinavian countries, which looked to Wittenberg for their theologians, there grew up the movement known as Lutheranism, often called the Lutheran Church or Churches. This is a misnomer. Luther opposed the word 'Lutheran'; the Church was Christ's, he argued, and could never bear another adjective, save in Rome where – he could not resist the sly dig – the Church was in the true sense 'papist' or 'Roman', for there it was the Pope's Church or the Roman Church. The theologians of what is improperly called the Lutheran Church support this view in that they do not consider Luther an 'authority' other than as a doctor of the Church, as he was in his own eyes and in the eyes of his contemporaries. By the same token Luther is no 'authority' as such in academic or ecumenical dialogue, though Lutherans have sometimes succumbed to the temptation of making him one.

Luther's authority rests in fact in his relevance to the whole Church, Catholic and reformed alike. In this connexion there is the plain historical reality of his impact on Christianity in the early sixteenth century. Historians will assess and reassess this in every generation. But there is a further relevance in that his protest cannot be exhausted in an historical estimation: it has an existentialist reference. His theology is studied in Roman Catholic circles, particularly in Germany. Moreover, the programme which Pope John called the Vatican Council to reflect on when he sought to make the Roman Church consider her renewal to fit herself for the demands of the twentieth century raised, among other things, some of the issues Luther called the Church to consider. In this sense Luther belongs not to

Lutheranism but to the whole Church. He is a pointer to Christ and the Gospel.

There is one further sense in which Luther is still a relevant figure, and that lies in the nature of his reformation. He saw religion as an activity as normal to man as wearing clothes or eating food. To him it was not a matter of visions and ecstasies and voices, but of normal men looking at normal evidence. Every point he made was open for all men to test and prove reasonably by the evidence of history, by sound critical scholarship, but above all by their own experience. He compelled men to look again and to look for themselves; in so doing they were convinced and converted. But he further showed why religion tended to turn sour, and why officialdom tended to preserve itself rather than a religion critical both of itself and of officialdom. The reason for this was that he saw the processes which both eroded and corroded Christianity as lying in the heart of every individual. Consequently, individuals as well as institutions found themselves opposed to evangelical Christianity in the interests of self-preservation, for the very same reasons, as St John and St Paul carefully declared, that the Jews opposed Christ. When Luther broke through to the dawn of his reformation consciousness, he realized (1) that the Gospel of freedom in Christ had been transmuted into a new law of servitude, (2) that the kingdom of all believers was now a quasi-spiritual tyranny and (3) that the true evangelical theology had been smothered under a human scholasticism which was no more than idolatrous intellectualism. The consequence of this was that countless souls were being lost for want of the saving truths the Church had been founded to convey. It would be utterly disastrous to think that the wrongs were peculiar to Rome, for Luther's protest means that these tendencies and failures do not belong only to the Roman Catholic Church but to all Churches all the time. Every Christian man has to come to terms with Luther sooner or later, and in this present ecumenical movement, the sooner the better.

Of course, Luther was not fully aware of all this at the time. He was simply a teaching professor concerned with truth; he did not think of himself in higher terms, nor did anyone else in those days. And that was just as well. He was afforded four precious years more, with a very light teaching load of about two lectures a week (although he had other duties, and preached more than three times a week) to strengthen his position. When Luther showed his hand (and his mind) in the matter of the indulgences scandal of 1517, it was no zealous youth who had allowed himself to become excited, but a mature man of unquestionable learning, unimpeachable life and granite integrity, who could hold his peace before God and man no longer.

CHAPTER 8

LUTHER AS TEACHER

LUTHER IN HIS STUDY

THE next four years were formative for Luther. A close study of his lectures from 1513 to 1517 reveals him forging his new evangelical insights on the anvil of scholasticism. We often find him using the old terms, but like a growing schoolboy crouching over his work, he is seen to be bursting at every seam. For example, he used the scholastic term for original sin and related ideas, but in a wholly different way from his contemporaries. He interpreted sin in the Augustinian sense of a self-centredness which destroyed the capacity freely to will the good. The will was enslaved to the self and had no true spiritual freedom. This bondage of the will Luther saw as man's supreme spiritual danger, always binding him to himself and his own interests, always blinding him to God and the needs of his brother man. When a man in this state, the natural man, as Luther called him, thought of religion, he did so quite understandably in terms of his own decency and goodness (acceptable enough in themselves), and believed that he would draw nearer to God in this way – a subtle idolatry, which was in fact plain unbelief. To Luther, unbelief was the fundamental sin.

All terms that he touched underwent a transformation. He talked of grace, as did the scholastic theologians, but he meant something wholly different and fresh. Ever since the days of the Apostles, grace had been increasingly regarded as some kind of proprietary medicine with supernatural properties, administered by the Church through her sacraments. This was a disastrous decline from the Apostles' doctrine. In the New Testament grace is a personal, living experience of Christ by which divine encounter a new creation is born. God was active in history; He had shown and shows His Hand. A man hears again, as the world did once before, of a God who 'so loved the world that

He gave His only begotten Son to the end that whosoever believes in Him should not perish but should have eternal life'. It was not a matter of works and what a man could do, but a realization that he had nothing at all to offer and there was nothing he could do; he had but to see this, and with this realization repentance would be kindled and faith begin to grow.

The scholastics, as well as Luther, spoke too of justification, but they were as far apart in their interpretation as Nicodemus was from Jesus. They thought of grace as infused into a man's soul like milk poured into a jug; Luther thought of it in the evangelical, personal terms of the New Testament which spoke of man the sinner unable to find the true God even with the help of the Law of God, and of God's work in Christ offering free unmerited salvation. When a man saw (and sees) the reality, even the enormity, of his own sin, and the work of God in meeting that sin in Christ, the response is one of obedience and surrender to a God gracious and merciful. A kind of buoyancy is born in the human soul, a trust and confidence in all God's promises. Faith is in no sense a human achievement or effort, a putting of something human into God's bargain, such as good works or efforts, as Judaism (and scholasticism) sometimes taught. It is an opening of the eyes. It is the birth of a new hope, a sober trust in God, and a joyful, hopeful expectancy of what the outcome will be. People sometimes speak of Luther's being in 'jocular' vein, but all his wit and humour and high spirits were symptoms of a glad, trusting, believing confident heart. 'A Christian man is always in good heart,' he said. He once commented on his dog Tölpel[1] cheerfully wagging his tail though not knowing where his next meal would come from, and marvelled at his pure trust in his environment, as he rubbed his ears and stroked his head. This was a parable of Luther's faith.

But faith must not be understood psychologically or subjectively. It arises not from man's work but from a gift of God (Ephesians ii, 8). The rebirth of a believing man comes about by contact with the preached or expounded Gospel, the Word of God. The preaching of the Gospel, as Paul described it, *is* the power of God. When the Gospel is declared, or read, or

1. A colloquial term of affection meaning a 'little clown', or 'young rascal'.

otherwise made known and communicated, the power of God is kindled at once. A man can no more work this up by himself than he could have done the work of Christ. He is justified by faith alone apart from the works of the Law. No other formula has ever expressed the whole matter so succinctly. Faith is like the response ·of a plant to the sun; the sunshine creates the activity of the plant. At no point is natural man more likely to misunderstand Luther than in his emphasis on justification by faith in Christ only. (In fact, it is Barth's awareness of this doctrine as applicable to the whole field of man's knowing as well as man's doing that is at the bottom of his theology.)

It was in a spiritual engagement of this kind that the Word of God came to occupy the central place in Luther's mind. He saw the Church's chief mission as the preaching of the Word rather than the administration of the sacraments, for the Word not only gave the Church her commission but preserved and governed it. As for Augustine, the sacraments to Luther were the Word made substance, the 'visible word'. The sacraments were central to Luther but were appropriated as Word. Christ was active and operative in the preaching of the Word, and it was Christ's active presence, not so much a scriptural passage, that made new believing men. A man was only what he heard from God.

This kind of theology gave him a biblical conception of the Church. The Church was the company of believers, the elect who had heard the Word. This was an invisible and spiritual community and not to be understood as coterminous with the visible Church. He took a view similar to that of Augustine, who had once said that there were wolves within the fold as well as sheep without. But clear as Luther was on this, and bold as he was in declaring it, he was equally clear that despite its wrong theology and grave crimes the constituted Church had not yet been forsaken by God nor yet had it lost the Gospel utterly. He had no sympathy with the sectarians who wanted to found a new, holy community, nor with the enthusiasts who appealed to their own special revelations, despising the Church, the Gospel, even Christ, in favour of 'the Spirit'. He would have said that the Church and the sacraments were derived from the Gospel, but emphasized that they were not normally dispensable but were part of God's saving plan.

A study of the lectures and disputations of these four quiet years shows Luther wrestling inwardly with all the basic themes of his later Reformation theology and to some extent anticipating and answering charges that were to appear later. His championship of faith sharpened the criticisms of his contemporaries, who had taught and were still teaching a theology of works, alleging that Luther taught that good works were unnecessary. But what Luther was saying was that a man could not *do* good before he *was* good, that good deeds were the natural, spontaneous and expected fruit of faith. He argued that the natural man was not good by nature and that the will to do good arose from his being re-created in Christ. Only then did he spontaneously, gladly, freely and voluntarily seek to do good. Only then was he free from the demands of the Law and the bondage of the Law. But, of course, Luther knew that though he lived in the aeon of Christ he stood all too solidly in the aeon of Adam, and, as Paul before him, was keenly aware of the perpetual tension of citizenship in two worlds.

As Luther's view on faith was utterly different from that which the scholastics taught, so also was his view on good works. Both would agree that good works could be summed up in the command to love God and love one's neighbour, but they would wholly disagree on what the command meant. Scholasticism taught that only the negative prohibitions of God were always binding; the positive commands were binding only when the original occasion of their being commanded was present. They did exactly as the Jews had done before them. The command to love one's neighbour suffered a vast casuistry as to who that neighbour was and was not, in what circumstances the command was operative and in what not, the process culminating in the declaration of the standards expected of monks and spirituals. Luther exposed this kind of argument for the humbug that it was and tore open the truth. He knew that a sin of omission might be as real as a sin of commission, even worse, and that the Law of God was good and unchangeable. The Law clearly demanded that we love God with all our being and that we do good to all men, friend or foe, good and evil. The qualifications, modifications and dispensations of scholastic casuistry had no authority, in fact no meaning. The distinctions between 'commandments' which were universally binding and 'evangelical counsels' which were not, between mortal and venial sin and so on, were meaningless and harmful; and these distinctions and refinements had the vice of multiplying.

Luther turned men back to the original sources which accepted the commandments and the counsels as true and valid for all, but helped them to see the vital distinction that a man must obey in that estate or calling to which God had called him and not in another. It was not true that there was a 'higher' ethic valid for monks, priests, nuns and spirituals, and a 'lower' ethic valid for married folk and those whose vocations lay in the secular world. It was not the character of the office that was operative but the character of the relationship with God in whatever office he had set a man, peasant or prince, potter or priest. The prince fulfilled a function different in kind from the peasant, the potter from the priest, but the same God over all saved them all in the same way by the same Gospel. It was in the sphere to which he was called (often simply set by birth) that a man knew what it was to obey God and serve those to whom God had related him. It was in this sphere only, and not in some supposedly holy performance, useless alike to God and man, that a man was called to obey the commandments and counsels.[1]

Luther was far in advance of Tauler and the monks. They all taught, of course, that a Godfearing layman could find salvation in his secular calling, but they regarded the monk's way as superior and his ethic higher. This was unwarrantable to Luther, and seemed true neither to the New Testament nor to common sense. Luther put the layman on his theological feet. Here was the beginning of the rediscovery of the priesthood of all believers. Here was the beginning of ideas which emptied the monasteries and convents of monks and nuns and set them seeking normal Christian employment. Here was the germ of that glorious

1. Luther developed this theme in his *On Monastic Vows* (1521). For a translation and discussion of the book see the American edition of Luther's Works, Vol. 44, ed. and tr. James Atkinson, Philadelphia, 1966, pp. 243–400.

quality of evangelical freedom which made a shy monk face un-
flinchingly the secular power of the Holy Roman Emperor and
the spiritual might of the Pope of Rome.

It is true that in his lectures he was now expressing himself
sharply against the corrupt Roman Curia as well as against the
institutions of the Church. Julius II, Duke George, Archbishop
Albrecht, all came in for criticism, even his own ruler, Frederick
the Wise, for his foolish interest in relics. Lazy artisans, cunning
merchants, drunken farmers, ignorant astrologers come into
Luther's purview, but his sharpest criticisms were directed at
what he called 'those sow-theologians'[1] and the indulgences
preachers. Already sharp comments are made on a theology that
holds prayers to St Apollonia for the relief of tooth-ache, to St
Anthony for the relief of erysipelas, to St Louis to prevent the
beer going sour; that deals with medals of St Christopher for
travellers, and all other idolatrous practices of his age. By these
criticisms Luther created no stir. Such censure was still conson-
ant with good Catholicism.

We need to remind ourselves that when Staupitz called Luther
to the professor's chair, it constituted a call to the pulpit. It is
interesting that Luther felt confident while teaching and lecturing, but when preaching was rather uneasy to find a Melanchthon in the pew or even his brother monks listening and thinking.
He seems always to have been shy in the pulpit, but of the power
and effectiveness of his performance on that divine square yard
there is all the evidence in the world. Of more than two thousand
of his sermons now extant, it is a pity we do not have one as
Luther delivered it or wrote it. They were noted down in Latin
shorthand by men who were struck by the content, and the
Word of God they sought to proclaim. With an arresting

---

1. A 'sow-theologian' or a 'theological sow' (*Sautheologe*) may be abusive
in the sense that we call a man an ass or a mule, and affix to him the vices of
the particular creature, stupidity, stubbornness, and so on! 'Sow' may
connote the wallowing in dirt. There may be a connexion with Luther's
reference to Tetzel the indulgences preacher. Luther said that he handled
Scripture like a sow a bag of oats. See p. 149. The word may simply be used
in the sense in which a Bavarian refers to bad weather as '*Sau Wetter*'.
What it means at the least, all associations removed, is that they were no
theologians.

command of language and image he poured out from his soul a cleansing and redeeming torrent of the saving biblical truths. The Germans had had a long and noble line of preachers, and not all of the same type either: Berthold, Suso, Tauler, Albertus Magnus, Eckhart, Geiler. Luther joined that noble line, but like a singer or an instrumentalist or a great actor whose magic dies with them, we can but imagine the great experience as those folk of Saxony packed in to their churches and sat up in hushed expectancy to hear Friar Martin.

It is interesting to ask ourselves *when* those near to Luther began to realize that he was no ordinary professor. In 1514 a Benedictine, Lange, compiled a *Who's Who* of German university life, but in the list of Wittenberg noteworthies Luther's name does not occur! By 1515 we know that the students had noticed the religious content of his lectures, as Wittenberg had noted the weight of his sermons. Early in 1515 we read of Mutianus writing to Lange about this 'sharp preacher of Wittenberg'. However, outside Wittenberg, Luther would be known only to members of his own Order.

But his influence was beginning to be felt. Spalatin, the court preacher, knew what was in Luther and regarded him with what was little less than veneration. (They had been students together at Erfurt.) In Spalatin, Luther had a friend at court. He always took Luther's part and 'explained' him to the Elector, who felt terrified at having this *enfant terrible* occupying a chair at his university. The Elector had to cross a theological minefield whenever he handled the Luther affair. Spalatin was the mouthpiece at court for Luther's ideas of reforming theological studies at Wittenberg. When Luther sought to abolish scholasticism in favour of Augustine and the Bible, and to found chairs of Greek and Hebrew, it was Spalatin who represented his views to the Elector. The world of scholarship has not yet made a full and proper estimation of the role Spalatin played as a spokesman for the Reformation at the royal court.

This progressive academic policy of Luther's kindled in the humanists much interest in his work, but it was hardly reciprocated. He had common ground with them in his honest pursuit of the authority of his sources, in the study of the ancient lan-

guages, and in his cool academic criticism of religious and philosophical authority, but absolutely no sympathy with their
approach to the religious question. Erasmus in his acuity perceived the difference from the outset, but hoped for some years
to win a valuable compromise without breaking the intellectual
and spiritual unity of Christendom. Similarly Luther was very
gentle with the French humanist Lefèvre, and certainly was not
only appreciative of the immense contribution Erasmus made
to the Renascence, and to the Reformation also in his edition of
a Greek text of the New Testament, but hoped at the beginning
for his support in the Reformation. Both were of one mind in
their opposition to late scholasticism, to the gross ignorance of
clerics and monks, and the bold scandalous immorality of the
leadership of the Church from the Pope down; both sought a
return to the oldest sources, and both championed the study of
Greek and Hebrew. But as early as 1517 Luther knew that
Erasmus's humanism and Christian ethic was not the real strong
meat of evangelical, theological Christianity, and that his own
emphasis on Christ, grace, revelation, sin, redemption, the
servile will, and all those doctrines that were once again to ring
across the world, would one day make an unbridgeable breach
between the two men. He wrote to Spalatin on 19 October 1516
that his gravamen against Erasmus was that the latter was unaware of the Pauline teaching on sin as well as unacquainted
with the great and authoritative theology of Augustine. Erasmus
even preferred Jerome to Augustine! As he was soon to express
it, 'Erasmus gives insufficient place to Christ and the glory of
God.' 'If I speak as a theologian rather than as a grammarian
I find a lot in Erasmus which is alien and unhelpful to knowledge of Christ.' To fail by this criterion was to fail altogether
as Luther saw it. At table he said, 'Erasmus is an eel. Nobody
can get hold of him; only Christ will. He is two persons in one.'
The final chasm between them yawned open in 1525.[1]

More important still was Luther's triumph within his own
faculty at Wittenberg. In 1516 he had engaged in a disputation
attacking the Ockhamist theology on the ability of man to fulfil
the commandments of God by dint of his own will and reason.

1. See p. 228.

Although his colleagues at first resisted his views, they were eventually converted to Luther's way of thinking, and with this began the fall of scholastic theology at Wittenberg and the rise of the Bible and Augustine.

The university regulations demanded of Luther that he should lecture on the Psalms and Epistles, and within five years we find that he had lectured on the Psalms and on the Epistles to the Romans, Galatians and Hebrews, and had begun again on the Psalms. Scholars still dispute certain niceties of the chronology but the following timetable is reliable enough for our purposes: *Genesis,* October 1512–July 1513; *Psalms,* August 1513–October 1515; *Romans,* Easter 1515–September 1516; *Galatians,* October 1516–March 1517; *Hebrews,* March 1517–March 1518; and *Psalms* again, April 1518–March 1521.

Luther threw himself into his task and after his monastic duties were performed worked at the sources into the long hours of the night in that silent cloister, till even the mice grew impatient at this new intrusion into their nocturnal liberties. He worked in the following way. He had his Wittenberg printer print the particular biblical text on which he was lecturing, with the lines of the text widely spaced and leaving broad margins. Between the lines and in the margins he glossed the text in the way of medieval exegetes, that is, he explained the text by means of grammatical and linguistic comment, by relating it to other texts, by reference to other authorities and by any aid at hand. These notes he dictated, so that the student then possessed his own text, duly annotated. In addition to the glosses we have 'scholia'. A scholion is continuous comment on significant parts of the text, and scholia cover the whole range of theological and related comment. For the Psalms, we have Luther's own manuscript, both of the glosses and the scholia, though in other cases we are sometimes dependent on the notes of a student.

LECTURES ON THE PSALMS (1513–15)

Criticism of the Church and of Monasticism

The source of the text for Luther's lectures on the Psalms (the Genesis lectures are lost) was the Latin Bible. He showed mastery both of the text and content, and only occasionally does the reader come across a mistaken reference or misquotation (doubtless because Luther was quoting from memory). In addition, he used the *Five-Fold Psalter*, the work of his distinguished contemporary, Lefèvre, the French humanist, who later put the New Testament into French (1523). This Psalter had five parallel Latin texts: the Gallic, the Roman, the Hebraic, the old Itala, and a collation of all four. Then there were the earlier commentaries: that of Hugo (thirteenth century); that of Nicholas of Lyra (1270–1340), the professor of the Sorbonne, who strove for a literal interpretation against the prevalent mystical flights of fancy;[1] the commentary of Paul of Burgos (1351–1435), the converted Jew who added much Rabbinical material to Lyra's commentary; and the work of Peter Lombard. For linguistic aid there was Reuchlin's *Rudiments of Hebrew*. Above all towers the work of the great Augustine. All these ancient authorities played a formative part in Luther's exegetical writings right down to his lectures on Hebrews in 1517–18.

He used at this time, though not invariably or rigidly, the traditional four-fold technique of searching out hidden meanings in a text. There was a Latin tag which ran:

> Litera gesta docet, quid credas allegoria,
> Moralis, quid agas, quid speres anagogia.[2]

This may strike one now as very artificial, but Rupp writes a spirited page in its defence.[3] He points out that this method captured the importance of the acts of God in history, their appropriation by us within the community of believing men, and the sense that all our knowledge is but human, anticipatory of the eternal Kingdom.

It is immensely difficult to estimate this vast range of material

1. A wit once discerningly said that if Lyra had not piped (*lyrasset*) Luther would never have danced (*saltasset*).

2. The literal meaning teaches you what actually happened; the allegorical what you ought to believe; the moral, what you should be doing about it; the anagogical, what you may hope for (i.e. the future life).

3. Gordon Rupp, *The Righteousness of God: Luther Studies*, London, 1953, p. 134.

on the Psalms (some 1,400 huge quarto pages of Latin text). Luther is obviously growing and using his terms with a content far fuller and often quite different from that of his contemporaries. Roman Catholic scholars such as Denifle and Grisar took the view that he stood on firm Catholic ground at this stage. Moreau writes more recently for example: '*Aucune proposition dans les* Dictata super Psalterium *ne s'oppose à la foi catholique.*'[1] (Not a single statement in the *Commentary on the Psalms* is contrary to the Catholic faith.) This is true as far as it goes. It is not unlike the assertion that the teaching of Christ could have been given by any Jewish rabbi of the period. This might satisfy a Jew or even a liberal Christian, but a person who knows Christ believes that it is true in one sense, yet false in the total sense. In the same way, the man who has studied Luther knows the limited truth of these assertions by Roman Catholic scholars. They accept Luther's criticisms of the abuses of the Church, for example his comments on Psalm 38, 'There is no soundness in my flesh . . . mine iniquities are gone over my head . . . I am troubled . . . my loins are filled with a loathsome disease,' etc., when he directs his words against the Church and her clergy. He speaks of the abysmal spiritual condition of the Church, and says: 'Throughout the entire Church the spirit is enfeebled and sins abound.' When the psalmist cries there is no peace in his bones, Luther replies: '. . . it is because of dissensions, sensual pleasures and all the other wretched extravagances with which the ablest and best in the Church are involved.' He speaks of the 'heavy odour of scandals everywhere', of 'foul corruption', and of churchmen who preach not a true theology but a human scheme of things. Luther says of the psalmist's lament that his loins are filled with illusions or deceits ('a loathsome disease' – A.V.):

The loins of Christ are those from whom he generates his children, i.e. the bishops, the priests, the doctors. It is not so much that these loins nowadays are filled with the deceits of carnal vice, fornicators and adulterers, but rather that instead of the holy seed they produce opinions, fables and nothing but schemes. They even do this from the

1. E. de Moreau, *La crise religieuse du XVIe siècle*, Vol. 16 in *Histoire de l'Église*, Paris, 1934– , p. 24.

pulpits. They do not produce the true seed, neither in intent nor deed, but spin webs of opinions, questions and nonsense.[1]

Roman Catholic scholars also accept his criticisms of monasticism, of the monks' concern with their own petty works and merits rather than with the work of Christ. He condemns the monks' attitude in the words Christ used when he condemned the Pharisees for their religious ostentation, with their large phylacteries and their great performances of prayer at the street corner:

These things [monastic works] are not tokens derived from the Gospel. All these performances are empty of content; there is nothing spiritual or vital about them. But because these men [the monks] love to do these things they re-establish and defend them even though the Lord disapproves of such performances. Even to the present day they are trying to establish them. . . . They are working against the Lord. . . . This zeal of theirs is utter folly. It is a zeal to establish their own righteousness. . . . Rend your heart and not your garment. Do not show so much external penitence, show it from the heart's core. . . . No one hears God except it be given him from Christ alone. . . . In Christ a man is clearly separated from those pharisees and literal-minded Jews, for God never heard them. God hears him [the believer in Christ] in His righteousness by giving to him righteousness: for a man discerns that he is devoid of righteousness and begs for righteousness. But because these men [the monks] are proud, they do not do this: rather they harangue the Lord, but He does not hear them. In fact it is less a matter of calling on God or invoking Him: it is more a matter of a penitent heart.   On Psalm 4 (W. A. 3, 61 f.)

They do not understand that it is in Christ alone they will be justified, and not by their own works. Those who seek to be saved without Christ are the very men who do not understand God's work in Christ. . . . They think those dreadful works of theirs are necessary. Else, have they ever understood the phrase 'the works of the Lord' . . . as the Apostles understood it . . . spiritual works of faith discernible by faith?   On Psalm 28 (W. A. 3, 155, 17 ff.)

The Psalmist is speaking, as did St Paul in Romans 4, against all those who want their sins remitted by God on account of their own works and merits, and seek to be justified by their own works. It is by this teaching that it could be said that Christ had died in vain, for

1. W. A. 3, 216, 24 ff.

these men want to be saved by their own works apart from the Death of Christ. This is false doctrine. Such men are Jews. Such men are heretics. All such are superstitious in their own particular way. They have thrown aside obedience and faith and establish their own righteousness, for they do not want the name of the Lord invoked above them. It is not the death of Christ that profits a man but their own exercises in humility. After all, every man that thinks he is above others is a man who denies Christ.

On Psalm 32 (W. A. 3, 172, 30 ff.)

There are pages and pages of material like this. Can anyone fail to see here the real evangelical Luther? If the Roman Catholics want to claim this as normal Roman Catholic doctrine, one can only say that Luther failed to convince them at the time.

In addition to his criticism of the scandals and abuses of the Church, Catholic scholars tend nowadays to accept his criticisms of the false humility of the monks. On the subject of true humility[1] Luther writes:

Unless a man is always humble, always distrustful of himself, unless he always fears his own understanding, his own judgement, his own passion, his own will, he will to that extent be unable to stand for very long without offence. For truth will pass him by. Light and goodness will evade him in a changing form and in an opposite kind. And then, wretched fellow, he will curse his humility, just as the Jews threw themselves against Christ because they did not recognize the wisdom hidden within Him. Do not condemn outright what you hear or see. Your strength is your weakness because you do not see rightly what seems not right to you. . . . Truth is hidden under another form to those who are unwise. But to the wise, that is, the humble and meek, it remains in its proper form. . . . In this way it turns out to all the proud and stubborn, to the superstitious, the rebellious and the disobedient, what is more, I fear, to our observant monks, who under the guise of a rule of life rush headlong into disobedience and rebellion.

On Psalm 92 (W. A. 4, 83, 3 ff.)

This was a key concept to Luther and came to dominate his lectures on Romans, where he says in the context of the goodness of man and of all his great achievements:

On that very account we must have humility in all these very matters. We must behave as if so far we had nothing at all, and wait for the

1. See p. 102.

mercy of God in all its stark nakedness. We must wait for him to reckon us as just and wise. And this is exactly what God does, provided a man does not get there before God, by justifying himself and thinking he is other than he really is.

On Romans i, 1 (W. A. 56, 159, 12 ff.)

Unless a man is always humble, always suspicious of his own motives, always afraid of his own view of things, his own judgement, his own appetite, his own wants, he will not be able to stand for long without stumbling. On Psalm 92 (W. A. 4, 83, 3 ff.)

The complementary aspect of this liberating truth is that pride in all its forms is the root of all evil and the origin of all sin, and that it is the proud and arrogant who insist on presuming on their own works and their own decency to save them, and so reject Christ and His work and have no faith in Him.

Luther's Concern not with Scandals but with Doctrine

(1) Justification in Christ alone

There is far more to these lectures than the criticism of contemporary religion. Above all, it was Christ and faith that were their subject-matter:

In holy and divine things we must listen before we see, believe before we understand, be comprehended before we comprehend, be captured before we capture, learn before we teach, be a learner before being a teacher or master of oneself. . . . Therefore he who wishes to be certain and faithfully to care for others must himself first be experienced. Let him himself first carry the cross and lead the way, and by this it will be proved that he can also help others. For that reason in the Church God visits a man every morning and tries him without warning, that he may learn from his own experiences what to teach others. On Psalm 94, 8 (W. A. 4, 95, 1 ff.)

On Psalm 89, 48 'What man is there that liveth and shall not see death?' he glosses:

'What man' means: unless Thou raise me; 'he that liveth' means: in eternal life, for there is no one who lives in a body except man, but all men are in the sight of God dead in their soul. They are not alive unless they have been raised from the dead by faith in Christ. . . . From this verse it is clear that the prophet is talking from beginning to end of the Person of Christ. (W. A. 4, 43, 7 ff.)

On Psalm 119 he writes in a gloss:

In the prophetic and literal sense this psalm is a petition for the advent of Christ and for the excellence of the Church of Christ, but in the moral and doctrinal sense it is the petition for the spiritual advent of Christ by grace and the excellence of his grace.

(W. A. 4, 281, 35)

Complaining that he has never seen this psalm expounded by anybody in its prophetic sense, nor was there anybody who had expounded it in its own form and order except by doing violence to the plain meaning of the text (4, 305, 3 ff.) he comments on verse 41, 'Let thy mercy come also unto me O Lord: thy salvation according to thy word':

The psalm refers to the advent of Christ, and the revelation of the Gospel and his grace. . . . The human race receives Christ not according to its own righteousness but according to the mercy of God. . . . He is given not as a result of the work I have done in getting ready for Him but as a result of the convenant of God.

(W. A. 4, 329, 14 ff.)

On Psalm 119, 76, 'Let thy mercy come to console me according to thy word to thy servant':

All things are given us not according to our merits but issuing from His promises. On that account he calls these things His mercy; mercy is given by covenant and promise, if His covenant and testimonies are kept. . . .

This can even be understood of the coming of Christ in the flesh. And thus it is a prayer of the prophet and of the people of the old Law for Him to come. This which had been prophesied by his predecessors was soon to come to pass. *Indeed let that be a general principle that wherever any verse is or can be expounded as applying to the coming of Christ in the flesh, it ought at the same time to be expounded as applying to his coming through grace as well as his coming in future glory. Christ's Advent is in fact three-fold. And in the second sense, that is the spiritual* [His coming under the form of grace], *in one way it is prayed by those beginning and in another way by those advancing in the spiritual life: granted it is the same words used. Because even those advancing are always beginners with regard to the things they do not possess yet, both in grace as*

well as wisdom, so that they may abound yet more and more in under-
standing as well as feeling. Because in this case nothing but the Gospel
and grace is ever asked for.[1]   (W. A. 4, 343, 34–344, 15)

Writing on Psalm 143, he adds the following footnote:

this Psalm in its spiritual and prophetic sense is the cry of the faithful
people of the synagogue, by now almost spiritually deadened by their
scribes and elders, at whose hands iniquity has gone forth into the
world and all dignity of spiritual understanding obscured. These
people are crying in the depths of their disquiet for the advent of
Christ in the flesh, that he might be made manifest to them as they
look for him. In this way the psalm is easy to understand. But because
the Church considers him for the benefit of sinners, therefore it is
taken in the moral sense as meaning the spiritual coming of Christ
into the human soul by grace.   (W. A. 4, 443, 18)

He begins to gloss the text thus:

O Lord, hear my prayer
   the prayer by which I seek to be redeemed of my sins and to be
   justified.
give thy ears
   that is simply repetition of and strengthening of the original words.
to my supplication
   which comes through something holy, as he says 'through thy
   mercy or truth', as follows,
in thy truth
   i.e. through the faithfulness of thy promise, by which thou hast
   promised mercy to the penitent and to those who seek it, not
   according to my own merit.

Luther then makes the following footnote to the word 'truth':

In Hebrew it says 'in thy faith' (as Reuchlin and our own A. V.
translators translated it), i.e. the faithful fulfilment of the promise, that
thou mayst be found true and righteous. In other words, delivering the
truth that had been promised, not as being owed to me from my own
deserts, but as owed to thyself from thy covenant.

Hear me in thy righteousness
   not in my righteousness, but the righteousness thou givest me and
   will give me through faith.

   1. The passage in italics is underlined in Luther's text.

And enter not into judgement
  in the matter of my own righteousness, but rather according to thy
  mercy.
with thy servant
  what will be the fate of an enemy if a servant is not justified?
for in thy sight
  in the presence of God or before Him.
shall no man living
  whoever thinks he is justified by his own righteousness.
be justified
  i.e. he will not be justified through his own righteousness.

Luther adds the following footnote:

Paul is saying the same thing in Romans vi. 'He that is dead is freed
from sin.' 'If ye live after the flesh ye shall die.' Therefore it behoves
us to be killed, and all our own wisdom, all our own righteousness to
be cast aside, that we may be clothed with the wisdom and righteousness of God. But in this life this does not come to pass completely:
therefore none is righteous upon earth, for no one is not a sinner.

(W. A. 4, 443, 5–36)

Closely related to this Christological interpretation of the
Psalms is his developing idea of the righteousness of God. As
God's righteousness terrified him, so did Christ in his purity
and righteousness. This was another of the points at which
Luther 'broke through', for he saw again that what Christ did
on the cross was the fulfilment of the righteousness of God that
we might be made the righteousness of God in him (2 Corinthians v, 31).

On the words 'judgement' and 'righteousness' (Psalm 72) he
wrote:

The old law properly prophesied only in the matter of the first coming
of Christ: when Christ would rule in a kindly and saving judgement,
because it is an advent of grace and mercy. Wherefore the Apostle
wrote, 'The righteousness of God has been witnessed by the law and
the prophets. But the righteousness of God is through faith in Jesus
Christ' (Romans iii, 21 f.). The new commandment prophesies properly of the judgement and righteousness to come. . . . That he speaks
of a merciful judgement in this context is plain because he says he

will judge the poor people. He condemns them to save them ... but he condemns the unrighteous in their unrighteousness. ...

The Gospel is called by many other names: the law of Christ, the law of peace, the law of grace: [Here Luther quotes examples from Isaiah, the Psalms, the Gospels] It is not to be marvelled at why 'grace' or the 'law of grace' (which is the same thing) is both judgement and righteousness. What must be seen is this: without a doubt, in that He judges, He justifies him who believes in Him.

(W. A. 3, 461, 20–462, 26)

It should be noted however, that when I say the Gospel is judgement and righteousness, that should be understood as referring to the Gospel in its entirety, i.e. as completely fulfilled. The Gospel itself fulfilled and made complete by the operation (*opus*) of God is judgement and righteousness, by which Christ rules the Church. [Because when the Gospel is fulfilled by this operation of God (*opus*), then it always means that the word of God is made flesh in a spiritual manner. For the work (*opus*) is as flesh. And the word is as the son of God. Wherefore the Gospel, when it is fulfilled, is judgement and righteousness, the work of God, the way of God, and all the rest of these terms, just as Christ in his person is all these things written of Him in the scriptures.]

(W. A. 3, 463, 21–8)

On Psalm 69, 6:

The Jews did not know in what way Christ was accursed. It is indeed true that he had been cursed by God: because the Father made him a curse for our sakes, and truly he died on account of sins. ... He was at one and the same time cursed yet blessed, alive and dead, sorrowing and rejoicing, so that he could absorb all evil into himself and confer all good things out of himself.

(W. A. 3, 426, 27 ff.)

In similar vein, on the subject of God's strange work and ways, he comments on Psalm 77, 19, 'Thy footsteps are not known':

Of course it is quite clear that in the context it refers to His footsteps through the Red Sea, but in the spiritual interpretation the same truth obtains. The natural man does not understand because this is the way of God which the saints tread. In fact it seems to them not to be the way of God, but foolishness and error, and a cause of offence. They see their own way, of course, and their own life, but they do not

see that this other way is the way of God, because the natural man does
not perceive the things which are of God and the Spirit. As Pharaoh
along with his countrymen saw quite well the road along which the
children of Israel went, but that this was the way of God, they never
understood – not until they went under.   (W. A. 3, 546)

This parallelism of God's 'alien work' and his real, intended
'proper work' fulfilled eventually in Christ, is a key not only to
the meaning of the Gospel but to the way the world treated
Christ and the way it treats and treated those chosen by God
for His purpose of redemption. God's 'proper work' was
effected through Christ's 'strange work'. It was this conception
of Christ's work that impelled a man to faith, the sole ground of
our justification. On Psalm 140 '. . . evil shall hunt the unrighteous man and destroy him', he glosses 'the unrighteous
man' as 'an unbelieving man', and says 'faith alone justifies'.
On v, 13, 'surely the righteous shall give thanks', he glosses 'the
righteous' as those 'justified by faith in Christ'.[1] On 'the
generation of the upright shall be blessed' (Psalm 112, 2) he
glosses 'the upright' as 'believing men' and adds 'for faith alone
makes a man upright'.[2] On Psalm 111, 3, 'his righteousness
endureth forever', he comments: 'That is understood of that
righteousness which is in us worked by God through faith. And
the work of faith is confession to God and his magnification.'[3]

On Psalm 119, 161, 'Princes have persecuted me without a
cause, but my heart standeth in awe of thy word', he writes: 'It is
only our faith that fails here. If faith were complete it would
make perfect our fear and awe for the words of God, so that this
happy boasting would come from faith alone, moreover faith
of the most robust kind.'[4] He adds on Psalm 58, 1: 'Do ye
indeed speak righteousness?' This is a righteousness that is
true and complete in the sight of God, and that means righteousness by faith alone.[5]

---

1. 4, 438, 3.   2. 4, 247, 21.

3. 4, 241, 24 ff. This idea of magnification is a favourite theme of Luther's.
He always seeks to make men 'confess' the wonder of the work God has done
for them in and through Christ, as part of a more reverent awareness of the
wonder and glory and majesty of God.

4. 4, 380, 5 f.   5. 3, 320, 20.

So strong is this Christological interpretation of the Psalms,
that Luther frequently heads his comment to a psalm with words
such as 'a word from Christ', or 'a prayer of Christ to the
Father', 'a confession of the Church on the benefits from God
shown through Christ', etc., and frequently refers to Christ as
speaking and prophesying in the Psalms. Christ is all in all to
him and the goal of all scripture. Throughout the commentaries
he continually identifies the non-believing Jews of the Old and
New Testament with the non-believers, the heretics, the per-
verters of his own day, the condemnation common to them all
being that they reject Christ. 'Every word of the Bible peals the
name of Christ.'

All the time the reader senses Luther's struggle for the truth
of the doctrine of justification in Christ alone. Therefore, over
and over again the question wells up to the surface, how does the
sinner attain this justification?

The fact that he shows mercy towards me, in itself justifies me. His
mercy is my justification.   (W. A. 3, 43, 9)

The idea of Luther's break-through as some lightning streak
of spiritual illumination is always attractive, for it dramatizes in
one moment what was a long and arduous struggle, and provides
a useful catchword – the *Turmerlebnis* (the tower experience).
But, as Paul's experience on the road to Damascus was but the
end of his career as a doctor of the Law and the beginning as a
preacher of the Gospel, a transition which needs the whole
Pauline corpus to explain it, so was Luther's 'break-through' in
the Psalms a parallel experience of an equally cataclysmic transition needing the Lutheran corpus to account for it. Many distinguished Luther scholars (Boehmer, Vogelsang, Scheel,
Wendorf, Stracke, Hermelink, Bauer – the list is long) have
sought with great learning, some to pin-point the moment of
Luther's break-through, others even to criticize any such pin-
pointing. More simply, we might reflect that Luther as a teacher
always *dramatized* his experiences (for example, the call to be a
monk, the tower experience, the confrontation by the Devil).
There is nothing against that. Many scholars interpret Luther's
break-through in terms of a process rather than of a cataclysm,

a line rather than a point. It takes a theologian, at least a religious man, to know the torment of that inner blasphemy against God and his ways. Luther's mind was exercised with problems of this theological dimension rather than with scandals, or even with the problems which seemed to exercise a St Benedict, who would roll his naked body in the thorns to quell lust, or of a St Cuthbert who stood all night up to his neck in that ghastly cold North Sea off the coast of Northumberland to subjugate the flesh. Luther cheerfully remarked once, 'Women never bothered me. I was always concerned with the really knotty problems.'

One of these 'really knotty problems' was that of predestination. In his wrestling with God he was like an amateur in the grip of an experienced wrestler; every move produced a firmer counter-lock. He sought for assurance but found none. 'No one could help me,' he cried. Staupitz did help him enormously here by liberating him from scholastic ideas of grace being given *pari passu* with human effort, and by assuring him of the wholeness of God's salvation in the first moment of repentance. He then began to think of God as a friend and helper pursuing him, 'whose strong feet . . . followed, followed after'.

It was his awareness of the work of Christ kindling faith in the heart that made Luther more and more aware of sin in the sense of what the scholastics (and he himself) called an accusation of self. This awareness of one's own sin (an awareness created by the Spirit not by the self) Luther described as 'humility'. Rupp discerningly pointed out[1] that this humility grew into what Luther was later to call faith, the passive waiting on the Lord, the jettisoning of every kind of self-righteousness and the apprehension in poverty of the overflowing mercy and righteousness of God. Rupp's view of faith as a master conception subsuming Luther's earlier conceptions is a profound summing-up of the meaning of these four years.

(2) The Law–Gospel Tension

There are two further conceptions of considerable importance to Luther, namely the Law–Gospel tension and the Wrath of God.

1. Gordon Rupp, op. cit., p. 149.

The Law–Gospel tension was not so prominent as it was very soon to become, but Luther was perfectly aware of that essential difference in the two ways God handled men, namely, under Law or under Gospel. Commenting on Psalm 85, 8, 'I will hear what the Lord God will say in me', he says of the words 'in me':

In this phrase the difference between the Gospel and Law is touched upon. The Law is the word of Moses *to* us, the Gospel on the other hand is the word of God *in* us. The former abides without; it speaks in figures and visible forecasts of things to happen. On the other hand, the latter comes to us within, and speaks of inward and spiritual things and of truth. The one speaks in us, the other speaks to us.

(W. A. 4, 9, 28)

It would be hard to arrive at a more succinct statement on the Gospel and the Law in any of his writings.

In connexion with this, Luther frequently discusses the theme which runs through the Psalms of how God handles his saints, and the meaning of all the sorrow and tribulation that comes to the faithful. He frequently refers to this mystery of God's 'contrariwise' handling of the righteous, and shows that it is part of the theology of the cross for God to kill in order to make alive, to destroy the natural man so as to bring to birth the spiritual man. This is exactly how he understood the Law. He referred to this activity as God's 'alien work' necessary to effect his 'proper work', which of course was one of love and mercy, seen at its purest in the Gospel.

On Psalm 44, which speaks of the deliverance of the children of Israel from the bondage of Egypt, he writes: 'Thou didst this freely because thou wast well disposed towards them. Thou showedst favour to them from thine own good will: not from their deserts' (verse 3): it is not the sword or bow that saved our fathers, nor will it be our human strength that will save us. 'Thou hast saved us from our enemies by preserving within us in our spirit faith and righteousness' (verse 7): but now thou has cast us off and put us to shame before the world and in the face of men, but not in our conscience where thou acceptest and glorifiest us. 'And thou goest not forth with our armies' (verse

9): God does not save us as he once saved these, that is in the flesh, but in the spirit. And then he adds the following footnote:

In this verse the same words can be taken to mean the rejection of the Apostles according to the flesh and the rejection of the Jews according to the spirit. The Apostles bewail both. Augustine is the first to follow. Isaiah also prophesied this: it is the alien work of God, that He might work his proper work (Isaiah xxviii, 21): He destroys in order to save, He condemns according to the flesh that He may glorify the spirit. What is more alien to salvation than destruction? And yet this is what Christ does to His own. And this is just what nobody understands, unless he has before him the education of the sons of Korah,[1] i.e. spiritual understanding. See the whole of this wonderful chapter of Isaiah. More true and more important is the opinion I now pursue. This psalm may be understood of the tribulation of the holy Apostles and martyrs though the original context refers to the rejection of the Jews. Therefore the lesson to learn is this: the Psalms teach spiritual truths. The temporal benefits [given to the Jews in the Old Testament] are not to be hoped for and sought after at the hands of God as once they were. The doctrine exhorts everybody who reads this psalm to know that in this world they are bound to be humiliated, cast aside and afflicted, even if they do good.   (W. A. 3, 244–6)

Nevertheless, though Luther always explained the Law in terms of the Gospel he never abrogated the permanent and universal authority of the Law, a principle that was to create many enemies for him in the shape of the radicals and enthusiasts. Not only was the Law abiding and applicable, but obedience to it meant not an unwilling, perfunctory, external compliance but a glad-hearted fulfilment of it. Speaking on Psalm 1, 2, on delight in the Law of the Lord, he writes:

It is not to be thought of so much as the hand forced by necessity, almost by fear, or the hope of reward, as something chosen without pleasure; but rather as delight which performs the Law of the Lord with a joyful unprompted gladness.   (W. A. 3, 17, 1)

See also on Psalm 19, 13 (W.A. 3, 129, 24) and on Psalm 84, 7 (W.A. 3, 649, 2 f.).

---

1. See Numbers xvi for the rebellion of Korah; cf. W.A. 1, 540.

(3) The Wrath

Luther was to develop his full theology of the Wrath later, but at this stage he held on to two important distinctions made by Augustine. The first was that God's anger should not be compared to or associated in any way with human anger, but should be interpreted rather as relinquishing self-centred man to his own devices, in much the same sense as Paul spoke of God's 'giving up' the heathen and leaving them to the wrath of their own creatureliness as well as that of all other created beings.

He interpreted 'Then shall he speak to them in his wrath' (Psalm 2, 5):

This means that in His wrath He makes Christ, and other saints, speak; for even the wrath or the vengeance executed by creatures is from God. The wrath is not God's in the sense that it is in God, but in that the creature, in whom wrath exists, is His, and that it is at His command and bidding that the creature afflicts the ungodly. God himself remains perfectly quiet and calm within: He is perfectly good and not perturbed.   (W. A. 3, 35, 11)

Similarly he expounded 'He sent them the wrath of His indignation' (Psalm 78, 50) (the plagues He sent to punish them not in kindness but in severity):

The Wrath of God is what God brings to pass in His punitive capacity. But the Wrath is not in Him. When I say the wrath of his indignation as it is called, or the effects of the Wrath of God, and describe this as wrath and indignation and tribulation, I am referring to what is in the people and their minds. That is to say, wrath may be taken in two ways. One: it is the Wrath of God conceived as brought to bear against them, by which He makes them angry and indignant. Two: because they themselves are angered by it. In this way the wrath and jealousy which burns within them (or if you prefer it of devils working against them) *is the Wrath of God*. In simple words it is the workings of the Wrath of God directed against them.   (W. A. 3, 591, 32 ff.)

A deeper meaning of the Wrath was the terrible *aversio dei*, when God just turned his back on a soul and let him go his own way. This inaction of God's was far worse than his reaction, his silence worse than his thunderings. On Psalm 59 (and 57 and 58), speaking on the theme of calamities and destruction and the prayer for deliverance, he wrote:

. . . what they are in themselves is destroyed that they might become what they themselves are not, i.e. sons of God and righteous. Happy is destruction of this kind! And the most unhappy thing of all is not to be destroyed in this way. God is most angry when he shows no anger at all. He then sends the godless to go their own way, to increase and further their own interests: he does not destroy these people.

(W. A. 3, 329 f.)

On Psalm 2:

Properly speaking God does not afflict a man by drawing near to him to do so, but by withdrawing from him and abandoning him to the natural world.   (W. A. 3, 35, 20)

On Psalm 69:

If thou askest a sign of the grace of God and whether Christ is in thee: behold, no sign will be given thee by the sign of Jonah. If then thou art in hell for the space of three days, then that is the sign that Christ is with thee and thou art with Christ. The worst thing to be afraid of would be if God were to say to you something like he said to Ezekiel: Let my fury against thee rest and my jealousy depart from thee (xvi, 42). But that is not the worst of Wrath! Because if jealousy is removed love is of necessity removed as well, since these are insepaable activities.   (W. A. 3, 433, 2 ff.)

On Psalm 69:

According to Bernard, the sorrow of the Church when it is under the heel of tyrants is bitter, under heretics more bitter, but when it is in a state of peace, the bitterest of all. Because in the opinion of all those devoted to the Church, and of those who really know, the worst temptation is to have no temptation. The worst adversity of all is to have no adversity. God is most angry when he shows no anger, again according to Bernard. For it is not when I do not feel Thee angry, but when I feel Thee angry, I am most greatly putting trust in Thy favour.[1]   (W. A. 3, 420, 14 ff.)

1. Bernard of Clairvaux, *Sermones in Cantica Canticorum*, 33, par. 13 (MPL, 183, 953–4).

On Psalm 90, 11:

Who knows the power of thy wrath? That man knows who believes that those very pains and death are so powerful and efficacious in earning reward and a crown. This is to say, Foolish people will not believe this, for they understand the ways of God in a human or carnal way. They do not think that things that are evil from a human point of view are from a God favourably disposed towards them. He can be understood even in severity, for the power of God is shown in His Wrath. He is angry with those whom He makes to prosper, even if He does not seem to be. And He is not angry in afflictions, even if it seems that He is. (W. A. 3, 52, 28)

Secondly, there was the distinction within the Wrath, of mercy and severity. Luther saw a 'hidden God' behind the Wrath, working out his irresistible purpose. God's Wrath appears different from what it really is, and this is its 'hiddenness'. It appears terrible but it is really merciful. It is a saving Wrath, in that it saves men from their sins. Luther peered through this darkness and violence of His Wrath and saw His Mercy. He heard, as he expressed it, under and above the 'No!' of God, the deep secret 'Yes!' that God speaks to a man. (See Psalms 6, 1; 58, 9; and 74, 1-2.)

There has been a tendency since Ritschl to explain the Wrath of God in psychological categories, to think of it in terms even of human wrath or anger. This is wholly alien to Luther's way of thinking and utterly misleading in itself. To Luther God was always and unchangingly *Eitel Liebe* (pure love): there was no wrath in Him. When sinful man in his freedom chooses to resist God and go his own way, God in His love uses that sin to work man's redemption. Man experiences the consequences of his own sin, or humanity's sin, and this in the Bible and in Luther is termed the Wrath of God. But the destructive power of the Wrath is always understood as the alien activity of God and not the proper activity which belongs to His real nature. God shows the stark reality of sin and its tyrannical power over men. God wrecks a man (or a society) by means of its own sin, but it is always a saving judgement, a divine teaching technique to free him from it. God desires not the death of a sinner but rather that he may turn from his wickedness and live. When God handles a man in Wrath He is showing man the horror of the world he makes when left to his own devices, and at the same time the prevailing power of His unchanging redemptive love. The supreme moment when the Love of God challenged the Wrath and routed it was on Calvary, and in this act God reconciled, and reconciles, a sinful humanity to Himself. When a man's eyes are truly opened to the tyranny of sin and its origin, and of God's undying and unchanging and undeserved redemptive love to champion him in the battle, he is at once delivered from its bondage. Wrath was terrifyingly real to Luther but it was a tyrant already vanquished in principle.

THE EPISTLE TO THE ROMANS (1515–16)

The Epistle to the Romans was the theological textbook of reformed theology, the charter of the Reformation. It is generally conceded by scholars that of all the classical commentaries on Romans Luther's has never been surpassed. This massive commentary is significant not only for its intrinsic worth but for its early date. It contains virtually the whole of the revolutionary theological thrust of the Reformation, though it appeared two years before the storm of the indulgences scandal (1517), some seven years before the break at Worms (1521). Yet this epoch-making document was not published until 1908, and owing to freaks of historical accident lay unnoticed and unread for four hundred years.

A study of the original document shows that the material had been accumulated with meticulous care and finally assembled by Luther himself with scholarly precision in the neatest handwriting. Luther's way of preparation, as with his Psalms, was first to have Grunenberg, his printer, print the text of the document with wide margins and wide spaces between the lines. In the case of this epistle there were twenty-eight sheets with fourteen lines per sheet. (Each student had the same twenty-eight sheets issued to him.) On the pages of this printed text Luther wrote in very small handwriting all his grammatical, philological and marginal comment. The essentials of these Luther dictated in class to his students to be written above or at the side of the printed text they were studying. But in addition to these notes, Luther had prepared his own extended commentary covering 23 sheets, only part of which he gave to his students. Consequently, all the existing student manuscripts which scholars have succeeded in tracking down give the text of Luther's lectures as given in class, but not the text in full of Luther's own manuscript. Luther saved his students from much of the then controversial material, certain passages criticizing the theology and pastoral practice of his day, and those sections where he was still formulating his theology. Consequently, what was lost for four centuries was not merely Luther's lectures on Romans but that priceless work of the young Professor Luther at this crucial moment of development and conflict.

In August 1518 Philip Melanchthon joined the faculty at Wittenberg, and to him were assigned the lectures on the Epistle to the Romans. Luther never again lectured on Romans, and as far as is known never referred again to his own lectures. They were never published. Whenever he was consulted on Romans he referred all inquirers to Melanchthon, whose responsibility it now was, though there is evidence that Melanchthon and his colleagues had access to or used copies of Luther's lecture manuscript.

The document was treated with considerable care by Luther's heirs. In 1582 it was bound in red leather and the covers impressed with the electoral coat of arms in gold. Luther's son Paul, physician to the Elector, refers to this document in a letter to the wife of the Elector in 1592, where he writes of his intention to have his father's early Latin lectures in his possession rendered into German. In 1587 the theologian John Wiegand referred to these documents, saying, 'I have held his own autographs in my hands and looked at them with admiration.'

Veit von Seckendorf (1626–92), the Church historian who had access to the archives of the electors, refers to this testimony of Wiegand but regretted that there was no trace of them in the archives and presumed them lost. He did not know that they had never been there but had been in the personal possession of Luther's family. The sons of Paul Luther sold all of Luther's manuscripts and printed books to Joachim Frederick, Margrave of Brandenburg, about the year 1594. The library of the latter came to be incorporated into the Royal Library of Berlin. The oldest catalogue of the library (dated 1688) lists Luther's manuscript on Romans, and it is recorded that on the three hundredth anniversary of Luther's death (1846) this manuscript was put on exhibition. It was later displayed in a show case in the public entrance but attracted no notice. In 1905 the librarian was moved to express his surprise that no Luther scholar had ever come to study it.

Yet Luther scholars had been spurred to a new search for this precious document believed lost, for a copy of it had been found in the Vatican Library. The Dominican Denifle, a virulent anti-protestant, published a learned and weighty attack on the evangelical theology entitled *Luther and Lutheranism* (1904), using this manuscript and others as the basis of his criticisms. Protestant scholars were pilloried before the learned world for their ignorance of the full nature of Luther's break with Rome.

This Vatican copy was a manuscript copy made by Aurifaber, the assiduous scribe responsible for much of the *Table Talk*.[1] Between 1570 and 1580 Ulrich Fugger, of the great banking house, a Protestant and collector of books and manuscripts, thought it of great importance to preserve and collect Luther's writings, and where there was no printed text in existence, assigned to this Boswell of the Reformation the task of making copies of the manuscripts, among which was that of the lectures on the Romans. These Fugger bequeathed to the Palatine Library of Heidelberg, and before his death saw to their careful removal himself. There they remained, all these priceless treasures, some 3,527 manuscripts, the finest collection in Germany, till the Thirty Years' War. When in 1622 Maximilian I of Bavaria captured the Palatinate, devout Catholic that he was, he handed over the entire contents of the library to the Pope, Gregory XV. It was in this collection that Denifle was to

1. See p. 323.

discover the lost manuscript on Romans three hundred years later.[1]

These discoveries, not unlike the chance discoveries of the Dead Sea Scrolls in 1947, generated an enormous literature which has been called 'the Luther Renascence'. In the last fifty years the whole understanding of what Luther said and did has authoritatively and decisively changed. All the romanticism which made of him a kind of Faust, all the nationalism which made him the type of Nordic hero, all the legends of his many Boswells, all the religious hatred and fanaticism which saw him as an arch-devil incarnate, are being rubbed off the canvas by both Roman Catholic and Protestant scholars alike, to set the solid professor in his true colours and in his real situation, the man of God with so much to say to the people of God. This Luther Renascence, now being caught up into the ecumenical movement, may well prove the determinative factor in the debate between Roman Catholicism and Protestantism. Certainly it was during these formative years of Luther before the disastrous break with Rome that the issues between Luther and the Pope, between Protestantism and Catholicism are seen at their clearest.

The Purpose of the Epistle

How can this mighty work of some five hundred odd pages be summarized or explained? As I look at my own copy on my desk now, scored, marked, commented on, with cross-references and underlinings on every page over years of study, teeming with concentrated profundities, bristling with critical discernment, it is certain there can be no adequate summing up.

Nevertheless, if it is hard to make a summary, it is easy to

1. In 1899 Pope Leo XIII declared the Vatican libraries open to the academic world. When a German scholar, Hermann Vopel, was seeking for material on Melanchthon, he found other manuscripts of Luther, one of which later turned out to be his lost commentary on the Epistle to the Hebrews, material used also by Denifle. For a translation with comment on this see James Atkinson, Library of Christian Classics, Vol. 16, London and Philadelphia, 1962.

make a start, for Luther shows his hand in the opening sentences not only of the scholia but of the glosses.

The sum total of this epistle is this: it is to tear down, and to pull out, and to destroy all wisdom and righteousness as man understands them. This is to happen whatever regard they may have in men's judgement, even in our own convictions, and no matter with what deep sincerity they are practised. After that its purpose is to set and establish, even to magnify, sin, no matter if we used to think that it was not there and could not be there. It was on this account that St Augustine said in his *Concerning the Spirit and the Letter*, St Paul 'contends valiantly against the proud, the arrogant and those who presume on their good works', etc. 'For that reason in the Epistle to the Romans this very investigation is almost its sole concern, fought for so bravely and in so many ways as almost to wear out the reader. But at the same time it is a fatigue that is profitable and health-giving. . . .' For God does not want to save us by our own personal and private righteousness and wisdom. He wants to save us by a righteousness and wisdom apart from and other than this. A righteousness which does not come from ourselves, is not brought to birth by ourselves. It is a righteousness which comes into us from somewhere else. It is not a righteousness which finds its origins on this earth of ours. It is a righteousness which comes from heaven. Therefore we must be instructed in this external and alien righteousness in every possible kind of way. That is why the first task is to pull out our own personal and petty righteousness. . . . As men without anything, we must wait for the pure mercy of God, for Him to reckon us as righteous and wise.

(W. A. 56, 157–9)

Or again, when he is about to gloss the text of Romans i, 1, he writes the following footnote to the title of the Epistle:

The sum purpose of the Apostle in this epistle is to destroy all righteousness and wisdom of our own, and the sins and foolishness which we thought no longer existed (i.e. we thought they no longer existed on account of such righteousness of our own); his purpose is to establish these once more, to increase them, and to magnify them. This means to effect a state of mind that can recognize that they still exist, and not only exist but are great and many. In this way we might come to realize that Christ and his righteousness are necessary for the real destruction of these. This he does down to Chapter 12. From there to the end he teaches us what things and what kind of things we

ought to do, once this same righteousness of Christ is accepted. Therefore, in the sight of God the case is not a matter of a man becoming
righteous by doing righteous works. (This is what the foolish Jews,
the heathen, and the seekers after righteousness foolishly believe in
their pride and conceit.) It is a case of a man being righteous doing
righteous deeds. As it is written, The Lord had regard to Abel and
his gifts (Genesis iv, 4) not first to what he had done [but to what he
was]. (W. A. 56, 3–4)

On Romans i, 16, referring to the 'power of God', he writes:

The power of God is to be understood not as that power by which he
in his own being is powerful in some definable way, but that power by
which he makes people powerful and strong. . . . He who believes
in the Gospel must become weak and foolish in the eyes of men so
that he may become strong and wise in the power and wisdom of
God. (W. A. 56, 169, 29–171, 10)

The Righteousness of God

On the key text of the 'righteousness of God' he opens up his
summary of the epistle:

In the doctrines of men it is the righteousness of men that is revealed
and taught. In other words, they teach who is righteous, in what way
he is righteous, and how he may become righteous, in his own judgement as well as that of his fellows. But the righteousness of God is
revealed only in the Gospel: in other words, who is righteous, how he
is righteous, and how he may become righteous, in the sight of God.
This comes about by faith alone: by that faith with which the Word
of God is believed. . . . The righteousness of God is the cause of
salvation. And here again 'the righteousness of God' ought not to be
taken in the sense in which God is righteous in his own nature, but
as that righteousness by which we are made righteous by him. This
comes about through faith in the Gospel. . . . According to Aristotle
righteousness follows from, and arises from, doing good works. But
according to God righteousness precedes good works and works spring
from righteousness. (W. A. 56, 169–72)

Again on the theme of righteousness he glosses Romans ii, 13,
in this way:

Not the hearers of the law
As those who say, 'Lord, we have prophesied in thy name'. They
are of the same kind as those who do the works of the law but have
no heart in it. To that extent they do not in fact keep the law.

are righteous in the sight of God
   i.e. are reputed righteous by God.
'To be righteous before God' and 'to be justified before God' are the same thing. It is not because a man is righteous that he is therefore reputed to be righteous by God, but because he is reputed to be righteous by God he is therefore righteous, as in Chapter 4. For no one is reputed righteous except the man who fulfils the law by his deeds. But no one fulfils the law except the man who believes in Christ. And thus the Apostle intends to conclude that apart from Christ no one is righteous, and no one keeps the law. . . .

but the doers
   they are only those who have grace, the effective conqueror of the will.

of the law will be justified.
   they will be reputed righteous before God.

(W. A. 56, 22, 5 ff.)

He returns to this central theme commenting on Romans iii, 7 and 26:

Every created being furnishes eloquent proof of the same point: it cannot happen that one who is full of his own righteousness can be filled with the righteousness of God. God only fills those who hunger and thirst after righteousness. Whoever, therefore, is full of his own truth and wisdom has no room for the truth and wisdom of God. They can be received only by the man who is without worth and without pretensions. Therefore, speak thus to God: O how readily we acknowledge our emptiness, that in thy fulness thou may dwell in us! Readily acknowledge my weakness, that thy strength may dwell in me! Readily admit I am a sinner, that thou mayest be justified in me! Readily admit I am a fool, that thou mayest be my wisdom! Readily admit I am unrighteous, that thou mayest be my righteousness!

(W. A. 56, 219, 3 ff.)

We cannot be justified by our own efforts. We draw near to him so that He himself will make us righteous as we confess that we are not in a state to get the upper hand of sin.   (W. A. 56, 221, 15 ff.)

As long as I recognize that I cannot be righteous before God . . . I then begin to ask for righteousness from Him. . . . The only thing that resists this idea of justification is the pride of the human heart, proud through unbelief. . . . It does not believe because it does not regard the word of God as true. It does not regard it as true because it regards its own understanding as true and the Word of God runs counter to that. (W. A. 56, 226, 7)

It is quite clear from this text that, according to the Apostle's way of thinking, God is called righteous in that he justifies men or makes them righteous. . . . And thus it is plain and evident from the Apostle's own explanation of himself, that 'the righteousness of God' is spoken of as that righteousness by which He makes us righteous, just as the wisdom of God is that wisdom by which he makes us wise.

(W. A. 56, 262, 19)

Luther further clarifies this distinction between righteousness understood as a human attainment, and righteousness understood as the righteousness of God working on and in a man, freely offered to him as a gift of mercy:

Two theses have to be borne in mind:

(*a*) *The saints are always sinners intrinsically and on that account are always justified extrinsically.*

(*b*) *The hypocrites* [in this context 'works-mongers' or 'works-righteous' people] *on the other hand are always justified intrinsically and on that account are always sinners extrinsically.*

When I use the word '*intrinsically*' I mean how we are in ourselves, what we are like in our own eyes and in our own estimation. But by the word '*extrinsically*' I mean what we are in the sight of God and in His reckoning. Therefore we are justified 'extrinsically' when we are justified not from ourselves or our own works, but by the reckoning of God only. His reckoning does not rest with us nor lie within our grasp. Therefore our justification lies neither in ourselves nor in our power. . . . Within thee is naught but perdition. But thy salvation comes from outside thee.

He paradoxically and tersely sums up:

Righteous thou knowest not how, though unrighteous thou knowest too well! Sinners in reality, yet justified in hope!

(W. A. 56, 268–9)

Or as Luther still better expressed it in a disputation at this time:

Every saint is a sinner to his certain knowledge, but righteous in a sense beyond his capacity to know [as God reckons]; a sinner in fact but justified in hope; a sinner indeed, yet justified by the reckoning of God showing mercy. *Disputation on Grace*, 1516 (W. A. 1, 149, 8)

Luther was always concerned that a man should appropriate this work of Christ to himself and not make of faith mere assent:

This is what the Apostle means when he says a man is justified by faith. It is to believe that this is spoken not only about the elect but rather about yourself, and it is to be appropriated by you (*assertive*): that Christ died for your sins and gave satisfaction for them.

On Romans viii, 16 (W. A. 56, 370, 11 ff.)

But Luther safeguarded his biblical position as many who succeeded him have not. Many have made of the doctrine of justification by faith alone a worse position than that of justification by works and effort. They have tended to interpret faith as a state of mind which allows them to appropriate salvation. They seek for faith and try to induce it. This, of course, makes of faith a very insidious work. The impelling power is not one's own faith, but Christ who occasions faith and restores the faith of sinful man in a good merciful God. It is not a matter of faith but faith in Christ:

They [people who presume on their faith] believe that they can have access to God without Christ, as if it were sufficient for them to have believed. They believe they can have access by faith alone. They will not go through Christ but alongside Christ. It is as if they no longer had any need of Christ after having received the grace of justification. ... These people who approach God through faith, and not at the same time through Christ, actually go away from God. ... Wherefore both must happen together: through faith, through Christ. Consequently let us do and suffer all we can, in faith in Christ.

On Romans v, 2 (W. A. 56, 298–9)

Scripture

On scripture he says:

The whole of scripture deals with Christ throughout.

On Romans x, 6 (W. A. 56, 414, 15 f.)

... every word in the Bible rings of Christ.

(W. A. 56, 414, 17 f.)

Sin

The deep diapason of sin can be heard beneath and behind every other motive.

Not as scholastics define it but as Paul and Christ teach it: the loss of all uprightness and of the power of all our faculties of body and soul, of the whole inner and outer man.

On Romans v, 14 (W. A. 56, 312, 8 f.)

It is not a matter of how a man stands in his own eyes or in the opinion of his fellows, but of how God sees him. There is the clear-cut stern tone of the prophet in Luther; even the righteous man is a sinner:

Look! Every saint is a sinner and prays for his sins. In this way the justified man is in the first place an accuser of himself. . . . Therefore it is the wonderful and most tender mercy of God that regards us at the same time as sinners, yet non-sinners.

On Romans iv, 7 (W. A. 56, 270, 6 f.)

The great evil and error is less that man is unaware of his sin than that he makes a wrong diagnosis of it and thinks he can cure this disease himself:

Here lies the error: in believing that this disease can be cured by means of our own works. All experience proves that whatever good work we effect, there remains in it that concupiscence toward evil and nobody is free from it, not even an infant a day old.

(W. A. 56, 270, 24 ff.)

Therefore 'actual sin' (to use the theologian's label) is more correctly sin understood as the work and fruit of sin. Sin really is that passion, that tinder [tinder in the sense that it is always there ready to be ignited], that concupiscence, that inclination to evil and the difficulty in doing good. . . . Now, if these work, then they are not works properly speaking. They work to bring forth fruit. They themselves are not the fruit.   On Romans iv, 7 (W. A. 56, 271, 6 ff.)

Law and Gospel

Therefore, closely related to Luther's emphasis on sin understood in its plain New Testament meaning was Luther's refutation of Law as an answer to the problem of man's sin. This carried with it the emphasis of Christ, that even though the Law was divine dispensation, no man could fail to see not only that no man could ever keep the Law, but that no man was spiritually free to do what he knew to be right according to Law (Matthew v, 17; vi, 24). Already we have Luther's clear distinction between the Law and the Gospel as methods of salvation, as well as his clear discernment, on Augustinian lines, of the bondage of the will.

He sees the problem as man's natural preference for the Law rather than the Gospel, and in his confidence that if he wills good and really loves God, he will effect the good and also know God.

> The sum total of this error is that it is a Pelagian[1] opinion. . . . They think if they have the will to do good, quite infallibly they will receive the grace of God infused. (W. A. 56, 502, 14 ff.)

But this is to think as man thinks and not as God disposes. It is to make the profound error of believing that a man comes to God by virtue of much striving, whereas it is not a case of man's striving to attain God at all but of a merciful God who comes all the way to man.

> Sin and the wisdom of the flesh are one and the same thing. (W. A. 56, 359, 1 f.)

To have kept the Law does not put us in a position of having a claim on God. It puts us in a position of really seeing our plight namely that we cannot even keep the Law:

> It is not true to say that the works of the Law can fulfil the Law, since the Law is spiritual and demands the whole heart and will. It is impossible to have these of ourselves. For this reason, they (who glory in performing the Law) do the works of the Law but do not fulfil its intent. (W. A. 56, 264, 31)

Law cannot be understood except in tension with faith. On Romans iii, 31, where Paul argues that it is he who is establishing

---

1. Pelagius was a fifth-century British monk who taught that man's initial steps towards salvation are without divine assistance. The derivative words 'Pelagian' and 'Pelagianism' are almost always used in a pejorative sense.

and not destroying the Law (as Christ argued before him),
Luther comments:

We establish the Law, i.e. we declare it fulfilled and confirmed by
faith. . . . The Law is established in itself and in us. In itself, in so
far as it is promulgated; in us, when we do it in will and deed. But,
apart from faith, nobody does this. Therefore we always make the
covenant of God void and of none effect, if we are without the grace
given by faith in Christ. (W. A. 56, 263, 17 ff.)

But Luther never despised good works as did the enthusiasts
who harped on their one string of faith. Arguing that good works
are not to be neglected, he points out that their danger lies in
our thinking that we measure up to God's requirements when
we do them. They are good only in that they prepare the way
of the Lord.

But good works are not the way of the Lord. The way of the Lord is
the righteousness of God viewed as the Lord present in us, who afterwards effects these good works through us. (W. A. 56, 233, 30)

And further on, discussing James and Paul on faith and works,
he writes:

Paul does not argue that faith alone justifies apart from the works
proper to it, but that faith alone justifies apart from the works of the
Law. Therefore justification does not require the works of the Law.
But it does need a lively faith which will effect the works proper to it.
On Romans iii, 19–20 (W. A. 56, 249, 5 ff.)

See also on Romans iii, 20 (255, 18); Romans ix, 6 (394, 30).

He carefully distinguished between the legal dispensation of
the Old Testament and the evangelical dispensation of the New
Testament. The students at those hard desks of Wittenberg
must have stirred when young Luther announced:

In the new law all things are free and nothing is necessary for those
who believe in Christ. Love is all that is necessary. . . . It does not
belong to the new law to set aside some days for fasting but not others,
as was done by the Law of Moses. Nor does it belong to the new law
to select certain kinds of foods and distinguish them from others, such
as meat, eggs, etc., as again the Law of Moses does (Leviticus xi, 4 ff.;
Deuteronomy xiv, 7 ff.). Nor does it belong to the new law to designate

some days as holy and others not. Nor does it belong to the new law to build this or that kind of church, or adorn them in a particular way or sing in them in a particular way; nor that we must have organs, altar decorations, chalices, images and all the rest we now find in places of worship. It is not even necessary to have priests and religious wearing tonsures and going about in distinctive clothes, as they did in the old Law. All these things are but shadows and tokens of reality. Indeed we have outgrown them. Every day is a holiday, every kind of food is permitted, every place is holy, every time is fasting time, every garment permitted. Everything is a matter of free choice, as long as moderation is kept in these things, and love, and the rest of the things the Apostle teaches.

On Romans xiv, 1 (W. A. 56, 493, 15–494, 17)

The Enslaved Will

Luther pursues this incapacity of man to fulfil the Law, his inability to do the good. He sees this as related to the bondage of the will and the necessity for a Gospel, rather than for a Law. Luther argues that a man cannot fulfil the Law and that his salvation is of mercy and grace.

[The natural man] seeks himself and his own interests in all things. He never seeks God. Only faith in love does that. . . . Unless faith begins to illuminate a man and love sets him free, no man can will or have or do anything good. He does evil to some extent, even when he is doing good.   (W. A. 56, 355, 13–26)

And this is scriptural teaching, which describes a man as curved in upon himself to such an extent that he hands back to himself not only physical but also spiritual goods and seeks his own interests in all things. Now this curvature is a natural crookedness: it is a natural defect and a natural evil.   (W. A. 56, 356, 4 ff.)

Grace sets before itself no object other than God. To Him it is drawn and to Him it directs itself. It sees Him alone. It seeks Him alone. It moves toward Him in all things, and everything else it sees in between itself and God it passes by as if it did not see it, and simply turns to God. . . . This is what it means to have a 'right heart' and a 'right spirit' (Psalms 7, 10; 78, 37; 51, 10). Nature on the other hand sets before itself no object other than the self. To this it is drawn and to this it directs itself. It sees itself alone. It seeks itself alone. It moves towards itself in everything. Everything else between itself and its own interests, even God Himself, it bypasses as though it did not see it, and directs its attention to itself. This is what it means to have a 'perverse' and 'wicked' heart (Psalm 101, 4; Proverbs xxvii, 21). It is first and last its own idol. . . . It values only those things that it can turn to its own enjoyment and advantage and interest. . . . It is happy and content in affluence, but when this is removed it is troubled and unquiet. Not so grace. This remains untroubled by either poverty or plenty, loving the will of God and observing it in all things. It is content whatever happens one way or another.   (W. A. 56, 356–7)

On the text of Romans vii, 18, 'to will is present with me, but how to perform that which is good I find not', Luther explains:

We must note, therefore, that the words 'I will' and 'I hate' refer to the spiritual man or to the spirit, but the words 'I do' and 'I work' to the carnal man and to the flesh. . . . One and the same man is both spiritual and carnal, righteous and a sinner, good and evil. . . . But these realities have no place at all in the carnal man. The entire man is flesh and nothing more than flesh because the Spirit of God has not taken its abode in him.   (W. A. 56, 343, 13–25)

. . . The Apostle does not mean to be understood as saying that spirit and flesh are two kinds of entities as it were. No, they are just one single idea, as wound and flesh are one. . . . The same man is spirit and flesh at one and the same time.   (W. A. 56, 350, 22 ff.)

A man's will is not free. In Augustinian terms he sees the entire person as curved in on himself, blind to God because of its own self-seeking; in rebellion against God and His ways by 'seeking itself and its own affairs'. It is a kind of ferment of egoism, a volcano perpetually grumbling:

The natural man enjoys everything with reference to himself and uses everybody else for the same purpose, even God himself: he seeks himself and his own interests in everything.   (W. A. 56, 361, 13 ff.)

This truth, this saving truth, about man is only revealed by God. To Luther the important thing is not what man thinks about God but what God thinks of man. In fact, the only path to grace is the broken will which alone can accept God in Christ without qualification. When the self-will is broken by the awareness of the terrifying reality of God as judge and the experience of His wrath, the soul cries out to God 'with no language but a cry'. This is very close to what Luther means by humility and it is already faith: a man who cries to God is already a believing man. And the reward of God is not vision and certainty, but quite simply faith increased; as Paul expressed it 'from faith to faith'. This is a movement, a direction, an activity, a working-out rather than a state. It is a kind of hidden process running contrary to man's normal human judgement or opinion. It is that invincible capacity for making fresh starts hopefully:

Paul is talking about progress and advancement. He is addressing people who are already Christians. Their life is not in resting quiet but in being on the move from good to better. They are like a sick man advancing from sickness to health. . . . It is no use to anybody for a tree to bud and blossom if the blossom does not develop into fruit. Many are the folk who perish in blossom. . . . A man's existence is always in a state of non-being, becoming, and being. . . . He is always in sin, in justification, in righteousness. Always a sinner, always penitent, always justified.

On Romans xii, 2 (W. A. 56, 441, 14–442, 17)

Sometimes Luther's strong views on the negation of the will are expressed in mystical categories, which were later to reach fulfilment in his mighty Theology of the Cross. His vehemence and despair give the impression of his own as yet unresolved conflict. There is, too, about the lectures a discernible influence of the practical mystics such as Bernard and Bonaventure and Tauler, though not the metaphysical mystics such as Dionysius. It was during the preparation of these lectures that the manuscript of *German Theology* came into his hands, and believing it to be the work of Tauler, Luther enthusiastically published it in December 1516 with his own introduction.

Predestination

Closely related to his emphasis on the bondage of the will is Luther's emphasis on predestination, a theme he handles more fully in his book written in reply to Erasmus's attack (see p. 228). He brushes aside the academic scholastic handling of the theme and makes Paul his starting point. To Paul this theme was one of comfort, always kept within the framework of the Promise

of God and the fulfilment of his evangelical purpose. It was to
Luther an aspect of the graciousness of God, a corollary of the
Gospel, purposed and intended by God for man. It was the perfect safeguard against any kind of works-religion or merit-
mongering; it was the fulfilment of the Law in the Gospel. It
preserved the theocentricity of the Gospel against the anthropo-
centricity of religion; it preserved the objectivity of the gift of
a gracious God and saved man from the subjectivity of his own
justification by works, his own merits and the belief in his own
fundamental decency:

To the elect and those who have the Spirit, predestination is the very
sweetest of all doctrines, but to the worldly-wise the bitterest and
hardest of all. . . . The reason why God saves in this way is to show
that he saves not by our merits but by election pure and simple, and
by His unchanging will. . . . We are saved by His unchanging love. . . .
Where then is our righteousness? Where our good works? Where is
our free will? What about this talk of the contingency of things?
On Romans viii, 28 (W. A. 56, 381, 18–382, 17)

It was a message of assurance and comfort to Luther. When
the doctrine torments a man, Luther says he should rejoice, for
God is then shown to be at work dissolving his own human
judgements, convincing him again that his salvation lies not in
his own works and efforts and plans, but solely in the election
of God.

Let him give thanks for such fear. Let him rejoice over his anxiety,
confident that God accepts the desperate heart (Psalm 51, 17).
On Romans viii, 28 (W. A. 56, 387, 21)

This experience was one of God's *Anfechtungen*, an assault on
the soul which brings salutary despair and thereby opens up a
man more fully to the Gospel and God's proper work in Christ.

No words are more effective in terrifying men, in humbling them,
and destroying their proud presumption in merits than these. . . .
People who are terrified and scared by this doctrine can take this as
the best of all signs, and a happy one.
On Romans viii, 28 (W. A. 56, 387, 4)

The Church and Society

Luther's horizon is wider than the lecture room. He criticizes the monks and the corruptions of the Church, the scandals of indulgences, the financial squabbles between princes and prelates, in fact all the ills of his day, not least the sordid materialism of the clergy:

Both the pope and the higher clergy who are so liberal in granting indulgences for the temporal support of the churches are more credulous than credulity itself if for the sake of God they are not equally or even more solicitous for grace and the cure of souls. They have freely received all they have, and they ought freely to give it. 'But they are corrupt and have become abominable in their ways' (Psalm 14, 1). They have been misled themselves and are now leading the people of Christ away from the true worship of God.
On Romans x, 6 (W. A. 56, 417, 27 ff.)

The monks are really Pelagians. They trust in themselves and their own works and consequently undermine both the Church and the faith.   On Romans xiv, 1 (W. A. 56, 501, 17 ff.)

Thou canst not live in that security conceived by thyself and found within thyself, but only in the mercy of God that you have prayed for and waited for. . . . To assume that the phrase, 'God unfailingly infuses grace into the man who does all that in him lies', means that a man may do anything and is able to do anything, is the most absurd of errors. It simply gives powerful support to the Pelagian error. The whole Church is absolutely undermined by its belief in this single idea.   (W. A. 56, 503, 1 ff.)

Speaking on the impenetrable darkness of the age he blames the spiritual rulers for their extravagances, for their quickness to defend the Church's rights, and for their fatal incapacity to consider themselves, rather than those they criticize, as enemies of the Church:

You may be guilty of pride and wantonness, you may be avaricious and contentious, you may be given to anger and ingratitude, and the whole catalogue of vices. . . . They may cry out to high heaven. But that is all right; you are the most pious of Christians if you protect the rights and liberties of the Church.
On Romans xiii, 1 (W. A. 56, 477, 7)

The ecclesiastical rulers . . . foster extravagance, greed, luxury and strife. It would be much safer if the temporal affairs of the clergy also were placed under the control of the secular arm.

On Romans xiii, 1 (W. A. 56, 478, 30 ff.)

My distress compels me to speak out, and my office demands that I do. Teaching is most properly understood when its relevance to present-day conditions is clearest. I must perform my duty as a teacher who holds his office by apostolic authority. My duty is to speak up on whatever I see happening that is not right, even in the highest places.

(W. A. 56, 480, 3–7)

He then refers to the war-mongering of Julius II and the shedding of innocent blood that his policy entailed, and says with irony:

That is no sin, the utterly scandalous collapse of the entire papal curia! It is the most revolting cesspool of filth of every kind, luxury, pomp, avarice, ambition and sacrilege. (W. A. 56, 480, 10 ff.)

Luther sought for a very careful demarcation of the role and responsibility of the secular authority on the one hand and the spiritual authority on the other. He saw clearly even at this early stage that the Church was disastrously involved in secular affairs and had overreached herself to the injury of herself and of secular authority. The State had authority over every man's life, according to Luther, an authority from which clerics were not exempt. That authority had to do with external and secular affairs only, with peace and property and law and order, with all powers, even of death, to punish its infringement. The role of the Church was simply to preach and teach, and care for the people as Christ cared for his. To confuse these was disastrous for both. When Luther put all power in the hands of the prince it was to a 'godly prince' (the great Reformation idea) who respected this distinction, who granted the Church full liberty and who sought to protect the Church in her spiritual tasks. He glosses Romans xiii, 1, in this way:

In the preceding chapter Paul taught that Church order had not to be upset; in this chapter he now teaches that the secular order must be preserved. For both are from God. The former is for man's instruction

and the maintenance of peace in his heart and his life. The other is for
the direction of the outward man and his affairs. For in this life you
cannot have an inner man without his outward counterpart.

(W. A. 56, 124, 9 ff.)

And in his scholion on the same text he writes:

Paul seeks to demonstrate that the man of faith is once and for all
exalted above all things, and yet is subject to all things. As Christ also
had, he has a kind of twin-like existence. He has within himself a
duality of being. According to the spirit he is lord of all things. 'All
things work together for good for the saints' (Romans viii, 28), also
as it says in 1 Corinthians iii, 22, 'All things are yours whether it be
in the world, or life, or death.' This is true because the man of faith
subjects all those things to his own advantage by faith, in the sense that
he does not let himself be affected by them and does not put his faith
in these things. He compels all these things to serve him as the raw
material of his glory and salvation. This is what it means to serve
God. This is what it means to be a lord in these matters. This is what
it means to live in a spiritual kingdom. This is what the text means in
Revelations v, 10: Thou hast made us a kingdom unto our God, and
we shall reign on earth.   (W. A. 56, 476, 6–12)

Luther has no doubt in his mind as to which serves which.

It is clear that by now Luther had found a firm theology.
He knew what it was to be justified by faith in God's redeeming
love and mercy. He knew what it was to be predestinated to this
saving mercy, 'overwhelmed by God's mercy'. He marvelled at
the righteousness of a God who did not charge man's unrighteousness to him. Luther knew himself to have been picked up at
the wayside of life and taken to His inn by Christ his Good
Samaritan, without whose intervention he would have perished.
He had a glorious conception of the mysterious and terrible
otherness of God, relieved by his evangelical doctrine of a God
seeking a sinner in love. Close as Luther was to God he resented
any familiarity with him, any easy mastery of the ways of God:
he would not have God treated as 'the cobbler does his leather'.
The great calamity of the theologians of his day was their
Pelagianism. Their theology was tainted with a reliance on man's
will to make headway against his sin, and it was their failure at
this point that deprived them of the cutting edge of the Gospel.

His interest in the mystics was that their teaching on humiliation and resignation to the will of God sharpened very much his conception of faith as reliance on God and His inscrutable will (an Ockhamist legacy) through all sorrows and afflictions; however, he was no mystic, but rather a man marked by faith.

THE EPISTLE TO THE GALATIANS (1516-17)

There was little more to Luther's lectures on Galatians (October 1516–March 1517) than has been indicated in his lectures on Psalms and Romans. They were rather rushed and we have only the manuscript of a student to work from. When he began, plague hung over the city and two hundred students had fled for safety. Luther lectured again on Galatians two years later, and again fifteen years later.

THE EPISTLE TO THE HEBREWS (1517-18)

The other academic lectures of this period were on the Epistle to the Hebrews (March 1517–March 1518). It will be recalled that this manuscript was found together with that on Romans in the Vatican Library, and, though published on its own soon after, it was not until 1939 that it was published along with Romans as Volume 57 in the *Weimarer Ausgabe*. Earlier scholars did not have the advantage of this text. All the evangelical theology found in the lectures on Psalms and Romans is here in one form or another but there are other emphases too.

Person and Work of Christ

First, there is Luther's fresh formulation of the person and work of Christ. It is his Christology that sets him apart from all others and it is his Christology that is the dynamic of his theology. Commenting on Hebrews i, 3, 'When he had purged our sins', he said:

By these words he forthwith makes short work of all notions of righteousness and every idea of penances which the natural man holds. It is the supreme mercy of God he commends. This means that it was

He who purged our sins and not we ourselves, and that it is our own sins He has purged, and not the sins of somebody else. Therefore we must despair of our own penances and our own purging of our sins, because before we even begin to confess, our sins have been already forgiven. I would even go on to say that it is not till then (i.e. until we despair of our own penance and purging) that Christ's own purging becomes operative, and produces true penitence in us. It is in this way that His righteousness works our righteousness.

(W. A. 57, 101, 16 ff.)

On the righteousness of Christ compared with human righteousness, he writes:

It has to be realized that this righteousness must be understood as the righteousness of God and not the righteousness of men (i.e. the righteousness acceptable to God and not a righteousness acceptable to men). . . . No one except Christ has loved righteousness. All others love money, or pleasure, or honour, or at all events if they despise these things they love glory; or even, be they the best of people, they still love themselves more than righteousness.

On Hebrews i, 9 (W. A. 57, 110, 14 ff.)

It pleased God to make Christ the perfect author of salvation and He used suffering as a means of fulfilling this work.

On Hebrews ii, 10 (W. A. 57, 126, 2 ff.)

In this way God promotes and perfects his proper work by means of his alien work, and by a marvellous wisdom compels the Devil to work through death nothing else than life itself, with the consequence that as the Devil is working his hardest against the work of God, he is by dint of his own work but working against himself and forwarding God's work. In this way he worked death in Christ, which Christ swallowed up into himself and rose again in glory.

On Hebrews ii, 14 (W. A. 57, 128, 13 ff.)

He is not like Moses who only shows sin, but rather like Aaron who bears sin. On Hebrews v, 1 (W. A. 57, 165, 24 ff.)

Sin

In his comments on the Epistle, Luther interprets sin as the love of self which prevents a person from loving Christ and therefore prevents faith in Christ. Sin produces works-righteousness and prevents faith in Christ.

As we are nothing and have nothing, then we ought not to puff ourselves up either with credit or praise of any kind, but on the contrary, accuse ourselves of every ignomy and make ourselves nothing in his sight.   On Hebrews xiii, 15 (W. A. 57, 90, 17 f.)

To fight against sin is to fight against the Devil, the world and oneself. The fight against oneself is the worst fight of all.
                              On Hebrews xii, 4 (W. A. 57, 76, 16 f.)

Law and Gospel

There is also present throughout the commentary Luther's distinction between Law and Gospel, particularly in the chapter headings, where he constantly reviews and sums up the argument of the Epistle. Discussing the meaning of the Law in ii, 1, he argues that it is imposed on a man because his heart is set on something else and therefore Law is always characterized by penalty. But there is also another difference:

... In the Law many works are enjoined, and all external, but in the Gospel there is only one, an internal work, and that is faith. For that reason the works of the Law make a righteousness which is external, but faith makes a righteousness hidden with God.
                              On Hebrews ii, 3 (W. A. 57, 113, 21 ff.)

In Chapter 7 he gives a long argument comparing the Levitical priesthood of the Law with Christ's priesthood in grace. On ii, 14 he describes the Law as God's alien work and the Gospel as His proper work:

God promotes and perfects his proper work by means of his alien work.   (W. A. 57, 128, 13 f.)

In Chapter 9, discussing the old sanctuary, he develops at every point the office of Christ in bringing in the Gospel, as compared with the work of the old Levitical priesthood under the Law. Referring to these differences, on ix, 8 ff., he says:

The sins, righteousnesses, sacrifices, holy things, promises, doctrines and priests of the old Law all pertained to the flesh. They did not sanctify as far as the conscience was concerned but only as far as the body was concerned. But now, under the dispensation of the Gospel, our sins, righteousnesses, sacrifices, holy things, promises, doctrines and our priest are all operative in the sphere of the spirit, and sanctify in matters of conscience. Nevertheless, both dispensations were given by God, but the old one was imposed until the time of the reformation.

> On Hebrews ix, 8 ff.

He differentiates between the Ten Commandments and the demands of the ceremonial law. The latter is about sin that does not really exist in its own right, but:

The Law of the Ten Commandments is the strength of sin because it creates knowledge of oneself.

> On Hebrews ix, 15 ff. (W. A. 57, 211, 9 ff.)

... the external ceremonies are commanded, not because there is salvation in them as such, but only in so far as they provide an occasion to exercise faith and love and are also a practical method of bringing pressure on sinners.

> On Hebrews ix, 24

Word of God

Never far away is Luther's emphasis on the Word of God, by which God intended and intends to address man.

A man may be said to depart from the living God when he departs from His Word, which is living and makes all things live. In fact, the Word is God himself. Therefore, when men depart from the Word, they die. He who does not believe is dead.

> On Hebrews iii, 12

If you ask a Christian what the work is by which he is made worthy of the name of Christian, he can give no answer other than hearing the Word of God, which is faith. Thus the ears alone are the organs of a Christian man, because not by the works of any other member but by faith is he justified and judged a Christian.

> On Hebrews x, 6

... the one and greatest demand which God makes upon the Jews (and indeed upon every man) is that they hear his voice. ... No one can cooperate with God unless he first holds fast to the Word, which takes place through faith, as a tool can effect nothing for the workman until it is taken in hand. On that account it is the height of perversity to hasten to perform good works before God has worked in us, i.e. before we believe.

> On Hebrews iii, 7 (W. A. 5 7, 142, 18)

Faith

Faith, too, receives the emphasis expected:

... all the works mentioned throughout the entire Bible are written up as works of faith. On Hebrews xi, 32

The sacraments are not effective simply by not obstructing them, they are appropriated only in faith:

If they believe and trust that at the sacrament they will receive grace, then this faith alone makes them pure and worthy. Such a faith does not put its trust in these works just described, but puts its trust in the most pure, most holy, most reliable word of Christ, when he says, 'Come unto me all who labour and are heavy laden, and I will refresh you'. Therefore, in confidence in these words they ought to go up to communion, and if they go up in this faith they shall not be confounded. On Hebrews v, 1

Faith, by which I mean the life of a Christian man, is more the work of God than ours. On Hebrews x, 37

On justification by works he writes:

To those who lived by faith, their works were good and meritorious, that is, they were keeping the inner meaning of the Law spiritually at the same time as they were keeping the letter of the Law outwardly. ... If you depend on these [external ceremonies] alone you transgress the Law in keeping it: thy circumcision is made uncircumcision. (Romans ii, 25.) On Hebrews ix, 24

Faith is closely linked to the mercy of God and to the grace of God. It is not a matter of subjective feeling, nor a matter of our earning it or meriting it, but wholly and entirely of divine activity, of divine initiation, of the mercy of God, an activity that is beyond the normal human value judgements. ... 'It was of His mercy alone, His grace, and the love He has towards us.'

The last words of the scholia are about the faith of Moses who on account of his faith was rejected and had to 'flee into Midian'. The professor closed his notes, the students looked up expectantly. They knew their professor had been summoned to Heidelberg to give an account of this theology of his. They saw his broad back fill the door: they later watched that sturdy figure set out on foot to Heidelberg. Would they ever see him again? The figure disappeared – in faith.

Events were moving fast. Within a few months this unknown scholar was to blazon forth on the grave scandal of indulgences; the Archbishop of Mainz was to lodge proceedings against him at Rome as a heretic; the Dominicans were to show themselves openly hostile. To the discerning reader the lectures are charged with all these issues which must certainly have been exercising the young professor's mind at the time.

LUTHER AS PRIOR

But the monk professor was more than a university lecturer. In May 1512 he had become sub-prior and director of studies when he had succeeded Staupitz. From May 1515 he had been the district vicar of eleven principal monasteries of the Meissen and Thuringian districts, including his mother cloister at Erfurt and important monasteries at Magdeburg, Dresden and Gotha, 'prior eleven times over' as he described it. This was work which demanded much pastoral care and oversight, and which he carried out with a sureness of touch as marked as his frank and firm kindness. The following are examples of his letters:

Dresden   1 May 1516

To the reverend holy father John Bercken,
Prior of the Augustinian Eremites,
Mainz.

Jesus

Greetings in the Lord! Reverend and worthy Father Prior, it is not good news to have heard that there is now staying with you one of my monks, a certain George Baumgartner, a member of our monastery at Dresden, who came to you for a shocking reason and in a shameful way. I extend my thanks to you for your faith and for your high sense of duty, that you took him in and so brought an end to his disgrace [i.e. he was no longer a vagabond]. That man is one of my sheep that I have lost. He belongs to me. Mine he is to seek out and return to the fold, please God.

I ask your reverence, by our common faith in Christ and our common Augustinian vow, that in some way you could in your charity as prior send him back to me either in Dresden here or to Wittenberg. Or better still, persuade him to go, induce him in friendliness and kindness to come of his own volition. I shall receive him with open arms, if only he presents himself. He has no cause to fear my displeasure.

I know, I know only too well, that scandals must arise. It is no miracle for a man to fall, but it is a miracle for a man to rise again and stand. Peter fell, that he might know he was only a man. Today even the cedars of Lebanon, reaching to the sky with their mighty tops, fall down. Wonder of wonders even an angel in heaven fell, and so did Adam in Eden. What wonder is it then, if a reed be shaken in the wind and the smoking flax be quenched?[1]

May the Lord Jesus teach you, and may he use you and perfect you in every good work.
Amen. Farewell.

> From our monastery at Dresden on the Feast of St Philip and St James.
> Father Martin Luther,
> Professor of Sacred Theology and Vicar of the Augustinian Eremites of the district of Meissen and Thuringia.
> (W. A. Br. 13)

23 June 1516

To the Reverend and holy father Michael Dressel,
Prior of the Augustinian Eremites at
Neustadt.

. . . You do indeed seek peace and ensue it, but altogether in the wrong way. You seek the peace the world gives, not the peace Christ gives. Are you not aware, my dear father, how God is so wonderful among his people that he has set His peace where there is no peace, that is in the midst of all our trials? As he says, 'Rule thou in the midst of thine enemies.' It is not therefore that man whom nobody bothers who has peace. That kind of peace is the peace of the world. It is that man whom everybody disturbs and everything harasses and yet who joyfully and quietly endures them all. You are saying what Israel said, Peace! Peace! but there is no peace. Say rather with Christ, Cross! Cross! and there is no cross. For the cross ceases to be a cross the moment you say gladly, Blessed Cross! of all the trees that are in the wood

---

1. Biblical references to the frailty of man. Isaiah xlii, 3; Matthew xii, 20.

there is none such as thee! . . . Seek this peace and you will find it. Seek for nothing else than to take on trials with joy. Seek them as you would holy relics. You will not find this peace by seeking and choosing what you feel and judge to be the path of peace.

Farewell and pray for me, my dear father. May the Lord direct thee.

> Wittenberg, the day of the ten thousand martyrs, 1516.
> Father Martin Luther
> District Vicar   (W. A. Br. 17)

Three months later we find Luther ordering this same prior to be deposed for having failed to keep peace and unity in his monastery and ordering arrangements for a new election. It is a very firm letter but he shows an unmistakable kindness and concern:

Wittenberg, 15 September 1516

To the venerable and holy father, Father Michael Dressel,
Prior of the monastery of the Augustinian Eremites at Neustadt,
as well as to the elders and chapter members of this monastery,
holy and affectionate greetings in the Lord.

Jesus

Greetings in the Lord! I hear with deep regret, as it is proper for me to hear, dearest fathers and brethren, that you are living without peace and unity, and though living in the same house you are not of one common way of life, nor are you of one heart and mind in the Lord. This wretched and useless kind of living arises either from a failing in your humility (for where there is humility, there is peace), or from my negligence. Quite certainly we both share the blame because we did not beseech the Lord who made us, nor pray to Him to direct our way as He saw fit and lead us in the way of His righteousness. The man who undertakes to direct himself, not to mention others, in the light of his own judgement, is wrong, plain wrong, dead wrong! . . . The entire cause, at any rate the cause of the disturbance, lies with you, for chapter and prior are in disagreement. This is worse than brother against brother. Therefore, by the authority vested in me, I order you, Brother Michael Dressel, to be relieved of your duties and to resign the seal of your office. By this authority also I release you from the office of prior in the name of the Father, the Son and the Holy Spirit. Amen.   (W. A. Br. 22)

He then proceeds to give instructions as to how the new election shall take place, issues directions on the matter of the novices, gives news of personalities who have died, and makes a poignant reference to the plague then raging in Wittenberg.

LUTHER SHOWS HIS HAND

About this time Luther began to feel he ought to give some public declaration of his theological views. This he did by drawing up Ninety-seven Theses against scholastic theology and philosophy, which declare his position in no uncertain manner, though also in a somewhat negative and polemical way. He first challenged both Scotus and Biel on the Augustinian doctrine of the bondage of the will:

The will is not free to pursue in the light of its own reason any good thing that has been made clear to it. (Thesis 10)

He argued that the natural man could not of himself love God, but only loves himself and his own interests.

For the natural man to love God above all else is a figment. It is but a chimera. (Thesis 18)

The natural man cannot want God to be God. Rather he wants himself to be God, and God not to be God. (Thesis 17)

He argued against the Pelagianism of the schoolmen. Goodness comes only from repentance which receives the grace of God, every man is depraved, redeemed only by God's grace:

The perfectly infallible preparation for grace, the one and only attitude, is the eternal election and predestination of God. (Thesis 29)

He argued against the disastrous influence Aristotle had had on Christian ethics and doctrine (at any rate the form that Aristotle's teaching had developed in medieval scholasticism). In particular, he criticized severely Aristotle's teaching that a man becomes good by training and disciplining himself to do good:

We are not made righteous by doing righteous deeds; but when we have been made righteous we effect righteous deeds. (Thesis 40)

The whole *Ethics* of Aristotle is the worst enemy of grace. (Thesis 41)

It is wrong to hold that the teaching of Aristotle on the highest good [happiness] is not repugnant to Catholic doctrine. (Thesis 42)

It is wrong to argue that a man cannot become a theologian without Aristotle. (Thesis 43)

The truth is that a man cannot become a theologian unless he becomes one without Aristotle. (Thesis 44)[1]

He gave a fine series of propositions on the Law and Gospel:

The Law and the will run counter to one another, and without the grace of God are irreconcilable. (Thesis 71)

He concluded with several propositions on the love of God and the love of self:

To love God is to hate oneself and to know nothing apart from God. (Thesis 95)

It is one of the mysteries of historical research that these revolutionary propositions seem to have had no effect on the learned world, although copies of them were sent both to Erfurt and Nürnberg.

Some weeks later, Luther compiled Ninety-five Theses against the scandal of indulgences about which he had always shown great concern. He had preached on the subject on the eve of All Saints a year earlier. Though couched in a difficult and academic form, these theses caught the imagination of the world, despite the fact that they were originally framed for a discussion with his fellow scholars, a discussion which none of them saw fit to attend. This publicity was largely the work of the popular Press, who, with that sense for good copy the Press and publishing men seem to acquire, at once saw the significance of the theses. As a result the presses poured them out in their thou-

---

1. See Library of Christian Classics Vol. 16, ed. and tr. James Atkinson, London, 1962, p. 269 ff., where the whole disputation is translated and annotated.

sands with consequences known to every schoolboy.[1] Luther had written far more important books and disputations and had preached far more disturbing sermons, but it was this document that dramatically fired the imagination of the Press. It was the printer's press that brought Luther out of the quiet secluded cloisters of scholarship. He now belonged to the world.

1. In the Black Cloister at Wittenberg a contemporary broadsheet of the theses is exhibited. A striking feature of the document is the gross number of misspellings and misprints there are: not even the numbers of the theses run in order. The impression given from a study of the sheet is that it must have been rushed off the press by a nearly illiterate printer (possibly the apprentice!) and certainly never checked by the master-printer nor read in proof by the author.

PART THREE

THE GREAT STAND
1517–21

CHAPTER 9

THE NINETY-FIVE THESES (1517)

CONTEMPORARY man with four centuries of Protestantism and four centuries of scientific education behind him does not readily appreciate the indulgences scandal of the fifteenth and sixteenth centuries. Unless he goes into a little detail he is apt to simplify and generalize the issues by thinking of the matter as a deceitful money-making device imposed on the credulous faithful in the interests of worldly clerics; further study reveals that the affair was neither as bad – nor as good – as was first thought.

First it is necessary to understand how it was that medieval man had little real fear of the eternal punishment of hell (however conceived), but a very real concern about the temporal punishments of purgatory (also however conceived). He believed, as is still good Catholic doctrine, that if he died forgiven by his priest and blessed he was thereby guaranteed entrance to heaven's portals, whose key the Church possessed. But the Church also taught carefully and assiduously that that same man had to face every consequence and punishment for every sin ever committed, known and unknown, before he reached heaven's gate, where only the pure or purified may enter. These punishments were called temporal in that there was an end to them; they had to be faced here on earth, but if necessary the full temporal punishment owing (known only to God) had to be endured in the pains of purgatory. Eternal punishment was reserved only for the man damned to perdition. Purgatory was very real and terrifying to the medieval man, and the Church kept him aware of his sin and its consequences, qualitatively with an intensity that portrayed it as diabolical, and quantitatively with such enormous time spans as to make time kiss eternity. Any means of shortening these pains were seized as a drowning man seizes a straw. Secondly, it is necessary to get a clear idea of the technical terms of the 'holy trade' (as it was then called), e.g. satisfactions, penances, the treasury of merits, attrition and contrition. Thirdly, the whole matter must be viewed in its historical perspective to understand its development and outcome in the light of its origins.

Indulgences do not mean the same thing to a modern Roman Catholic as they did to a contemporary of Luther's, or to a man a thousand years before Luther. Indulgences were not always discreditable. In the early Church, lapse into sin involved separation from the fellowship. Re-admission was gained by public confession before the congregation and true repentance shown by certain 'satisfactions', a word found as early as Tertullian (d. 220) and Cyprian (d. 258). These satisfactions might take the form of fasting, or alms-giving, or the manumission of a slave, depending on the nature of the sin and the status of the sinner, but they were always imposed by the congregation in the interests of the sinner and for his salvation. The nature of the satisfaction was always open to mitigation or even abolition on merciful grounds, if the congregation thought fit, in the light of a penitent's sincerity, or sickness, or any other material or spiritual change in his condition. These gracious and pastoral mitigations were the honourable beginning of the system which came to be known as indulgences and they must be reckoned as sound psychological and spiritual practice.

In the course of time, public confession before the congregation changed to private confession to the priest. It was then left to the discretion of the priest to impose the satisfaction to meet the sin. To arrive at common and fair practice, books were issued listing sins with their appropriate satisfactions related to the status and responsibility of the offender. This came to be called 'doing penance'. From the seventh century there developed a system of commuting penances which could take the form of a payment of money, or of a pilgrimage to a church or shrine with some payment towards its funds. This obtained in Germany, especially as the legal code there had familiarized the idea of commuting punishments by payment of cash. Another factor which influenced the practice in Germany was the idea that in certain circumstances a penitent might be relieved of his punishment which could then be met vicariously; thus a servant might do the penance for the penitent in whole or in part.

In the year 1030 several French bishops conceived the idea of promising to penitents some partial remission of penance as a reward for some particularly pious work. This caught the imagination of the people. The popes particularized the idea and in 1063 a total remission was proclaimed for the good work of engaging in a war against Islam. By 1187, under Pope Gregory VIII, this was transmuted into an arrangement whereby a full indulgence could be granted to anybody unable to go to the wars but willing to pay the cost of a soldier to do the work vicariously. Thus the concept began to be besmirched with the sordidness of money-making. When the campaigns to the Holy Land ceased, the popes and their advisers felt the necessity of devising an alternative scheme which would have the same appeal to the people as well as the equivalent financial appeal to themselves; to this end Boniface VIII established the jubilee indulgence.

This promised a full remission of penance to all who visited the graves of the Apostles in Rome once a day for fifteen days during the jubilee year 1300, an indulgence decreed only possible once in a hundred years. But Clement VI reduced the period to fifty years (in 1343), and before the century was out (1389) Urban VI made it thirty-three (in remembrance of the thirty-three years of the earthly life of Jesus). The next century saw Paul II reduce it in 1470 to twenty-five years (in view of the brevity of human life). It followed the same pattern as the jubilee indulgence. By 1490 the indulgence could be secured for money. At the same time the popes assumed a general power to grant plenary absolutions at any time for any purpose. The right to commute, a wholesome and godly duty, had moved from the hands of the congregation through the hands of the priests and the hierarchy until eventually it was in the hands of the Pope. In the transition a spiritual activity had been transmuted into a commercial transaction (*merx sancta*) and people now spoke of the whole business as a 'holy trade' (*sacrum negotium*) without so much as a blush.

But there was one drawback to these 'sacred commodities'.

They were not available at all times. The popes were well aware of this disadvantage, and in 1294 there began the issue of confessional letters which a soul of gentle birth might keep in reserve. These letters enabled the holder to procure complete absolution from any priest of the penitent's choice once during life and once 'in the article of death as often as it shall threaten'. This was both insurance and assurance at its best: it insured against sin and offered an assurance of eternal life when temporal life had ended. The holder was saved in either eventuality. Trade was so brisk that they were eventually granted to anybody who could pay enough. Further refinements of these letters soon appeared. They came even to be parcelled out as favours.

As soon as the idea of indulgences caught on, the innocent layman became anxious to procure this advantage for his poor relatives in purgatory. There was and is something touching about the practice in that it purported to be for the advantage not of self but of another; such is the view of Roman Catholics today. The popes, who were essentially jurists, drew the line at applying them to the dead, but their resistance held only until 1476, when Sixtus IV established an indulgence for the dead. There was a real rush on these. The popularity of this kind of indulgence surprised even the organizers. Rome was quick to meet the demand. Further inducements were devised. The purchaser of an indulgence was usually granted in the first instance a confessional letter; secondly, a 'butter' letter (allowing the holder to eat butter, eggs, cheese and milk on fast days); thirdly, the right to substitute good works for vows; fourthly, the right to increase his spiritual capital by transference of a credit balance from the treasury of merits (see p. 145); and lastly, for a further charge, permission to use illegally acquired goods whose owner could not be found.

Luther did not attack the simple pastoral system of indulgences, the merciful mitigation of penances for sin imposed by the Church. He shared the pastoral view that what the Church had imposed she had the right to commute. But there had always been those who had protested at the whole idea. The Waldensians and the Cathari would not touch indulgences. Of the theologians, only Abelard rejected them until Wyclif showed his hand. In the fifteenth century eminent professors in the universities (Ruchrath of Basel, Martinez of Salamanca, Gansfort of Gröningen, Laillier of Paris and Vitrier of Tournay) declared firmly against them. And of course wherever there was no belief in purgatory, as in the Orthodox Church, the disease never took hold.

But there was more to the problem than the disastrous worldliness of an institutionalized Church. Three main quasi-theological factors complicated the issue: the treasury of merits, the change brought about by the elevation of penance to the dignity of a sacrament, and the distinction between *attritio* and *contritio*.

The idea of a treasury of merits was first formulated in the thirteenth century by Alexander of Hales or Hugo de St Cher. It took the form of a heavenly capital conceived as a treasury of the surplus good works of the saints and of Christ. The idea was that the good deeds of the saints had built up a great spiritual capital available to everybody, and that the sacrifice of Christ was sufficient to wipe out the debits of all. These merits were stored in heaven and could be dispensed by the Pope to the faithful. A plenary indulgence transferred enough merit to deliver the holder from all penalties on earth and in purgatory, a partial indulgence delivered from a matter of days to millennia, either on earth or in purgatory or both. It will be readily seen how this served to increase the vague sense of supernatural powers possessed by the Pope. By Luther's time, indulgences were no longer a matter of gracious relaxation or merciful mitigation, but a mitigation of penalties in return for money. The indulgences' certificates had proper theological qualifications written into them, but these were ignored by seller and purchaser alike.

When the institution of penance developed into the sacrament of penance, the natural sequence of sorrow, confession, satisfaction and absolution fell into the indefensible sequence of sorrow, confession, absolution and then satisfaction. It was taught that guilt and the eternal punishment of hell were avoided by absolution, but that the sinner had of course always to face the full temporal punishment consequent to the sin. Heaven would never be entered before the full temporal punishment owing had been endured.

Temporal punishment was of two kinds, the punishments in this life and those after death. The penance which the priest imposed became the equivalent of the temporal punishment due, but if the assessment were not exact the pains had to be completed in purgatory. It was at this point that the new idea of indulgences came in, to secure the sinner against the pains of purgatory. The valuable indulgence was the one which because of the merits from the treasury was an equivalent in God's sight for the temporal punishment due for sins. The value of indulgences was that they procured remission of the temporal penalties which a penitent had still to face after absolution, even though absolution had assured him of his place in heaven.

The third idea which influenced the development of indulgences, though indulgences were always primarily related to satisfactions, was the distinction which grew up between attrition and contrition. Down to the thirteenth century the belief had been that contrition (the true sorrow prompted by love) was the one and only thing required by God in pardoning sin. Theologians of the thirteenth century began to recognize attrition (a lesser sorrow prompted by fear) and to accept this in place of contrition, teaching that attrition could be up-graded by means of ecclesiastical discipline and by the sacrament. It meant, in effect, that a requirement as little as attrition was sufficient to achieve absolution, and therefore the blotting out of eternal punishment with the certain possession of heaven. This was not taught by the best theologians and cannot properly be described as official doctrine, even though it was official policy. But it was taught by the Scotists as well as by the mischievous pardon-sellers and, human nature being what it is, it was welcomed by the vast majority of indifferent Christians. The whole scheme increased the power of the spiritual hierarchy, as well as the amount of papal revenues. The scheme of salvation in effect resolved itself into attrition, confession, indulgence.

The most disputed question was whether an indulgence gave remission of the guilt of sin, or only of the penalties the sin incurred. The universal answer, of course, was that guilt (*culpa*) and eternal punishment (*poenae aeternae*) were dealt with in the sacrament of penance and that indulgences related only to temporal punishments (remembering always that that category included also the pains of purgatory). But this hardly exhausts the problem. The usage of the Church which theologians were attempting to defend as well as to define made little distinction between *culpa* and *poena* in that the phrase 'remission of sins' denoted both remission of guilt and remission of penalty. (No less a person than Dante was under this impression.)

The discussion of these theological points is necessary to a full understanding of the problem of indulgences in the early sixteenth century, though Luther's approach was not theological but essentially practical. He saw the matter from the pastoral point of view, considering the effect of such practices on the soul of the ordinary man. The latter believed that an indulgence did in fact remove the guilt of sin and the theory of the theologians hardly affected popular belief. Once penance was instituted as a sacrament, the idea was that all guilt of sin and eternal punishment were remitted in the absolution. Penance safe-guarded the sinner from hell and guilt. But there still remained the actual sins to be satisfied because God's justice demanded it, and these were purged in purgatory. This loomed large in men's eyes, for the punishment might last thousands of years. In fact the figures bandied about were astronomical. One needs a unit similar to a light year to apprehend them![1] A man had but to buy a papal ticket, perform the good deed required and he was assured that the punishment was remitted and God's justice satisfied. The indulgence meant remission of guilt as well as of penalty, and this was the disastrous consequence against which Luther fought.

Luther had shown a pastoral interest in the problem before it came to a head in the scandal of 1517. As early as 1515 we find him perturbed about the abuse, but significantly and characteristically his concern was for the soul of the indulgence receiver who in buying an indulgence had thrown aside the re-demptive value of God's punishment and hardened himself

---

1. The relics of the Castle Church on whose door Luther nailed his theses were reputed to earn by one estimation 1,902,202 years, 270 days.

against true evangelical repentance. This theme was touched on in sermons in October 1516 and February 1517. Luther saw that indulgences indulged the sinner and tended to turn his mind from Christ and divine forgiveness. Belief in indulgences gave a man a false sense of security (*securitas de salute futura*) which Luther found irreconcilable with evangelical salvation in Christ (*certitudo salutis*). It was at this point that Luther's interpretation of the Gospel showed itself sharply opposed to the accepted piety of the Church. His contemporaries knew at once that he had touched the exposed nerve not only of the institutional hierarchical system but also of the everyday practice of religion. When they began to oppose what Luther saw was inescapably true, he carried his criticism further and further, until one day he woke up and found to his astonishment that he had irrevocably broken with popery.[1]

Let us see how the issue came to a head in 1517. The house of Hohenzollern was seeking to gain control over the ecclesiastical and civil life of Germany. The young Prince Albert, though only twenty-three and not of age, already held the two sees of Halberstadt and Magdeburg. In 1514 the possibility of the Archbishopric of Mainz and the Primacy of all Germany opened up to him. To gain this coveted prize he had to pay the Pope the enormous fee of ten thousand ducats for permission to accumulate unlawfully such a prize collection of benefices, and in addition twenty-one thousand ducats as pallium fee. The Pope met him in this impossible financial strait by promising to issue an indulgence in deferred payments over the next eight years on the understanding that half the revenue would go to the Fuggers, who had footed the bill, and half would go to the Pope himself to help build St Peter's at Rome. There were four privileges attached to this indulgence. First, subscribers would enjoy a plenary and perfect remission of all sins; secondly, they would be given a letter allowing the penitent to choose his own confessor; thirdly, they would participate in the merits of the saints; fourthly, they would relieve the poor suffering souls in purgatory.[2]

1. See letter to Spalatin, 24 February 1520 (W. Br. 2, 48, 20–49, 2).
2. There is an original Tetzel indulgence in the British Museum.

Albert carefully safeguarded himself by demanding auricular confession from a contrite heart, but in the hands of the experienced Tetzel, a man who demanded and got a salary twenty times that of a university professor plus expenses, such scruples were brushed aside in the interests of the nefarious traffic. In his preaching urgent appeals from dead souls languishing in the agonies of purgatory crying out for relief were cunningly deployed:

The dead cry, 'Pity us! Pity us! We are in dire torment from which you can redeem us for a pittance. . . . Will you leave us here in flames? Will you delay our promised glory?'

As soon as the coin in the coffer rings
The soul from purgatory springs.

Will you not then for a mere quarter of a florin receive these letters of indulgence through which you are able to lead a divine and immortal soul into the fatherland of paradise?

So Tetzel preached and so they believed, proclaiming his written authority from the Pope 'to shut the gates of hell and open the door to paradise'. But the authority was challenged: and not only by Luther. There is evidence of a mountain guide asking why the Pope had to have payment before he would release souls from agony; of a penniless student publicly demanding an indulgence without fee according to Catholic doctrine; of another who, anticipating Tetzel's sermon for St Michael's Day, stole from the reliquary the feather of St Michael's accoutrement, replacing it with a piece of charcoal, and who was to witness Tetzel dramatically open the box and with some presence of mind divert his sermon from the Archangel and his feather to the subject of the charred remains of poor St Laurentius. True, Wittenberg itself was forbidden Tetzel by order of Frederick the Wise, but the pardons were nevertheless readily available just over the border.

Luther reacted. 'I'll knock a hole in his drum,' was his ominous remark on learning of Tetzel's activities. He actually chose the traditional and universally acceptable course for investigating truth, the academic disputation. Rather than put up a student to argue the theses as was normal procedure, however, he elected to stand himself and argue out the truth from his own theses. It would appear from the fact that Luther sent printed copies of the theses both to the Archbishop and to his own diocesan, as well as from his correspondence of the time, that his main concern was not only to shake his colleagues into a heightened awareness of the scandal and of their theological responsibilities in the matter, but to make both the Archbishop and Bishop show their position. This first Reformation act of Luther should not be exaggerated. It was more the concern of an academic monk, deeply committed to his Church, that truth should prevail and that true Christianity should be furnished for the souls in the Church's care. As he wrote to Spalatin: 'It was the love of truth that drove me to enter this labyrinth and stir up six hundred minotaurs.' The theses were essentially a pastoral criticism by a professor of theology of the Mainz instruction and of the Mainz indulgence preacher. The document was posted on the church door, as was usual, on the eve of All Saints' Day, the day the university attended church in its official capacity as a university and the day the crowds always flocked to view the famous relics of the good Frederick. The drama attached to these theses lay in their subsequent history.

These Ninety-five Theses are strangely uncoordinated, rather remote and academic, not well thought out, even disappointing, compared with the mighty writings whose thunder was to reverberate throughout Christendom. Luther was quite shocked when the matter was taken out of his hands, and what had been intended as an academic disputation among scholars was literally shouted from the house-tops. He grumbled and said that if it had been a criticism of indulgences they wanted he could have written a proper one, but that had not been his purpose. It should always be remembered that the Theses are pithy aphoristic Latin paradoxes, such as were normal to academics discussing issues at universities.

The content of the Theses can be summarized in this way, though they do not lend themselves to summary: Theses 1–4 showed what true New Testament penance really was. Repentance was not 'doing penance' nor was it the kind of mercantile transaction Tetzel was making of it. It was an inward and continuous process of dying to self and rising again to righteousness, a turning of the entire man to God. The motive of indulgences in its desire to evade punishment was directed against any true understanding of repentance, since it actually prevented repentance. Sorrow, suffering and sin, tasks, trials and tribulations were the divine erosion which broke down the hard rock of self into fertile and productive soil. These were to be welcomed, understood and seen as God's activity, not bought off. They served true repentance and therefore the meaning of the Gospel.

In Theses 5–7 Luther taught that the Church could remit only the penalties she had imposed: only God could remit guilt. In Theses 8–29 he turned to the indulgence for the dead and (in agreement with the medieval popes) denied the Pope's power over purgatory. In Theses 30–40 he discussed the indulgence for the living and related it to true forgiveness which a believer always had, with or without indulgences. Theses 41–52 compared true Christian works of mercy and love in everyday life with the waste of money on indulgences for the rebuilding of St Peter's; Theses 53–80 the preaching of indulgences with the preaching of the Gospel to which the Church was committed, arguing that the bishops, clergy and theologians would have a great deal to answer for in making this unwarrantable substitution. He offered some trenchant remarks on the interest shown in money rather than in souls, and made a plea to raise and discuss all these matters so as to strengthen a questioning and concerned laity. Nine times do the Theses ring out at this point with the opening words 'Docendi sunt Christiani!' (Christians must be taught!). This is as good a summing-up of Luther's mission and message as can anywhere be found. Theses 81–91 argued the grave pastoral responsibility of the Pope for this scandalous state of affairs and he concluded with four powerful theses based on his own Theologia Crucis. It was at this point that Luther's clear religious motive appeared and his limpid evangelical theology shone forth:

92. Let all those prophets clear off who say to the people of Christ, 'Peace! Peace!' when there is no peace.

93. Let all those prophets make this their right course of action and say to the people of Christ, 'Cross! Cross! When accepted it is no longer a cross.'

94. Christians must be exhorted to follow Christ their head with utter devotion through punishment, through death, through hell.

95. In this way let them have confidence that they will enter heaven through many tribulations, rather than through a false assurance of peace.

This theology was not new, but it was the first time it had been used in criticism of the practice and theology of the Church of the day.

True, no academics came to the disputation; yet in the short space of four weeks, before Luther could procure the opinions of scholars and ecclesiastics, the Theses were printed and circulated all over Germany and Switzerland. Most people praised them. Dürer sent Luther some of his woodcuts as a mark of appreciation. Many who were sympathetic were nevertheless afraid of where it would all lead. The Dominicans were sure he was as good as on the stake. Luther realized that neither friend nor foe had got the issue clear; all that he had proposed were 'talking points', not established truths. He wrote to his bishop giving him an explanation of his Theses (February 1518). But this document (called *Resolutions*) went far beyond any mere explanation of the Ninety-five Theses. It was in fact an independent scheme of reform. Luther actually demanded a reformation, and that it should be the concern not only of the Pope and cardinals, but of the entire Christian world. He discussed the authority of the Pope which he accepted in external matters of order but not in internal matters of faith. He spoke of true historic Catholicism as opposed to the unfounded claims of Rome. He discussed forgiveness as a promise of God and argued against the ecclesiastical and professional possession of it as a priest's to give or withhold, and distinguished sharply between evangelical penitence and ecclesiastical penitence. Indulgences could remit a canonical penalty only, and their use served to screen a soul from the therapeutic power of genuine contrition and to prevent it from finding any real penitence. The treasury of merits he ruled out; the Church had but one treasure, and that was Christ.

Luther's concern was to make Christendom aware of her wholesale defection from New Testament Christianity and of her appalling theological ignorance. He thought that if men's hearts and minds were opened to an awareness of this, God would instigate a reformation in and through that awareness. Luther's explanations show scholarship and ability, as well as a grasp of canon law, church history and the writings of the Church Fathers.

Luther's Archbishop was eventually constrained to make a move against the 'rash monk of Wittenberg' as he called him, though the move was little more than a wriggle out of his responsibilities. He reported Luther to Rome on the grounds that he was spreading new doctrines (not for heresy!), and told his advisers not to bother him any more about the matter but to have Luther inhibited. Rome seems at this time to have issued a warning through the Vicar-General of the Augustinian Eremites, Gabriel della Volta, who was sent to 'soothe and quieten down the man' as well as to secure a formal recantation from Luther through Staupitz. The prelates still hoped to dismiss the matter as a monkish quarrel.

Staupitz sought to protect Luther at this juncture and to preserve peace if possible, but the Dominicans in Saxony were after Luther's blood and had a vociferous and willing champion in Tetzel. In January 1518, a chapter of the Saxon Dominicans met at Frankfurt-on-Oder, where Tetzel debated one hundred and six Theses (written for him by Conrad Wimpina, a professor at the university) primarily directed against Luther's Ninety-five Theses. They were anxious to secure their victim and thought he was as good as burned. They decided to report him to Rome for heresy, a very clever move, for the most influential theologian at Rome was Cajetan, and as he was a Dominican the charge was bound to be followed through. (Luther was soon to face Cajetan at Augsburg.) Tetzel was very pleased with these developments and sent a bookseller to Wittenberg with hundreds of copies of his one hundred and six Theses. The student body sized up the position with that lively mixture of realism, humour and action characteristic of them, and gave the poor fellow very short shrift. They made sport of him in the market-place in the afternoon and burnt hundreds of copies of his Theses. Luther disapproved of this conduct officially, but doubtless the robust humour of the students would bring a smile to his lips privately as he contemplated the rude fall of error and pomposity.

The wide circulation of the Theses, the Dominican counter-thrust, the many and varied reactions in Germany, the fear of his friends in Wittenberg, all served to convince Luther that he ought to make his standpoint clear. He had written a deferential letter to his bishop, explaining that his views were not mere 'assertions' as they were called, but genuine academic points for discussion, and showing that his authorities were scripture, Church canons and the Fathers. This document had lain on the bishop's desk for weeks without any action having been taken, so Luther decided to write a sermon on indulgences and grace to initiate the laity into the meaning of these academic issues. This showed a noteworthy and fresh characteristic in Luther, a characteristic which was to mark his entire career as well as later to provide the dynamic of Protestantism; he charged the layman with the responsibility of thinking all things through, and of opening himself to God and the reform and revival God was seeking for the Church. This little German tract penetrated into places a thousand academic disputations would never have reached. Luther went much further in this tract in disapproving altogether of indulgences and indeed of talking about purgatory at all. The sermon was probably not preached, but was printed and propagated. In it he says:

Let none of you procure tickets of indulgence. Leave that to the lazy Christians dozing half asleep. You go right ahead without them. . . . I know nothing about souls dragged out of purgatory by an indulgence. I do not even believe it, in spite of all the new-fangled doctors who say so. But you cannot prove it to them. The Church has not even made up its mind in the matter yet.

He concludes:

On these points [against indulgences] I have no doubt at all. They [indulgences] are not properly based on scripture. Therefore, have no doubt about them, regardless of what the scholastic doctors say. . . . I pay no attention to that sort of drivel, for nobody engages on it except a few dunderheads who have never even smelt a Bible nor read any Christian teachers.

If the Latin tract did not make the bishop move, the sermon certainly did. When it fell into his hands, he sent a personal message to Luther post-haste by a senior abbot, begging him to withhold his sermon from the people until a decision should be taken.

Frederick began to show signs of anxiety about this new young professor of his, anxiety which his chaplain Spalatin shared completely. They were both very concerned at the fact that in this delicate situation Luther was preparing to walk all the way to Heidelberg in order to appear before the chapter of his fellow Augustinians to give an account of his theology. Frederick knew that anything could happen and feared the worst; Luther was not afraid and set off with a firm stride.

On his return, or even possibly just before he set out, he sent his 'explanations and proofs' to the printer. In these he develops and enlarges every one of his Ninety-five Theses. He is cautious and courteous, but there is about them a courage born of certainty. Underlying the work is the clear call for the reform of the Church. Discussing the early Church and comparing it with the contemporary, he writes on Thesis 72:

The Church was not then what it is now, a Hydra, a monster of many heads, an underworld of simony, lust, pomp, murder and all the rest of the abominations [of the papal curia].

On Thesis 89:

The Church needs a reformation. This reformation is not, however, the concern of the Pope alone, nor the concern of the cardinals; this fact was plainly demonstrated by the recent council [the Fifth Lateran Council of 1512–17]. It is the concern of all Christendom, or better still, of God alone. Only He knows the hour of this reformation.

The explanations are strong meat, and rehearse all that he has so far said on Aristotle and scholasticism, the bad practices and corruptions of the Church, as well as on his developing *Theology of the Cross*.

From this you can now see how, ever since scholastic theology began (illusory theology it is, for that is the connotation of the Greek), the *Theology of the Cross* has been emptied of its meaning, and everything else has been turned upside down. The theologian of the cross (that is, one who speaks of the hidden and unfathomable God) teaches that punishments, crosses, and death are the most precious treasure of all and the most sacred of relics, relics which the Lord Himself, the creator of this theology, has consecrated and blessed. This He did, not only by the touch of His most holy flesh but by the embrace of His most holy divine will. He has left these relics here to be kissed, sought after, embraced. Indeed happy and blessed is the man who is considered by God worthy to receive these treasures of the relics of Christ! Nay rather, who understands that they are given him! For to whom are they not offered?   (W. A. 1, 613, 21 ff.)

Despite the rigid academic framework the reader can sense Luther shattering the shackles without, as he had already shattered them within.

As was to be expected, Luther did 'knock a hole in Tetzel's drum'. The whole scheme collapsed financially and was transmuted into a skirmish in the long battle for evangelical freedom. Tetzel was finished. He was later to be handled very severely by the Church, in the person of the otherwise kindly Cardinal von Miltitz, for having bungled the whole affair. Soon he was unable to appear on the streets for fear of being lynched. In fact, the whole affair killed Tetzel. It should be remembered that within the space of one short year as he lay dying in Leipzig, rejected, ignored, broken and alone, it was Luther alone of all men who wrote to him in comforting words, explaining that after all Tetzel was not to take upon himself the whole blame; he had not fathered the scandal but had been its victim.

But this is to anticipate our story. We left Luther setting out from Wittenberg to walk to Heidelberg to face his Order and give an account of his theology. The indulgences controversy was now virtually behind him, but he was well aware of the storm that was brewing and how very much alone he was. The storm when it broke was to divide Christendom, not as when she fell apart into East and West in the eleventh century like a cell dividing into two like parts, but in a far more dangerous sense; it was a theological split from top to bottom, like the rending of the Temple vail or the split in the New Testament between Judaism and Christianity.

CHAPTER 10

THE HEIDELBERG DISPUTATION
(APRIL 1518)

JUST after Easter, on 11 April 1518, Luther left Wittenberg to attend the triennial chapter of his Order. In addition to routine business, part of which was to render an account of his own office as vicar-general, there was to be a disputation, also customary, and on this occasion Staupitz selected Luther to formulate the theses and to preside. He asked Luther to be non-controversial. Consequently the theses are silent about indulgences and penance, and handle the mighty themes of original sin, sin, grace, free will and faith.

Luther set off with a Brother, Leonard Beier, for companion, as the rules of the Order required. He walked through Leipzig, Coburg, Würzburg to Heidelberg, a journey which he found too strenuous. But he wrote cheerful letters to Spalatin *en route*, and though he travelled incognito we know that at one place he was recognized by a former pupil and that throughout the journey he was treated with kindness and respect. Frederick had done all he could to make the journey safe. One official when he looked at Luther's papers, carefully compiled by Frederick, exclaimed, 'By God! You've got marvellous credentials!' At Würzburg the prince bishop received Luther with great friendliness and insisted that he should at least get a wagon to help him on his way. Luther declined because he had just met the Erfurt contingent and they had offered him a lift on their wagon. The good bishop was later to write to Frederick in great concern lest Luther should be unfairly treated: 'Do not let them take away from you this devout man Doctor Martin. He is being treated unjustly.' At Heidelberg he was received with honour by the Palgrave.

Luther took over in the great hall of the monastery, crowded not only with friars and professors of theology, but with courtiers and burghers. It was a triumph for Luther. In a sense a theological watershed had been reached. Ten years' hard study and lecturing stood behind him as well as the fact that he had shown his hand in the Ninety-five Theses. He said he might be beaten at logic but none could gainsay his theology. Further he stood among friends, interested even if critical, a theologian before theologians.

There are forty theses – twenty-eight of them directed against scholastic theology, his main concern, and for good measure twelve more directed against Aristotelian scholastic philosophy. This disputation receives too little recognition generally. Here Luther deals with the great theological themes he had been making his own: God's righteousness and man's righteousness; Law and Gospel; sin, grace, free will and faith; justification by works and justification in Christ; man's inability to will and do the good on his own strength; in particular, his powerful theology of the cross. Here are all the essentials of Luther's mighty evangelical theology, and in many cases they are carefully developed.[1]

Luther begins at once with the determinative distinction between Law and Gospel:

The Law of God, that most wholesome doctrine of life, cannot bring a man to righteousness. It is a hindrance rather than a help. . . . How much less can man's works. . . . They may look splendid, but in all probability they are sins. . . . The Lord humbles us and absolutely terrifies us with the Law and the prospect of our sins so that we . . . seem to be nothing but fools and evil men. The truth of the matter is that is exactly what we are. . . . This sense of our own deformity arises in us when God flays us or when we accuse ourselves. This is what Isaiah calls the strange work of God that he may effect His proper work (Isaiah xxviii, 21), that means that He might humble us in our own eyes and make us despair of ourselves, so that in His mercy He may exalt us and make us men of hope.

Luther dismisses all the petty distinctions and modifications men make to evade this truth such as 'free will after the fall', 'doing what in one lies', 'mortal and venial sin', etc.

1. For a complete translation of these theses with comment, see the Library of Christian Classics, Vol. 16, pp. 274–307.

The Law works fear and wrath; grace works hope and mercy. . . .
When God makes a man a sinner, He does it to make him righteous.
. . . Sin is not known except through the Law. It is clear that not
despair but hope is preached.

With this he turns to man's knowledge of God. He argues that
men abused their knowledge of God by attempting to draw
nearer to Him through their good works, thinking thereby to
attain a closer knowledge of Him. But this was not how God
had determined it. He was to be known in suffering, humility and
shame – a *Theology of the Cross* as opposed to the prevalent
Theology of Glory.

In Christ crucified is the true theology and the knowledge of God.
'No man comes to the Father except through me.' 'I am the door.'
As long as a man does not know Christ, he does not know God as
hidden in sufferings. Such a man prefers works to sufferings, and glory
to a cross.

This knowledge of God means, of course, a *saving* knowledge
of God revealed by God Himself and is not the same kind of
knowledge which philosophers may talk about when they argue
whether it is possible to know God at all.

From this point therefore he turns to righteousness:

The righteousness of God is not acquired by acts frequently repeated,
as Aristotle taught, but is imparted by faith. . . . The good man knows
that the good works he is doing are the outcome of this faith and are
not his own at all but God's. . . . Christ is his wisdom, his righteousness, his all. . . . The justified man is surely the work and instrument
of Christ.

Luther attached to the disputation a memorandum on the
scholastic doctrine that a man could love God above all things
by his own power and could in a sense fulfil the Law. He says
that this makes of the Gospel a more refined or difficult Law,
arguing from scripture and from his own experience and reason:

This is the sweetest mercy of God that it is not imaginary sinners he
saves but real sinners, upholding us in our sins and accepting our
works and our life, worthy as these are of total rejection. He does this

until he perfects and consummates us. . . . We escape his condemnation because of his mercy and not because of our own righteousness. . . . Grace is given to heal the spiritually sick, not to decorate spiritual heroes.

The simplicity of it all is striking as Luther turns away from scholastic theologians and philosophers, rejects the ways of the mystics and spiritual place-seekers, for the simple incarnational, revelational work that God did in Christ. He likes neither their technical terms nor their highly intellectualized mystical way. Christ is the author and object of faith. With Him and in Him we are given the meaning of all the suffering and affliction innate in the godly life, but amid the humiliation and shame and weakness and scandal we peer through the mist to see the smile of God. He is a hidden God indeed, but when we see Him in Christ the very hiddenness is his revelation.

Luther's twelve philosophical theses, like his Ninety-seven Theses of September 1517, were directed against the Ockhamists, who were well represented in the audience not only in numbers but in distinction. His old teacher of Erfurt days, Usingen, was there to hear this attack on the metaphysics of Aristotle, when he played off Pythagoras, Anaxagoras, Parmenides and Plato against Aristotle. Luther did not develop these themes, however, and though he was to refer to them occasionally in later life, he now virtually left them aside in favour of biblical and Augustinian themes.

Staupitz insisted that Luther have the privilege of a wagon for his return journey. He sat in the cart next to Usingen but left the old scholar theologically exhausted by the time he reached his destination. Luther was willing to hold a philosophical disputation at Erfurt on his way back but his old philosophy teachers were quite literally 'saved by the bell', for three fast-days followed their return and made a debate impossible. This was virtually the end of Luther's connexions with Erfurt, and his teachers, Usingen, Truttvetter, even Nathin, all turned out hostile to the new theology. Luther was hurt but undeterred.

The disputation must be reckoned a great success. The young theologians, three of whom, Bucer, Brenz and Billicanus, came later to exercise great influence on the Reformation, were positively captivated by the new theology. Schwarz, again a young man, was the only Heidelberg professor to support Luther. His older colleagues remained courteous but aloof and noncommittal. The Count Palatinate of the Rhine wrote to Frederick:

Luther has acquitted himself so well here with his disputation that he has won no small praise for your Grace's university and was greatly lauded by many learned persons.

That same day the young Martin Bucer, then at Heidelberg, wrote to Rhenanus at Basel:

Although our chief men refuted him with all their might, their wiles were not able to make him move an inch from his propositions. His sweetness in answering is remarkable, his patience in listening is incomparable, in his explanations you would recognize the acumen of a Paul, not a Scotus; his answers so brief, so wise, and drawn from the holy scriptures, easily made all his hearers his admirers. On the next day I had a familiar and friendly conference with the man alone and a supper rich with doctrine rather than with dainties. He agrees with Erasmus in all things, but with this difference in his favour, that what Erasmus only insinuates, he teaches openly and freely. . . . He has brought it about that at Wittenberg the ordinary textbooks have all been abolished, while the Greeks and Jerome, Augustine and Paul, are publicly taught.

Luther's comment; 'I went on foot and returned in a cart', says much.

On his return to Wittenberg his old friend and counsellor Staupitz prevailed on Luther to write to the Pope to assure him of his orthodoxy and of his loyalty to the Holy See. This document called *Resolutions* bears every sign of having been worked over by a courtier for presentation to the Pope, and reads differently from Luther's first draft, which we still possess. It is also very different from his normal work. At this time Tetzel rose to the conflict and published fifty theses which aroused Luther to make a vigorous counterthrust. The document, in powerful peasant German, says little new. Luther never really wanted to write it, for he felt he was wasting his shot on pompous fatheads, and was too aware of the gravity of the situation to be found 'playing this game'. He referred to Tetzel's words as paper flowers and dry leaves to be cast to the winds, and said, 'I shall deal only with the cornerstones of his house of cards.'

According to Luther, Tetzel asserted that he found satisfactions and penance grounded in scripture and supported by thousands of uncondemned teachers. Luther argues that this vast number can be reduced to three, and that the rest were simply imitators. Men like this shall be slain with their own sword, to which he likens their glosses of scripture. They destroy the authority of scripture. Luther did not greatly mind Tetzel's abuse of his own person, but added:

I won't put up with it for one minute when he handles the scripture, our comfort, as a sow attacking a bag of oats. We shall soon see about that! Every day they invent new kinds of keys. What for? To empty all our purses and coffers, and after that, unlock hell and lock up heaven. These men are worse than the Turks at the gate, for they are inside.

Not that Luther rejects the scholastic doctors without qualification. They served their purpose in their day. He only rejects those opinions held by them which were unwarranted by scripture, and this mainly for the sake of the simple laity who are led by these opinions and ideas into indulgences and other unreasonable and unscriptural practices. In a diatribe entitled *Freedom to Preach* he discussed Tetzel in popular language:

At last the storm is about my ears. Now am I an arch-heretic, a heretic, a renegade, a false teacher, a miscreant, a blasphemer and all the rest. ... When such people, who do not know the Bible, nor understand what words mean either in Latin or German, and furthermore insult me with such extreme slander, they make me sick. They bray at me like some brute ass. I can't stop him, poor brother, getting punishment and prison, water and fire ready for me. My advice to him is that he keeps to the water from grapes and the fire that roasts the goose, which he knows something about. ... What they are shouting about has nothing to do with faith and salvation, human need and God's Law. They are worthless causes, nothing to do with heresy. ... When these men abuse the scriptures and give the lie to the Word of God, they call it improving and honouring Christianity. But when one teaches that it is not necessary to buy indulgences and that it is not right to skin poor folk of their money, that is dishonouring the Church and sacrament and vexing Christians. I only say this so that from now on their language and their new thieves' slang may be understood. . . . He [Tetzel] boasts he will defend his views at Frankfurt-on-Oder. The sun and moon will be struck at the brilliance of their wisdom. I dare say that they [Tetzel's theses] are for the most part true. I would be quite prepared to put up with them, except that where they state 'Christians must be taught that . . .' I would want to put, 'Indulgence sellers and inquisitors of perverse and heretical tendencies must be taught!'

O God, help the truth alone and nobody else.

Amen.

I don't think I can fly over the fir trees, but I have no doubt I can crawl over dry grass.   (W. A. 1, 391, 16–393, 24)

Meanwhile the Dominicans were by no means idle. They exalted Tetzel by giving him a doctorate, and espoused his cause, at the same time pressing the charges against Luther in Rome. Sylvester Prierias, himself a Dominican and a long-established theological adviser to the Pope, formulated them. He simply dismissed the Theses as false, and then with coarse invective developed an unpleasant polemic against Luther under the title *Dialogus*. This document, together with the citation to appear in Rome within sixty days, was sent to Cardinal Cajetan in Augsburg, who dispatched them to Wittenberg where they arrived on 7 August 1518. Both Erasmus and Eck severely castigated Prierias for his arrogance and impertinent handling of the Luther affair. Luther at once wrote to the Elector, requesting his trial in Germany and not in Italy, in circumstances and before people beyond suspicion. To Prierias, who had said superciliously that he had needed only three days to write his criticism of him, Luther replied with an eighty-page answer that took two days to formulate. Prierias was no match for a man of Luther's ability and experience; nevertheless Luther's intellectual energy is staggering. In reply to his critics he took the view that there was nothing that he was saying or writing that had not already been said before: by Augustine, for example, or even by Ockham and d'Ailly. He was not attacking Catholic dogma at all (by which he meant doctrine that had been clearly and formally defined by Pope and council), only doctrines such as indulgences, which he was entitled as a doctor of divinity to bring up for disputation as well as to discuss. Even this matter of indulgences was still technically *sub judice*; he was waiting for the doctrine to be decided. True, Luther showed his own fresh theology in no uncertain terms in the process. He saw the Church as present in Christ rather than in an institution. Pope and council might both err; only scripture was infallible. The Catholic faith had always maintained the authority of the Bible and the Fathers, but Rome now virtually disregarded both.

In addition to writing, Luther was preaching. On his first Sunday back from Heidelberg, he preached a powerful sermon against the ban. As he expressed it, he 'put a bell round the cat's neck'. The ban was originally a disciplinary measure, but it had now deteriorated into a policy of extortion. If a man was unable to pay his church dues, he was banned without mercy. If he failed a second time, his whole family was put under the ban and barred from the fellowship of the Church. This meant exclusion from all the sacraments, penance, baptism, the Eucharist right through to extreme unction, and embraced all other pastoral ministrations, such as Christian burial. Further, it meant exclusion from all normal business relationships, such as buying and selling. If he died when under the ban, he was thrown into the ground like a dead cat. If the ban continued to be ineffective it was extended to include all neighbours and associates. The truth was that if the poor folk could not come to terms with their taskmasters they might as well run away like vagrants and leave everything behind them. The issue was a very live one. At harvest time when the big tithe fell due these bans 'were flying around in hundreds, like bats', to use Luther's phrase. This power was used freely not only against individuals but against corporations too, and civil authorities which had had the courage to convict clerics of crime were heavily penalized.

The pericope contained the passage, 'They shall put you out of the synagogues' (John xvi, 2, translated – 'They shall put you under the ban'). The Wittenbergers were startled at the vigour of his attack on the ban.

They had had perforce to tolerate a practice they considered illegitimate and were rather aggrieved, but Luther looked upon it as a grave spiritual scandal injuring the souls of men. He argued that it confused the conscience of simple folk to see petty transgression treated with the utmost rigour and severity, while on the other hand grave moral crime was perpetrated by the Church for money and committed with impunity. It caused men great spiritual distress when any of their friends or relatives was put under the ban, for they believed that if a banned person died he was consigned to hell for eternity. But Luther had other ideas on who was likely to find himself on the road to hell! Here again it is important to discern the issues as Luther engaged in them and analysed them. It is fatally easy to see him as a socialist, as some even of his contemporaries tried. But Luther was as interested in social problems as such as Paul was in colonialism or slavery; both men spoke only of God and His dealings with men.

The ban he describes as a mere exclusion from outward fellowship, not from that inward fellowship of true believers. No man but God only sets another in this fellowship, and no man but only sin can exclude him from it. If a man is unjustly banned for the sake of right he must not therefore cease doing the right on the grounds of his exclusion from the sacrament, even if he knows his corpse will be torn out of its grave and cast into the river. For him who has died faithful unto righteousness there awaits only the crown of life. This sermon did much good. Many called for a public disputation, from which Luther desisted only at the urgent request of the Bishop of Brandenburg.

Sitting under the pulpit that morning were agents of the Dominicans, and unknown to Luther they reported a twisted, controversial version of the sermon, which they developed into theses. Later, when preaching at Augsburg, Luther was led into a discussion after dinner with a Dominican. He could always be relied on to talk, but he did not know that the whole affair had been planned to draw him out and so entrap him, nor that a Dominican was hiding behind a door, taking everything down.

The Dominicans moved fast, still unknown to Luther. They sent this report to Cajetan, who immediately forwarded it to Rome by imperial messenger, requesting that Brother Martin should be banned not only for his teaching on indulgences but for his sermon on the ban. This spurred Rome to action. Luther was declared a notorious heretic; the Elector was requested to hand over 'the son of perdition' to Cajetan, who was ordered to arrest him and hold him pending further orders. Volta was asked to send an Augustinian monk to seize Luther, bind him hand and foot, and throw him into prison. For good measure, Volta summoned Luther to Rome two days later.

Luther's fate seemed sealed, but a political affair stayed Rome's hand. The old emperor, Maximilian, wanted his young nephew, Charles of Spain, elected to succeed him. Frederick refused to subscribe. Charles was the very last man the Pope wanted, and quite suddenly Rome began courting Frederick and offered him its highest distinction, the award of the Golden Rose. But Frederick was Luther's prince, and Luther was his best professor at his own young university. Frederick suddenly achieved a position of importance in the political game. Luther did not know of all these schemings, but was keenly aware of the peril of his position. Frederick was determined that justice should be shown to Luther, to the extent that he actually said that God expected this of him as his prince. But he was equally determined that if Luther were condemned by the Pope it would be his own responsibility as Luther's lay lord to effect the punishment. The whole affair validates much of Luther's protest, in that the grave spiritual crisis in Christendom could be so lightly set aside for material interests.

Frederick sympathized with Luther's insistence that his case should be heard on German soil before competent and impartial judges, and actually wrote to Maximilian asking him to have this done 'in a place beyond suspicion and before judges beyond suspicion'. It was an astute move made at the right moment. Before the Diet at Augsburg broke up, Cajetan had received orders authorizing him to command Luther to appear before him at Augsburg and empowering him to pronounce absolution or condemnation when he had heard Luther's case. Frederick, the layman, thought of a 'fatherly handling and not a judicial', which, if it failed to produce agreement, should be followed by a fuller hearing before impartial authorities. Cajetan, the church-

man, regarded anything other than Luther's unqualified submission as leading to his own condemnation as a responsible
Catholic theologian and statesman.

All this was known only to a few of the protagonists. Rumour
ran high. People were apprehensive. Luther's colleagues on the
faculty made public protestation of their support for his cause as
well as for his orthodoxy, though he might have disputed 'somewhat too freely!' They wrote to Cardinal von Miltitz assuring
him of their colleague's piety and erudition, begging him as a
fellow German to support Luther before the Pope. Luther knew
he was in the gravest danger. Looking back on these days, he
said: 'I clearly saw my grave ready, and kept saying to myself,
"What a disgrace for my dear parents!"'

Even when he learned that the hearing was to be in Germany
he knew that this was not everything. John Huss, with a more
powerful lay protection than Luther had, had openly gone to
Constance, to be destroyed by faggots piled high by Dominican
hands. Albert, the count of Luther's birthplace who was a convert to evangelical theology and who had a kind of proprietary
interest in Luther as a local boy grown famous, begged him not to
leave Wittenberg, for he had heard talk in high places of plots to
waylay him on one of his journeys and have him strangled or
drowned.

At this juncture Luther wrote to Link at Nürnberg in very
serious and sombre tones to the effect that what he was now
experiencing had always been the Christian pattern of life. Had
not Christ set him in office as an unconquerable preacher of this
truth? The more such people threatened him, the more for his
part would he trust in Christ. He had already given up everything.

He continued:

There is only one thing left, my weak and broken body. If they take
that away, they will make me the poorer by an hour of life, perhaps a
couple. But my soul they cannot take.

I know perfectly well that from the beginning of the world the word
of Christ has been of such a kind that whoever wants to carry it into
the world must necessarily, like the Apostles, renounce everything
and expect death at any and every hour. If it were not so, it would

not be the word of Christ. By death it was bought, by deaths spread abroad, by deaths safeguarded. It must also take many deaths to preserve it, or bring it back again. Christ is a bloody partnership for us.   (10 July 1518)

These are the words of a man fully apprised of his dangerous position and of the issues he was prepared to defend with his life.

CHAPTER II

BEFORE CAJETAN IN AUGSBURG
(OCTOBER 1518)

HISTORY will always recall the dramatic nailing up of the
theses against indulgences in 1517 and the still more dramatic
stand at Worms before Church and State in 1521, but the trial
at Augsburg was equally dramatic and probably more momentous
than either. In 1517, virtually unknown outside his Order,
Luther stood on the safe ground of his own university; in 1521,
now famous, he had the certain support not only of scholarship
but of society – possibly of half Germany. In 1518 when he set
out to face Cajetan in Augsburg he was a solitary, beggarly monk,
unaware either of how the Church or the Empire would handle
him, or even what they were doing about him at the very time
he was walking there. If ever a man set out in faith alone,
Luther did. Influential lay friends warned him that he would
never be allowed to return; Staupitz begged him to escape while
he could. He answered, 'Christ rules in Augsburg, even in the
midst of His enemies.' Once more he started on foot for Augsburg, again with Leonard Beier. He thought he would never see
his beloved Thuringia again. At Heidelberg he was gravely
warned that the Italians sought only to burn him, to which
Luther answered with a wry humour as invincible as his faith,
'If my cause is lost, the shame is God's.' It was in this
spirit that he journeyed to Augsburg and indeed faced his life's
mission; it was God's cause, not Luther's, and if Luther failed,
the cause could not. The journey overtaxed him. He suffered
great pain in his digestive system, a certain symptom of nervous
strain and exhaustion, and collapsed with fatigue three miles
from the city. He was taken on in a cart and so shabby was his
appearance he was obliged to borrow a cowl from his old friend
Link to appear before the Cardinal. Luther was a little taken
aback when he found that the Augsburg laity were adamant in

refusing to let him meet Cajetan before they had secured written guarantees from the court of officials (assembled at this time in Augsburg for the Diet), assuring Luther's safe return. Serralonga, a court diplomat (known to the Saxon court, too), called on Luther in the role of Mr Worldly Wiseman, advising him to withdraw and not to argue with the Cardinal. Luther answered that he would of course withdraw if it could be shown that his theology was not what the Church recognized as true. Truth had as much interest for the diplomat as it had for Pilate. He asked Luther sarcastically if he toyed with the illusion that Frederick would take up arms for his cause.

'Of course not,' said Luther.

'Where will you be then?'

'Where I am now – in the Kingdom of Heaven.'

There was no answering this man with his single-minded belief in God.

Cajetan was a Dominican, and a theologian of some substance. Protestant history has been critical of Cajetan, but Luther respected his sincerity. The Cardinal had none of the corruption of so many of his colleagues and contemporaries, and was moreover a strong critic of ecclesiastical abuses. He was a good Aquinas scholar, had always opposed the conciliar movement in favour of papal absolutism, and in the judgement of his contemporaries might well have filled the papal chair had Clement not lived. He certainly set out to treat Luther in a 'fatherly way', and unlike many other critics had the intelligence to read some of Luther's writings before facing the author. But he never had the slightest intention of talking things over with Luther and offering pastoral and theological guidance; he was simply going to tell this 'shabby little friar' the course of action expected of him – recantation.

Cajetan announced that the Pope required three things of Luther: first, that he repent of his errors and recant; second, that he promise never to teach them again; third, that he do nothing to disturb the peace of the Church. Luther replied that he had not come all the way from Wittenberg to be told what he could quite easily have been told at home, and asked what his errors were. Cajetan instanced Thesis 58 on the treasury of merits, and Thesis 7, where in the Resolution Luther states that it is not the sacrament which justifies, but faith. These were highly intelligent criticisms and not altogether unfair; to deny the treasury of merits put Luther in the position of denying a papal decretal of 1343, while to defend the second necessitated a nice balance of views. Cajetan demanded immediate recantation. Luther answered that scripture took precedence over decretals. Cajetan argued that the Pope was above councils and scripture. 'His Holiness abuses scripture. I deny that he is above scripture,' answered Luther bluntly. The Cardinal exploded and shouted at Luther, telling him not to come back unless to recant. There was no ground common, and sensing the impasse Luther asked for time. He appeared the next day with a statement and argued that he had neither been convicted nor refuted and therefore could not recant. He was not aware of having taught anything contrary to the Bible, the Fathers, the decretals or reason. He offered to submit himself to open debate or to the opinions of the combined universities of Basel, Freiburg, Louvain and Paris. In this he showed a want of tact, for the remark was a slight to Cajetan and his ability to deal with the matter. Luther found that all Cajetan could talk about was 'Thomas, notions, and scholastic theology'. He thought his theology vague, obscure and unintelligible, and believed him as fit to understand the issues raised as 'an ass to play a harp'.

The written 'justification' presented on the third visit is a defence of his position with respect to the two points the Cardinal criticized, the treasury of merits and the necessity of faith to justification. Luther now clearly subordinated all papal decretals to scripture and begged the Cardinal to respect his conscience in this matter, to show him truth rather than force a recantation. On the treasury he writes:

The Pope does not have this treasure in a purse or treasure chest as it were. . . . Christians virtually believe that they obtain an actual positive good as if it were a gift, or grace, when in actual fact they receive the ministry of the keys, the forgiveness of sins. . . . When a man becomes one spirit with Christ by His love, he thereby shares all his benefits.

On the subject of justification by faith, Luther issues eleven good arguments from scripture and the Fathers. In one place he says:

No person is justified save him who believes in God, as stated in Romans i, 17, and John iii, 18. . . . Therefore the justification of the righteous man and his life as a righteous man, constitute his faith. . . . Faith is nothing else than believing what God promises or says. . . . Whatever remarkable thing we read about as having happened in the Old or New Testament, we read that it was done by faith, not by works, not by a general faith, but by faith directed to the matter in hand.

I cherish and follow the Church in all things. I resist only those who in the name of the Roman Church strive to erect a Babylon for us . . . as if holy scripture no longer existed.

The Cardinal promised to send this 'justification' to Rome, but again commanded Luther to recant. High words were spoken. Spalatin persuaded Luther to beg pardon for his rudeness and, further, to promise silence if his enemies could be silenced. Cajetan thought he had vanquished Luther and said haughtily, 'Luther will have to come to market with fresher eggs.' Staupitz sensed danger. The dear old man combed the town of Augsburg in vain to borrow money to get Luther to Paris, believing that in such a strongly anti-papal milieu Luther would be out of the Pope's clutches. He wrote to his Elector, saying Cajetan was threatening to break Luther and himself and to throw them into prison. Staupitz was in great distress. He released Luther from his vow of obedience so that he would be a free agent, able to act without regard to his Order, and hastily withdrew with Link without taking leave of Cajetan. But before he departed he said the kindly comforting words, 'Remember you have begun this affair in the name of our Lord Jesus Christ.'

Luther now stood dangerously alone. There was no answer from the Cardinal to his apology. He had also written an appeal 'to the Pope ill-informed who thought to be better informed', as he expressed it, demanding a hearing elsewhere than in Rome, and making the point that as the Pope himself had only narrowly escaped assassination in Rome the previous year, the chances were that he, Luther, would not. He again wrote to Cajetan taking formal leave, but no answer was returned. Luther's supporters feared the ominous silence. Very ugly rumours were circulating about what was in store for him and suddenly he was whisked out of a side gate in the city wall at dead of night by a well-wisher, set on a bare-boned nag, and without breeches or boots was ridden to Murheim without stop (a distance of some forty miles). When he reached his destination he fell off his horse too weak and sore to stand, too tired even to crawl to a bed. He dropped down in the straw and slept off his fatigue in the stable. Then he continued his ride to Wittenberg. At Nürnberg he fell in with true friends and there received from Spalatin a letter containing a copy of the papal arrest, a letter which brought home to him the narrowness of his escape. On reaching home he wrote and published an account of all that happened at Augsburg under the title of *Acta Augustana*. This included an account of the interviews, Luther's written statement in defence of his theses on the treasury of merits and justification by faith, the text of Leo X's *breve* to Cajetan of 23 August 1518, and Luther's reflections on the *breve*. Apart from its intrinsic truth, the strength of Luther's case lay not a little in his open appeal to lay judgement. In him the Christian layman was again re-established and the Christian religion declericalized.

Luther quietly awaited the expected bull of excommunication, intending when he received it to leave the country, perhaps for Paris. But in the meantime Cajetan had written to the Elector blaming Luther for the breakdown. In his letter he said: 'I exhort and beseech Your Highness that you take counsel of your conscience and either send Brother Martin to Rome or banish him from your country.' Frederick sent a copy of the letter for Luther's comment and within one day he returned a spirited and firm answer, long and complete, the central point of which was that he had been called to question on the matter of indulgences, and that the points he raised (as the Cardinal well knew) had never been formally or finally determined by the Church, but were debating points. Cajetan neither pointed out the errors nor proved Luther heretical; he was merely asking his prince to hand him over to the tender mercies of Rome. Luther was writing for his life, but made no effort to seek the support of his university or his Church. He was always splendid before a clear and visible opponent, but he knew the abysmal uncertainty of standing alone. He thought his end had come. In a letter to Spalatin he wrote:

For the rest I await my excommunication from Rome any day now. On that account I have set all my affairs in order, so that when they come I shall be ready for them with loins girded. I shall be like Abraham not knowing whither I go. Yet I am most certain whither I go, for God is everywhere.[1]   (W. A. Br. 2, 253)

He called a farewell supper party. At the beginning of the meal he received from the Prince a letter expressing surprise that he had not yet fled the country. It was all up now that Frederick had refused lay protection. Yet before the end of the meal a second letter came asking him to stay. This must have been one of the happiest second thoughts of all time, but it shows how slender Luther's chances really were. Frederick eventually resolved to send Luther neither to Rome nor into exile unless he was given a fair trial and duly convicted. He never changed his ground. Humanly speaking, he saved the Reformation.

The delicate political situation forced Rome to set aside this grave theological problem and to pursue a political course, which she did very cautiously. The policy was to woo Frederick, and to this end Cardinal von Miltitz was sent, for he was a Saxon nobleman, known to Frederick and Spalatin already as well as to the Saxon court. He was well armed with bribes and rewards. For Frederick he had a Golden Rose, a coveted papal honour, and special letters rendering legitimate the inheritances of Frederick's illegitimate children. He carried powers to confer titles of count, poet laureate and doctor of theology. But the main purpose of the expedition was to neutralize Frederick's protection, so he was carefully instructed to leave the Rose with Cajetan and make its actual conferment dependent on Frederick's compliance with Cajetan's advice in the Luther affair. Miltitz was provided with letters to Spalatin and to the chief magistrate at Wittenberg ordering them to give every assistance to the Cardi-

1. 25 November 1518.

nal in dealing with the heretic, together with similar injunctions to the towns on the route back, with a view to enabling Miltitz to get away with his victim and bring him to Rome. It was all very carefully planned, but Miltitz was a young, pompous and sentimental palaverer without any understanding of the real issues of the matter; in fact, he was little more than an ecclesiastical gossip. Feigning frankness and friendliness he complimented Luther on his youth and vigour. Later he was to say of his mission that he could not have got Luther out of Germany with 25,000 men. The upshot of the conference was that a truce was to be observed on both sides and that Luther would submit to the learned judgement of a bishop of the Pope's choice, and if convinced of error, would recant. Miltitz then turned against Tetzel as the real villain of the piece and issued charges against him for embezzlement and immorality.

Miltitz managed to persuade Rome that Luther was ready to recant but that he would never recant to the Dominican Cajetan, who, he alleged, had bungled the whole affair. Rome adopted new tactics. Vague allusions were actually made to the possibility of a cardinal's hat being offered to a friend of Frederick's (to Luther, obviously). But at this time Maximilian died (12 January 1519). Within a few months it became clear that Charles was in any case to be the new emperor so it was pointless for Rome to woo Frederick any longer. Thus the courtship ceased, and the Luther affair was left unresolved for the time being.

Meanwhile, a former friend of Luther's, the redoubtable if rather disreputable John Eck of Ingolstadt, had chosen to make a strong theological attack on the Wittenberg School. This attack he cunningly directed at its weakest member, Carlstadt, a feint which Luther recognized. Carlstadt, being Luther's senior, took up the cudgels on behalf of Wittenberg but Luther insisted on taking part in the debate in person and defending what was being attacked, namely his own theology. The outcome and significance of that historic debate need another chapter.

CHAPTER 12

THE LEIPZIG DISPUTATION (1519)

CARLSTADT has suffered much at the hands of historians, owing largely to his later lapse into enthusiasm and socialism and his consequent confusion of the Gospel with these movements, but he was an earnest and sincere scholar of no little weight. He made the same sort of spiritual pilgrimage from scholasticism to an Augustinian biblical theology as had Luther.

John Eck was no light-weight either. He was the most feared disputant in Germany. He had all the faults of the clerics of his day, all their worldliness, all their bombast, but Catholic scholars have shown convincingly that he was a scholar in his own right, strong, fearless and independent.

The very sight of Luther's Theses was like the smell of gunpowder to an old war-horse, and the two men Eck and Luther engaged on a passage of arms in writing, after which both seemed prepared to let the matter drop. Carlstadt on the other hand (when Luther was absent at Heidelberg) impetuously went forward with 405 Theses which were in effect a radical formulation of the new theology of Wittenberg, more radical than Luther would have allowed. This aroused Eck to refute Carlstadt point by point.

Carlstadt and Eck were eager for disputation, and when Luther met Eck on his visit to Cajetan in October 1518, they agreed in a friendly way to the disputation being held not at Rome, but at Erfurt or Leipzig. Luther preferred Erfurt but Eck finally settled for the more favourable ground of Leipzig. When Eck sent his theses to Wittenberg Luther saw at once that all save one were directed at him, not at Carlstadt, and in particular, at his assertion that papal authority was based on nothing but late decretals. Luther set out the theses he was going to defend, even sharpening the point Eck singled out:

That the Roman Church is superior to all others is shown by the insipid decrees which the Roman popes have put forth during four hundred years. Against these are the historical evidence of 1,500 years, the text of divine scriptures, and the decree of the Council of Nicaea, the most sacred of all.

But Luther had to go to considerable pains to secure permission to attend the debate, and when the permit finally came it did not mention him as one of the principals, but only under the heading of those whom Carlstadt might bring with him – a deliberate and rather mean affront. Meanwhile, Luther was not idle. He was making an intensive study of the papacy. When he arrived in Leipzig, he had mastered a mass of historical material which caused him to question the decretals altogether, and to see the medieval papacy as a recent and false imposition on Christendom, almost as an alien and secular power. He seemed critical of any view of the Church as an organization, believing it to be rather a community composed of believers called of God.

Eck arrived a few days before the Wittenbergers. He was given a horse and groom for his daily rides, and received every courtesy and consideration; but when the Wittenbergers arrived they were largely ignored. The Wittenberg theologians, Carlstadt, Melanchthon and Luther, came in two carts escorted by some two hundred students in helmets and halberds. It was an exciting sight, so exciting that the town council hastily called out the town guard, but unfortunately as Carlstadt's cart entered the town the wheel broke throwing him, Carlstadt, and his books into the mud. The fall gave the older man much pain and was taken as a bad omen by the bystanders.

After a pompous start at the Pleissenburg Palace¹ on 27 June, Carlstadt and Eck debated for a week, giving Luther some peace and rest. When Luther looked round the churches, the priests of one church broke off the mass they were celebrating

---

1. The Pleissenburg Palace was demolished at the end of the nineteenth century and the new Rathaus built in its place. On the site of the house where Luther stayed there is now a department store. The church in which he worshipped and the church where he preached still stand. Luther's pulpit is there, too.

and ran out with the vessels under their arms. Armed men had to stand in the inns where the Wittenberg students were meeting. There was more excitement in the town than in the debating chamber. Carlstadt was a total failure in debate and was utterly out-classed by the able and ready-witted Eck. He was like the 'paper preacher' – no use without a manuscript, no use even without a load of reference books. Eck won by a first-class memory and a ready tongue. The first Wittenberg dragon was neatly slain by the new St George and everybody was waiting to see how the second would fare.

Luther stepped on to the rostrum on 4 July. He expressed regret that none of his accusers was present. (The Dominicans had refused to attend the debate.) He sought to argue his case on the authority of scripture, the orthodoxy of the Greek Fathers and the authority of Nicaea, but Eck very cleverly sought to provoke Luther by the taunt that he was simply Huss *redivivus*, maintaining that his views on the papacy were purely Hussite and condemned by council. The cleverness of this constant play on Huss lay not only in that there was a close affinity in the evangelical theology of Huss and Luther, but also in that it was at Leipzig that Huss had been convicted. History would repeat itself. Luther rejected Eck's insinuations. His views were, in fact, conciliar and Catholic. Eck then wanted to know why he had not used his gifts to attack the Hussites rather than the Holy Father. Luther angrily replied that many of the views of Huss were evangelical and Christian, and could not be condemned outright. This created an uproar. Duke George, the ruler of Albertine Saxony and an avowed enemy of evangelical theology, was moved to swear aloud. Eck pressed home his point in the sympathetic atmosphere. Then Luther doubted a Catholic council? A Catholic council had condemned Huss, had it not? Luther replied that councils might err. A further uproar! He had now shown his hand. The debate continued on the subjects of purgatory, indulgences and penance, but not at the white heat of the argument on the Pope and councils. Magnanimously, Carlstadt was allowed to reinstate himself when he was given two days at the end of the debates to discuss the freedom of the will and grace.

How shall we assess the debate? Eck believed that he had in-flicted a crushing defeat on the Wittenberg School. A great number of the witnesses, impressed by manner rather than argu-ment, were of the same opinion at first. Yet it is clear that skilful as Eck was in debate, and ready as he was with his undoubted weight of learning, he did not meet the arguments of the re-formers. Nor was this all. In character and demeanour he fell far short of the purity and sincerity of the learned Carlstadt, the fire and earnestness of Luther, and the theological acuity of the shy young Melanchthon quietly sitting at the side taking notes.

It is interesting to compare the behaviour of Luther and Eck after the debate. Eck stayed on in Leipzig sunning himself in his glory, writing bombastically to the world at large of what he had done, enjoying gifts of food, clothing and wine. His taste, not plebeian enough to enjoy the Leipzig beer, was sophisticated enough for the city's 'voluptuous prostitutes'. The university put on another debate for their champion disputant, providing a nice easy victim to whom Eck delivered a thundering verbal flogging. He was fêted and feasted. He enlisted the chief German inquisitor to his side, preached a farewell salvo against Luther, wrote an article against the little 'grammatist', Melanchthon, and returned to Ingolstadt 'in triumph', as he expressed it. Like almost all his contemporaries from the Pope down, he hardly understood the deep and tragic issues raised by Luther, the scholarly, God-consumed monk. He could not see what it meant when the universities were refusing to pronounce judgement against him. Luther, on the other hand, returned home at once, quiet, thoughtful, bitterly disappointed, in order to work, think and pray. The victory was really his, as certain neutral observers and intelligent laymen were well aware. As one expressed it, only the learned saw the truth of the Wittenberg argument; the rest who applauded Eck were as fit to assess the issues as a don-key to play the harp.

Gradually the atmosphere changed. Eck found out that there were not so many on his side after all. And then these Witten-bergers did not seem to realize they had been trounced, but went on quietly writing. This was utterly intolerable! The

despised, unassuming Melanchthon wrote a crushing reply to
his attack on him as a 'grammatist'. Further, the humanists had
found that attack gratuitous and distasteful, and realized that
they were not on the Catholic side at all. Oecolampadius also
dealt Eck a crushing blow from Basel. A poet ridiculed him. He
sought to have a public bonfire of the Wittenberg writings; he
sought to disparage that miserable little upstart of a university
at Wittenberg. But the writings flowed out in an ever-increasing
river, while the students flowed in like invading hordes. Even
the universities of Paris and Erfurt, on which Eck had relied for
support, withdrew, though Louvain and Cologne (under the
power of the inquisitor) still held out against Luther. Yet
Eck had made Luther declare himself, and that was his main
purpose.

As was his practice, Luther wrote an account of the debate for
the German people, so that the layman could be informed of the
issues. He showed that the Pope's supremacy was but four hundred years old and did not exist in the eastern half of the Church
at all, and had never existed there. The Greek Church had nothing to do with the Pope, and the great councils which had formulated the Catholic faith knew nothing of papal supremacy.
Luther showed himself in line with the great Fathers of the
Church. His was the soundest Catholicism by far.

Leipzig made Luther see himself more clearly. He now realized
that in his attack on the traffic in indulgences he was not merely
striking a blow at an abuse but thrusting a dagger at the heart of
priestly mediation which denied the right of every individual
believer to approach God. The humanists turned towards him.
The burghers saw that opposition to priestly tyranny was not
necessarily irreligious, and that a Germany independent of Rome
was a religious possibility. Luther felt a new freedom and turned
with fire and fury to his pen. He never seems in later life to have
accorded to Leipzig the significance for the Reformation it undoubtedly had. He had a blind eye about Leipzig, and seemed
always to bear a grudge against it, even against its people. Be
that as it may, Luther made it plain for the first time that he
denied the divine right and origin of the papacy as well as the infallibility of a general council. He left three main points:

scripture, responsible private judgement and faith, all of them to be attested by sound, rational, historical, informed judgement. As it was once vividly and dramatically expressed, at Leipzig the ship of the Reformation was launched on the high seas and Luther found himself at the helm.

CHAPTER 13

LUTHER'S WRITING

MENTION was made in the previous chapter of how Luther turned to his pen. His method was clear from the start. To quote his famous words as he looked back on these days:

I simply taught, preached, wrote God's Word: otherwise I did nothing. And then, while I slept, or drank Wittenberg beer with my Philip or my Amsdorf, the Word so greatly weakened the papacy that never a prince or emperor inflicted such damage upon it. I did nothing. The Word did it all. Had I desired to foment trouble, I could have brought great bloodshed upon Germany. Yea, I could have started such a little game at Worms, that the Emperor would not have been safe. But what would it have been? A mug's game. I left it to the Word.[1]

Luther was not only a prodigious writer, but wrote with a readiness, effectiveness and colour that has perhaps never been excelled. He is responsible for nearly a hundred massive volumes, each containing several major works. He averaged a book a fortnight over the rest of his life, all the more remarkable when it is remembered that he was nearly forty years old and his health ruined with foolish monastic disciplines before he began to write. Whether in Latin or German, he wrote in a style facile and fluent, full of humour and homely truth, of poetry and simplicity. He wrote to the point every time. His power rested in that he felt he had something from God to say and felt called by God to say it. There was nothing mealy-mouthed about him. The tragedy within the Reformation was the failure of Rome to give any proper answer to Luther. They condemned him, yet never answered his arguments. As Israel in that dark hour turned a deaf ear to Jeremiah and thereby forfeited her destiny, so did Catholicism, in rejecting her noblest son, choose for herself a disinherited

1. Quoted by Gordon Rupp, *Luther's Progress to the Diet of Worms, 1521,* London, 1951, p. 99.

and disunited existence. Nevertheless, Luther left more than a message; he conserved a remnant of the true people of God.

Let us take a brief glance at some of the things Luther was saying and writing at this time. On his return from Leipzig he learned that Frederick was ill from overwork, and at the request of Spalatin, he wrote the Prince a small book of spiritual comfort. This bore the odd name of *The Fourteen*, the reason being that, instead of inculcating the help of the fourteen patron saints of medieval devotion, whose alleged powers were supposed to defend the suppliant in time of illness,[1] Luther looked at the problem of evil in relation to the Gospel under fourteen headings. He set human suffering in relation to Christ's suffering, and discussed the problem of suffering and sin in this context. Against evil he set the inexhaustible grace and mercy of God, the power of faith and Christ, and the invincible goodness of God. The Elector was much helped by the book, and Spalatin begged Luther, who had rather naïvely asked for his manuscript back, to let it be published. In itself the work is remarkable enough, but when one considers the savage onslaughts Luther was undergoing and his distress of mind, it shows the deep piety within him and that peace of soul that passeth all understanding.

On his recovery the Elector asked Luther to produce a book of sermons for the Sundays of the Christian year. These were called *The Postills*. In addition Luther wrote a quite enormous number of spiritual tracts and articles on prayer, sacraments, confession and the ban. He tackled the economic problem of usury. He produced his commentary on the Psalms. He wrote polemical tracts. He was working out his views on sacraments. He began to see that a sacrament was a gift which could be appropriated only in faith: baptism was forgiveness of sins and a covenant with God; the Lord's Supper was an inner communion with Christ which grew out of faith in Him and the forgiveness of sins. He gave up the Catholic doctrine of transubstantiation but held on to the real presence. On the sacrifice of the mass he was silent at this stage, but wanted communion in both kinds. At this time he believed in three sacraments, penance, baptism,

1. To quote one example from the fourteen: St Blasius was the defender against sore throats.

mass, but later was to drop the first on the grounds that it had not been instituted by Christ.

Of special interest is his book *On Good Works*,[1] a subject on which Luther, then as now, was misunderstood. His principles are clear. Good works are good only in that God commands them, and are never those which we opt to do as good, for example fasting. As Christ taught, the first and only work is faith, from which stem all the good works God requires of us. This is in no sense a contribution we put into the bargain, something we do or offer, something we struggle to attain, for then faith would be a human work or striving. Faith is confidence in God, an assurance, almost a reassurance, of His favour towards us, which takes root in the soul when the news of the Gospel has been given or preached to us. It is something that was not there before; it is something wholly new; it is something that God created, that man cannot create; it is a gift of God (Ephesians ii, 8). Anything that is done in response to this faith is a good work, anything that is done by this faith is transformed into a good work. Good works are not specifically 'religious'. The work may simply be mother washing the baby, the little miller's girl putting the corn on to the ass's back, the farmer tending his beasts or ploughing his ground, the cobbler at his last, the scholar reading his book and teaching his students, the prince governing his people, and so on. These are the good works. These are the works God wants His people to do for one another, and He calls them to do these in His sight so that His world may continue in peace and harmony. Going on pilgrimages, reciting paternosters, paying for masses as holy merchandise, counting beads and all the rest are not good works at all. Moreover, once faith has taken root in the heart, a man never needs any telling as to what work is good and what is not. He knows it instinctively and intuitively, as a husband who is loved by his wife does all things large or small for her (and the home) in utter faith and without distinction. Only where there is doubt does he seek to please her and curry favour and approval by devised deeds rather than the ordinary good works of daily life. For those who are young and for those

1. See the translation with introduction in Vol. 44 of the new American edition, ed. James Atkinson, Philadelphia, 1966.

who have not grown to the stature of knowing this truth, God gave the Ten Commandments, and these Luther then proceeded to elucidate for his readers.

This writing has rarely been accorded its due weight, possibly because it was never classed with the *Reformation Writings* of 1520.[1] Yet in showing the ethical meaning of life it wrought a transformation. It utterly turned upside down (or better, the right way up) the dualism, the intellectualism and the absurd arbitrariness of medieval ethics. The distinction between the so-called sacred and secular, characteristic alike of ancient and classical religion as of medieval religion, was removed by Luther. In his view, all that the man of faith did within the framework of his relationship of faith towards God, was holy: all that a man did who had not this relationship of faith to God, was unholy, even the accepted religious activities such as fastings, pilgrimages, etc. Consequently, monkish morality was not higher than secular morality.

He also wrote a book on the mass, entitled *Treatise on the New Testament*. The title is significant. The essence of the mass to Luther was the new covenant, the forgiveness of sins, which Christ confirmed under the signs of bread and wine. 'This is my body, this is the cup of the new testament in my blood which is shed for you for the forgiveness of sins.' In the first instance, this was God's gift, but now it had been made into a gift from man to God, a sacrifice, a meritorious work, though the only sacrifice a Christian man can make is of himself and his prayers. Of the souls in purgatory, Luther argued that it was neither scriptural nor reasonable to believe that a celebration of a mass could release a departed soul from his misery. Where a mass did not serve to underline the new covenant, that is, the forgiveness of sins, it was otiose. Endowed masses should be reduced, the institution made audible and in German. If the sacrifice of the mass was that of oneself and one's prayers, all believers might make such a sacrifice, not only priests. Faith made everybody a priest. (Luther, of course, unlike the sectaries and enthusiasts, allowed the place of ordained clergy, commissioned and called by lawful authority, to preach and teach and minister.)

1. See p. 187.

Not the least important, Luther had clarified his attitude towards Rome by 1520. In May he wrote a book entitled *The Papacy at Rome*, in which he showed that the Church was not to be identified with the institution Rome had made of it, but was to be thought of as that congregation of men of faith who are called of God and listen to His Word. At this moment, Prierias's 'Answer' to the thirteenth of Luther's Leipzig theses reached him. Prierias argued that every decision of the Pope on matters of faith and morals is infallible because it comes from God, and has to be accepted by everybody under pain of temporal as well as eternal death. By now Luther, who had earlier suspected the authenticity of the papal decretals (notably, if uncertainly at Leipzig), had received certain proof, arising from the publication by von Hutten (1517) of the researches of Valla, who had demonstrated in 1440 that the Isidorian decretals were a forgery, as was the alleged Donation of Constantine. It was shown to the world that the authority of the papacy based on these ancient decretals and the alleged gift of the Western Empire to the papacy by Constantine were based on common fraud and plain deceit. Luther was like a young man returning home from abroad to find the fiancée he loved fallen to the level of a street woman. He was filled with dismay. To him the Antichrist was now in command at Rome.

But it is as important to see how Luther understood this term as it is to know how he combated the reality it represented. His grasp of the situation was far more profound than John Wyclif's or that of any of his predecessors. He did not think of the Antichrist as some person or being who would appear at the end of time. Nor did he identify the papacy with the Antichrist. The Antichrist was to him some sort of demoniacal power which had gradually infected the court of Rome, and in the course of centuries thoroughly corrupted it. He saw its worst manifestation not in its striving after earthly power and riches, nor in its moral depravity, intensely aware as he was of these vices. It lay essentially in the papal claim to infallibility. In Luther's eyes the worst feature of this claim was that it meant that the papacy set itself above scripture, thereby claiming an authority over God and His Word and holding the faithful in spiritual bondage and tutelage.

Luther also found great offence in the way in which the papacy arrogated to itself the right to release men from oaths and vows. Still worse, the closer knowledge of ecclesiastics which recent events had given him had convinced him that few of these agents of the papacy seemed to believe what they were professing. He was forced to the conclusion that the papal curia consisted of religious nihilists, even atheists. History has shown that Luther was largely right in this belief.

This state of affairs at Rome convinced Luther that he was living 'in the last days', understood in the real New Testament apocalyptic sense. He fought the Roman Sodom as a devilish institution, as an enemy of the Gospel, as a city set against God. It was to responsible laymen he wrote his book, *An Open Letter to the Christian Nobility of the German Nation Concerning the Reform of the Christian Estate*, as a call to resist the papacy. Clearly Rome would not reform herself, so Luther appealed to lay Christians. He began writing his book in June and it went to the press in August. It was an enormous success. Even his staunch enemy Duke George was fascinated by it. This was the first of those works, all written in 1520, which subsequently earned the title *The Reformation Writings (Die Reformationsschriften)*.

Luther appealed to the leaders of Germany, to the young Emperor, the princes and knights and cities, though warning them that they must never imagine that they could heal Christendom by force of arms. They were dealing not with flesh and blood but with the princes of hell, who could fill the world with war and bloodshed but never themselves be overcome by them. It was faith in God that they must have. He struck at once at the quasi-divine power supposed to be inherent in the Church and priesthood, a power which had cowed Europe for centuries. Rome had entrenched herself behind three walls: (1) the claim that her spiritual power was superior to the temporal power of kings and princes, (2) the claim that no one could interpret scripture but the Pope, (3) the claim that only the Pope could summon a general council. Luther set about demolishing these three walls.

The Romanists asserted that there were two estates of man, the spiritual and the secular. The Pope, bishops, priests and monks constituted the spiritual estate while the princes, lords, artisans and peasants constituted the secular. But the whole idea that there was a higher spiritual estate and a lower secular estate was a disastrous delusion. The real 'spiritual estate' as such was constituted not by the clerics but by the whole body of believers in Jesus Christ, clerical and lay alike, for God had called all such, and all such were alike kings and priests by the calling. There was only one body under Christ the Head. All Christians belonged to the same spiritual estate. Baptism, the Gospel, faith, these alone made a Christian and spiritual people. We were all kings, all priests (1 Peter ii, 9; Revelation v, 10). A farmer belonged to the spiritual estate as much as a bishop. The clergy were not distinguished by some indelible character given them at ordination, but simply because they had been set apart to do the particular work of a priest by and on behalf of the community. What all could do, not all might do; only the men properly called and duly set apart might perform the office and work of a priest in the Church of God. The spiritual priesthood of all believers blasted to pieces the first wall of the Romanists.

The second wall tumbled just as readily. To allege that scripture needed interpreting before it could be understood and that only the interpretation of the Pope was valid was absurd. If this were true, then there was no need of Holy Scripture at all. 'Let us burn the scriptures and be content with the unlearned boys at Rome!' Holy Scripture was plain to all, and could be interpreted by all 'who have the true faith, spirit, understanding, word and mind of Christ'.

The third wall collapsed with the other two. There was no historical foundation to the pretension that only the Pope had the power to call a council. The Church itself might call a council, as it did in Jerusalem in Acts xv; even the Emperor might call a council, as happened at Nicaea in 325. Certainly the calling of an ecumenical council had never been the prerogative of a Pope.

In the second part Luther chastised the worldly pomp of the Pope and cardinals, their greed, their exactions. It was a very telling indictment. He referred to the three thousand papal secretaries at Rome, and called the whole lot a swarm of vermin misappropriating the wealth of Germany and other countries. The details of the annates, the buying and selling of benefices, plurality, simony, make very dismal reading to Christian men, but doubtless quickened the interest of the self-interested masses in the consequences of a religious reformation. The latter is an important point. Luther's only concern was religious: to declare God and bring souls to Him in Christ. When he refurbished the house of God, there were too many influential people interested in what would happen to Church endowments, lands, properties and resources, rather than in the establishment he sought to re-build. One of the tragedies of the Reformation is what worldly men made of it. Much of Luther's wild anger in later life was aroused by the men who refused to accept the spiritual and theological nature of the Reformation, and whose self-interest made of his mission a kind of socialism, a new kind of libertinism, the end of which he saw as disastrous for society as well as for Christianity.

In the third part Luther gave a long, practical list of reforms which needed to be carried out. A few are listed here: the abolition of annates;[1] of the buying and selling of benefices; of the extravagant papal court and all the customs that gave adulation to the Pope, such as kissing his feet and carrying him on men's shoulders; of saints' days and wakes; of interdict and ban; of masses for the dead with the concomitant carnivals and processions. He further advocated that the Pope should renounce temporal power and re-dedicate himself to prayer and the Word;[2] the restriction of mendicants; that every town should have its own parish parson elected by the congregation and that he should be free to marry or not as he chose; that schools and universities should be reformed; that common life should be simplified and luxury and prostitution abolished; that drinking should be controlled; that care should be taken of young people.

What Luther sought in the main was the complete abolition of papal power over the state, the creation of a German Church

1. The first year's revenue of an ecclesiastical benefice paid to the papal curia. In England Henry VIII transferred them to the crown in 1534.

2. In this context he exposed the forged papal decretals of Isidore as well as the Donation of Constantine.

with its own court of final appeal, together with a religious and ethical reform of the whole of Christendom. He wrote to Spalatin at this time, 'I am beyond injury. Whatever I have done and do, I do under constraint, ever ready to keep quiet if only they do not demand that the truth of the Gospel be quiet'[1] (W. Br. II, 135, 41 ff.). The effect of the book was instantaneous.

At the end of the Appeal Luther promised another book, and this was to be the *Prelude on the Babylonian Captivity of the Church*, a book written for the clergy and the humanists which appeared in October 1520 within a matter of weeks. It had far-reaching consequences, for it severed the tap root of Romanism, namely, the sacramental system by which Rome controlled the life of every member from birth to death under the power of the priest. It should not be assumed that Luther had no sacramental theology. There was nothing of the radical or liberal about him; he was intensely sacramental in his theology as well as in his religion. When he severed this tap root he was cutting not sacramentalism but clericalism in the guise of sacramentalism.

Luther first discussed the sacrament of the Holy Communion and exposed three errors of Roman practice as a three-fold bondage: the exclusion of the laity from the cup, the doctrine of transubstantiation, and the sacrifice of the mass.

With regard to the withholding of the cup, Luther proved from the Gospels of Matthew, Mark and Luke, as well as from Paul, that early Christians not only partook of the cup but were intended to partake. 'Drink ye all of this.' It was the Romanists who were the heretics and schismatics in excluding the laity.

The doctrine of transubstantiation he regarded as a product of scholasticism. He disbelieved in any miraculous change of the substance of bread, but maintained the coexistence of the body and blood in, with and under the elements. He was a total believer in the real presence, but thought that the Body of Christ could be included within the substance without the substance having to be transubstantiated, rather in the manner of the Incarnation when Christ dwelt in a human body without any transubstantiation of human flesh and blood. Luther's views are generally described as 'consubstantiation' as distinct from

1. Letter of 9 July 1520.

transubstantiation, but this is misleading. He never used the word, which implies 'inclusion' or 'circumscription'. This view he never held. He thought of Christ in terms of an illocal presence. In other words, Christ was present, but that presence was not to be thought of in terms of a place or a thing.

The sacrifice of the mass meant the offering to God of the very body and blood of Christ by the hands of the priest after consecration. It was a repetition of the atoning sacrifice of the cross in an unbloody manner. This institution is central both to Roman Catholic and Greek Catholic worship and theology. Luther argued that the original Lord's Supper was instituted by Christ to serve as a perpetual and thankful memory of the atoning death of Christ: to it a blessing was attached, namely the forgiveness of sins, a blessing to be appropriated by faith. The burden of the sacrament was the promise of forgiveness and its appropriation by faith. But of course this promise was larger than the sacrament proper, and was not restricted to the sacrament. It was established and proved in Christ's total ministry, and was true even without the confirmation of the sacrament. This promise is the Gospel, and the sacrament its acted Word. It is something God is offering, not man. We have nothing whatever to offer. It is exactly like baptism, to be received not given. The Romanists had changed all this into a good work of man, an *opus operatum*, by which they imagined they pleased God. They had surrounded it with vestments and incense, gestures and ceremonies, so that its original evangelical meaning was beclouded. According to Luther it is God who is doing all the offering, and who gives the free gift of undeserved forgiveness. All man can do is respond with thanks, with all that he has and is. Luther never sought to abolish the mass but rather to reinstate the true mass. He also quite sensibly wanted the service in the vernacular.[1]

Luther then turns to the sacrament of baptism. Here is a clear example of how he was more of a sacramentalist than the Romanists themselves. He was thankful that this sacrament at any rate had largely remained untouched by avarice and unspoilt by bad theology. The only serious theological difference was

1. See p. 259 for a discussion of Luther's liturgical reforms.

that Rome diminished baptism by relying much more on 'the second plank' of penance, the plank that saved a man from drowning. Luther objected to this. Instead of placing his confidence in priestly absolution, a man should rely on the remission of sins offered in baptism. A penitent man should return to faith in his baptism, where he received and receives the promise of remission of sins. Luther preferred immersion as a better significance of death and resurrection of the old man. He also accepted the baptism of children as an ancient and justifiable practice of the Church. There is no satisfactory way of reconciling Luther's clear teaching on justification by faith alone with his views on baptismal regeneration. His contemporaries saw this chink in his armour, and so have many radicals who succeeded them. Perhaps the least unsatisfactory way of resolving the problem is to recall Luther's simple defence of the example of Jesus in blessing the children and the long practice of the Church in bringing up the young. Further, it emphasizes that in a sacrament what comes first and matters most is God's work not ours.

Finally, Luther attacked the number of the sacraments as then held. He believed that there should be baptism and bread, in that both of these were instituted by Christ, and both promised remission of sins. Penance he used as a means to return to the grace of baptism. The rest of the seven sacraments he rejected on the grounds that they were common to the heathen world, or were not taught by Christ, or could not be proved from scripture.

Although Rome had finally condemned Luther, Miltitz persuaded him to write once more to the Pope. This was Luther's third and last letter. With the letter he sent a book entitled *The Freedom of a Christian Man*. Written in some twelve days, it is in effect a popular summing up of the Christian life. The leading idea is a kind of dual paradox, namely that the Christian man is the lord of all and subject to none, by virtue of faith; and that he is also the servant of all and subject to everyone, by virtue of love. A Christian's life is made up of faith and love: faith expresses his relationship to God, love his relationship to man. Man is made free by faith which alone justifies, but faith manifests itself in love to one's fellows and in good works. The person

must first be good before he can do good works; good works proceed from a good man. Faith, as it makes man a believer, by the
same process makes his works good; but works in themselves
do not make a man into a believing man nor a justified man. The
error of good works is in seeking justification in doing them.
Faith unites the soul to Christ in perfect union, therefore whatever is Christ's is the soul's also. This is more than communion
as such; it is victory and redemption and freedom. By faith we
are all kings and priests. It is not sufficient to preach the words
and works of Christ in a historic manner, but rather (as St John
did) to promote faith in Him, so that Christ is Christ for us.
We must preach why Christ came; He has given us liberty and
made us kings and priests – kings in that we are lords of all
things, priests in that we stand continually in His presence.

Luther then turns to his second principle, that a Christian
man is the servant of all. Faith issues in works, for a Christian
enjoys that most free of all servitudes in which he serves others
of his own will and for nought. He should empty himself and
serve his neighbour, in the same way as he sees that God has
acted and is acting towards him through Christ. A Christian
lives in Christ and in his neighbour, in Christ by faith and in his
neighbour by love. What Luther criticized in the Romish doctrine
was that Christian men were there taught to seek merits and rewards, so that Rome turned the Gospel into Law.

What the Pope thought of the book we do not know. He was
much too worldly to like it, or even to read it. The letter
accompanying it destroyed all prospects of reconciliation. In
his first letter to the Pope (1518) Luther threw himself at his
feet, in his second letter (1519) he addressed him as his humble
servant but would not recant, in his third letter (1520) he addressed him as an equal and pitied him as a poor Daniel in a
den of lions. He made the devastating remark that the Pope was
called the vicar of Christ for a vicar was there because someone
else was absent, and it was Christ who was absent from Rome.

CHAPTER 14

THE PAPAL BULL (1520)

EARLIER this same year (1520) it was realized in Rome that Miltitz had utterly misjudged the Lutheran affair. It was realized equally clearly that for all Frederick's unquestioning loyalty to the Pope he was not going to hand Luther over to the tender mercies of the papal curia. A condemnation was therefore drawn up in Rome. The gentle and scholarly Cajetan suggested that only some of Luther's statements need be instanced as indictable and the rest merely described as offensive to Catholic truth, and that Luther himself be once more asked to recant. But the burly Eck prevailed against Cajetan's sensible and kindly course of action, and made short shrift of the whole affair by writing a bull of condemnation which he submitted to the Holy Father at his hunting lodge when he was hunting for wild boar. He began his bull with the pompous sally, 'A wild boar hath entered thy vineyard, O Lord . . .!' From Luther's writings they haphazardly drafted forty-one articles which they condemned as heretical. It was a shockingly irresponsible piece of work. They had not read Luther's writings and even instanced as heresies such opinions as 'to burn heretics is contrary to the will of the Holy Spirit', and 'secular and spiritual princes would do well if they put an end to mendicancy'. Others were torn from their context, others were unintelligible. All rulers were forbidden to believe, teach, favour or defend them. All Luther's works were to be burned (though in another place only those containing the forty-one heresies were instanced). Luther and his followers were excommunicated, and given sixty days in which to recant.

Even Eck thought very little of the final form of the bull, still less of the knowledge the curia displayed. He could not understand why so many harmless articles were included. There was no real refutation of Luther's alleged errors at all, and at that moment of time the bull was utterly without point. It was the real wild boars in his reservation that interested His Holiness. For the so-called 'wild boar' of Saxony he cared as little as he did for the 'vineyard of the Lord' the wild boar was alleged to be invading. Not the least support for Luther's case must surely lie in the casual, irreligious, flippant way in which Rome handled the whole affair.

On 17 July 1520 the Pope appointed Aleander and Eck as his two nuncios who were to execute the bull in Germany. Eck's area of activity was to be mainly in Saxony, Aleander's the west. Eck proceeded in his usual blustering manner, even taking the liberty of adding to the bull names of sympathizers. He received a rude shock when only three places allowed him to publish the bull. Even in Leipzig, the home of his glorious triumph but one year previously, he found disenchantment and coolness. Of course he received his gift of wine, of course he was offered soldiers, but it was a bitter experience when the university refused to publish the bull and Duke George approved their action. And then the students made his life a mockery, taunting him with that rough, inimitable, penetrating humour common to students the world over. Eck had to flee to a monastery for peace and protection. The students penetrated even those formidable walls by the simple expedient of the post!

This delighted Miltitz who had great pleasure in saying, 'Serves you right! I told you so!' He accused Eck of proceeding without his (Miltitz's) authority, and of wrecking the whole scheme of mutual rapprochement between Rome and Wittenberg so delicately, so hopefully and so unobtrusively pursued by himself. Miltitz rose to the situation. He persuaded his fellow-countryman Luther to write but once more to His Holiness, a letter which was too outspoken to serve the cause of reconciliation.[1] Meanwhile Luther wrote a vigorous manifesto against the new bull, wherein he traced the hand of Leo but the voice of Eck. He translated the bull into German in an approximate version for the layman to read and understand. He reissued his appeal for a free, general council, at the same time calling on lay responsibility – emperor, prince, knight, councillor and the rest – to see that this was done. Luther now had the ear of Germany.

1. See p. 192.

Meanwhile the other papal nuncio in the west, Aleander, the pope's librarian, was doing rather better than Eck in his campaign against the 'new Arius and Mohammed'. In Antwerp he elicited an order from the young Emperor for an edict against heresy in his lands in Burgundy, and in Louvain managed to arrange a bonfire of Luther's books. In Cologne, there was a different intellectual climate. There Aleander received very short shrift. Even the Elector, in Cologne at the time, refused to see him, and Aleander had to suffer the indignity of having to buttonhole the Prince whilst at church. Erasmus, too, was then in Cologne, and it was on this occasion he uttered his famous remark when consulted by Frederick, that Luther had committed two wrongs: he had hit the Pope on his crown, and the monks in the belly. Erasmus argued that it was in everybody's interest to give Luther a fair hearing before expert and impartial judges. He made the further very important point that, of so many universities, only two had condemned Luther and none had refuted him.

When the Elector returned home Aleander pursued his bonfire tactics, but neither the Archbishop, the chapter, the town council nor the university would join in with him. All the pomp and force of the occasion was taken out of it by this non-cooperation, and a little mockery put into it when ribald students handed over to the hangman to consign to the flames not the works of Luther but old scholastic tomes and ancient collections of dry sermons. What is more, in Mainz the hangman bluntly refused to burn Luther's books at Aleander's command. They found a grave-digger who was willing to do so, a not inappropriate substitute, but here again students stole the show by piling in anti-Lutheran tracts for the illiterate grave-digger to consign to the flames, which he did with bucolic determination. Nevertheless, this feverish activity of Rome's seemed to impress the common folk; they began to believe that Rome meant business.

Luther made like reply. On 10 December he and the other professors with their students marched out to the carrion pit where Agricola had already kindled a fire.[1] Agricola threw in the volumes of the Canon Law, the *Summa Angelica*, together with

1. An oak tree marks the spot today, just outside the old city wall.

some smaller volumes of Eck's and Emser's. The Canon Law embodied for Luther the confusion of Gospel with Law, of politics with religion, the making of the Kingdom of God into a temporal kingdom, the secularization of all that was spiritual, the setting up of the Pope in the room of God. It was the Alcoran of the Antichrist. The *Summa Angelica* embodied the intellectualization of this casuistry, the perversion of pastoral care into jurisprudence, the corruption of clergy into judges. Luther stepped forward. Quietly and unostentatiously he put the bull on the fire. He watched it burn, then turned on his heel and left the scene.

A thrill went through Europe when it learned that an obscure monk, a man with no more weight behind him than his faith in God, had burned a papal bull. It was the fiery signal of emancipation. The individual soul had discovered its true value. If the Reformation can be dated, that date must be 10 December 1520. If eras can be dated, our modern era began at nine o'clock that morning.

CHAPTER 15

WORMS (1521)

ALEANDER did all he could to arrange for Luther to be put under the ban at once and unheard, and when he was foiled in this plan he insisted that, in the event of Luther's going to the Diet of Worms, the Lutheran affair must not be raised with the German national grievances, but that Luther must be summoned not to argue his case but to make public recantation. As the world knows, Luther was in fact summoned to appear before the Emperor at Worms and was granted for that purpose an imperial safe-conduct. It is odd, looking back on this, to recall that none of the principal parties was very happy about the prospect of this appearance – the Emperor was not, Frederick was not, their advisers were not, Rome was not. Only Luther was clear about his course – he had to go. He saw the whole affair against that general pattern of history when error seems always with power, and truth on the scaffold. He knew he had God's Word, and he knew equally clearly that his opponents had only their own. 'I simply say that true Christianity has ceased to exist among those who should have preserved it – the bishops and scholars.' Meanwhile his pen flew over the folios; not only continuous polemics against his adversaries such as Emser and Catharinus cascaded off his desk, but splendid spiritual documents such as his *Advent Postills*, his Magnificat and his writings on the Psalms. In the three months before Worms he published fifty works and kept three printers going, all in addition to heavy pastoral preaching and university teaching.

When the time came for him to go, the council generously provided him with the luxury of a covered cart for the long journey, and his university offered him twenty guilders for his expenses. For company Luther had the theologian, Amsdorf, a fellow monk and a young noble. With no less a personage than the imperial herald himself in front, the retinue threaded its way

to Worms.[1] In every place the 'populace poured out to see
Doctor Luther', and everywhere he was received with honour.
At Erfurt, the place of his old university and the monastery
where he had taken his vows, the whole university came out to
meet him as a body, an experience he movingly described as his
'Palm Sunday', a prelude to his own 'Good Friday'. Here and
elsewhere he was called on to preach, and it was on this occasion
that the crowds were so tumultuous that the church porch
bulged with the press and collapsed in the middle of his sermon
on faith and works, a situation he calmly capitalized in the content of his sermon! In Eisenach, his own Eisenach, he fell
dangerously ill, but persevered, undaunted and undismayed in
his borrowed strength. The whole affair turned out to be a
triumphal procession, to the consternation and chagrin of
Aleander. After Frankfurt, the crafty Glapion, father confessor
of Charles himself, contrived at the eleventh hour to deflect
Luther by means of a 'conference'; but Luther saw through the
trick, for the purpose was to cause him to fail to appear at Worms
on time and so lose his case by default. Bucer too tried unsuccessfully to arrange a conference at the Ebernburg with Sickingen and Hutten, the two nobles leading the cause of reform,
though on humanist and nationalist lines. A letter reached Luther
from Wittenberg at this time saying that the Elector was of the
opinion that it was all up with Luther. Luther's courage was
superhuman. He was later to say, 'Even if there were as many
devils in Worms as there are tiles on the roofs, I would enter
anyway.'

There were more devils rampant in Worms than ever the
young monk imagined. There were colourful wares and wealth
on the streets and gargantuan indulgence in the taverns. There
was jousting in the fields by day and drinking in the inns by
night. An observer wrote of the leading prelates spending most
of their time banqueting and drinking (Lent though it was), and
of one who lost sixty thousand guilders[2] at one sitting. Another

1. The route lay through Leipzig, Naumburg, Weimar, Erfurt, Gotha,
Eisenach and Frankfurt. See map, p. 13.

2. Reckoned on the basis of earnings at that time this figure amounts to
over £2,000,000 today.

commentator said that murders were averaging three to four a night, even though a hundred folk had been executed for these offences. It was a humanist who described Worms during the Diet in these words: 'It goes on here quite as in Rome, with murdering, stealing; all the streets are full of whores; there is no Lent here, but jousting, whoring, eating of meat, mutton, pigeons, eggs, milk and cheese, and there are such doings as in the mountain of Dame Venus.'

Luther entered the town on Tuesday, 16 April 1521, at ten in the morning in company with a great number of nobles who had come to meet him, together with a hundred horsemen. Two thousand people awaited him. As he entered his lodgings he glanced at the crowd, which ever remembered the deep black flash of his falcon eyes. He was heard to say to himself as he stepped down from the cart, 'God will be with me.' And God was.

On the next morning Luther heard the confession of a knight who lay dying and granted him the sacrament. Informed that he was to appear before the diet at four o'clock, he went for a haircut to have his tonsure clearly defined. He was then taken to the palace by a devious route owing to the throng of people.

After a wait of two hours, he was brought in to that august assembly in the packed and suffocating hall. He was asked two questions: firstly, was that pile of books his? (the Emperor could not believe that one man had written so many!); secondly, would he renounce them? To the first question Luther acknowledged quietly in German and in Latin that he had written them. To the second, he replied that he needed time to reply, for it involved faith, salvation and the Word of God. Doubtless he was playing for time before he showed his form, for he knew the world was watching and waiting, and he knew the power and subtlety of the Empire and the Church arrayed against him. He was granted a further twenty-four hours on condition he made a verbal answer only and brought with him no written statement.

The proceedings had not gone as Luther expected. He had been under the impression that he had been summoned to present his case, not just to make a recantation. The reserve of the first appearance should not be interpreted as meaning that he

was contemplating the possibility of recantation. That he could
never have done nor even contemplated. 'Truly, with the help of
Christ I will not revoke even a dot in all eternity.' But Luther
was shy, humble, nervous and utterly alone. He needed time to
think over the mood at Worms. His advisers equally needed time
to see the course their enemy sought to pursue. All night long he
worked out his statement, the manuscript of which we still
possess. He needed desperately to talk it all over with his friends,
but his only friend with him in Worms, Amsdorf, was in hiding,
for Aleander had threatened him with imprisonment on the
grounds that he had no safe conduct even if Luther had. The
next day at four he appeared again. But it was a different Luther:
utterly restored, completely self-composed and reassured about
what God demanded of him. To the same questions now set him
again after his twenty-four hours' reflection, he replied in fearless
German that he was sorry for any breach of etiquette, for he was
a monk and no courtier, and that he acknowledged authorship.
He put his works into three classes: (1) devotional, which not
even his enemies would want him to recant, (2) polemical works
against the papacy, which he would not recant, (3) polemical
works against private persons who defended this papal tyranny,
which though perhaps too vehement, he could not recant.
Nevertheless, he was open to conviction, and if he were refuted
from the Bible, he would be the first to cast his books into the
fire.

He went on to say how well aware he was of the dangerous
dissensions that had arisen owing to his teachings. But it was the
Word of God that had excited the controversy; as Christ had
said, He had come to bring not peace but a sword. It would be an
ill start to the proceedings to begin by condemning the Word of
God, for that would bring a flood of evils on the reign of the
young Emperor whom he loved next to God. Luther owed it to
God to take the course of action on which he had embarked in
the interests of Christendom.

It is as important not to over-dramatize this appearance at
Worms as it is to notice that Luther humbly asked to be set
right. The princes did not know what to do. All this seemed to
them reasonable enough. But the spiritual princes argued that

Luther had already been judged by the only competent authority there was, namely Rome, and that the task of the princes was not to hear his plea or make their own judgement, but as guardians of the Church to uphold the decision the Church had already clearly made. It is also true to say that neither Luther nor Frederick would have chosen the appearance to take place before a body so heterogeneous and unwieldy. They would have preferred a small, competent, fair-minded court under the temporal protection of the diet.

To resolve the dilemma Luther was asked to give a plain answer to a plain question. 'Will you retract? Yes or no?'

Luther gave a plain answer, as he described it, one 'with neither horns nor teeth' (presumably meaning an answer that did not put a man on the horns of a dilemma and which also was not an attack in reply). He replied that unless he were proved wrong on the basis of scriptures and sound reason, for popes and councils had erred and might err again, he was bound fast by his conscience to the Word of God. He could not and would not retract. He added in German, 'May God help me, Amen!'[1]

The princes made to depart, for the last word had obviously been spoken. Dr Eck[2] tried Luther once again. He told him to forget his conscience, adding rather maliciously that it could err as perhaps a council might err, though he would grant that possibility in the case of a council only with respect to matters of discipline, never faith. Luther rose to the argument. 'I can prove it!' he cried. But the young Emperor by now had had enough and could not bear the thought of further argument from this

---

1. The accounts which relate the famous words, 'I can no other! Here I stand! May God help me, Amen!', published that same year in Wittenberg, and the earliest account of the diet, were not from Luther's hand, and there seems to be a consensus that, though they summed up Luther's stand at Worms, they might not be his exact words. Further, the great 1546 edition of Luther's works, published immediately after his death, do not include those seven words, 'I can no other! Here I stand!' For a translation of the proceedings at Worms see *Luther's Works* (American Edition), Vol. 32, ed. George W. Forell, Philadelphia, 1958, pp. 103–31. For the original: W. A. 7, 814–57.

2. Not the opponent at the Leipzig Disputation but the chancellor of the diocese.

intense monk. He made a sign for Luther to be taken away. This was interpreted as a signal to lead him off to prison and a tumult arose, but it soon became clear that no such order was intended. The Germans felt they had won a great victory, though the Spanish underlings hanging about outside thought the whole affair was *chose jugée* and called out when Luther's figure filled the frame of the door, 'To the bonfire!' – fortunately for them in Spanish, so that the words escaped the German bystanders. 'I've come through! I've come through!' Luther cried in deep emotion on reaching his lodgings.

It is true that he always regretted the way he had handled the appearance at Worms. His advisers strongly urged him to go cautiously, play for time, and see which way the cat jumped. This advice, carefully followed (to the letter on the first appearance), put him in a straitjacket. If he had been his real, large, natural self, Worms might have had a more dramatic influence on events. He ought to have been allowed to play the role of an Elijah rather than a Pashhur at court.

There was more to Worms than the official proceedings. With a speed that took their breath away, the Emperor summoned the Electors to meet him the next morning at eight o'clock, and when they assembled he asked them what they intended to do next. He told them, on their asking time for reflection, that as far as he was concerned there was nothing to think about; he was prepared to stake his life, his soul, his dominions, his all, on the vindication of the Roman Church. He wished he had tackled Luther earlier, but now that he had appeared at the diet, it was his intention to send him back home at once on a safe-conduct. A single monk could not be right against one thousand years of Christianity, he argued. Charles's mind was made up. But certain posters of an alarming and inciting nature began to appear in the town. One of these proclaimed that four hundred nobles and eight thousand men were determined not to abandon Luther, as well as being prepared to fight princes and Romanists, in particular the Archbishop of Mainz, to maintain their cause. The placard bore the dreaded sign of the peasants' *Bundschuh*. This was rebellion.

Terror struck the Archbishop's troubled heart. He begged the

Emperor to allow Luther a hearing. Charles answered that his mind was made up, but as a concession he allowed the estates three more days in which to tackle Luther and get him to recant. Unfortunately, all the men involved were avowed opponents of Luther; not even Frederick showed the slightest support for his professor. It is sometimes difficult to know whether he was simply neutral, or feigning neutrality to protect Luther. The latter seems to be nearer the truth in the total view. At the hearing Luther again made it clear that the basis of his doctrine was scripture and reason. Even in private conversation Luther was heard to criticize the decisions of councils, that of Constance in particular, which he believed had condemned Huss wrongly.

Then Cochlaeus came along with a private proposal from the nuncio to the effect that if Luther would be willing to recant only those points which were generally agreed to be in contradiction to the Catholic faith, then the questionable points could be considered in due course by an authority competent to do so, and his writings amended accordingly. Luther answered that now he was but one voice among many. Even if he were to recant all his writings, nothing would be gained by such personal recantation. Evangelical theology was in other hands far abler than his own. It was no longer a question of one man, but of a cause.

Negotiations still went on. Two jurists, who wanted reform anyway, kept negotiations open, and it seemed at one time as if Luther was prepared to leave the whole thing to a general council to be called as soon as possible. The Archbishop sent for him hopefully, but it became clear that Luther would never leave his basis of the Word of God and submit that principle to a council. There was no more to say or do.

Popular memory has forgotten the conferences subsequent to the diet, but they were not unimportant. It can truly be said that it was there that the real decision was taken, and moreover it was there that an earnest effort to come to an understanding with Luther was really made. The Romanists began to see that the cleavage was abysmal. It was not a matter of Church politics or Church order, it was fundamentally a difference in the interpretation of Christianity. But the conferences were important for yet another reason. The documentary evidence of these meetings shows a Luther different from the generally accepted picture of the Titan at Worms – a Luther sitting on his bed talking to Cochlaeus, or in a small conference chamber, warm, emotional, modest, hoping everything may yet work out as God would have it. His convictions were so deep that not even all of his devoted supporters entered into them and understood them, to say nothing of his enemies. But they all stemmed from one root, whether it was his view on the errancy of councils, the papal pretension to temporal power, canon law, a works theology, or any other of the themes of his thought and work over the past few years; that root was his confrontation by God, his seizure one might almost say, when in the hands of God he was made aware of his total impotence and sinfulness, and when that confrontation set coursing in his veins a faith no circumstances could destroy and no person remove.

The imperial messenger then called to inform Luther that the Emperor, as guardian of the Roman Church, intended to take action to prosecute him. He granted him twenty-one days in which to return to Wittenberg, on condition that he did no preaching, teaching or writing on the way. Luther then thanked the Emperor and the estates formally for granting him a hearing, as well as a safe-conduct, saying that all he desired was a reform according to holy scripture. He declared his loyalty to the Emperor to the end of his life, but reserved the right and freedom to testify to the Word of God.

The next morning two wagons pulled out of Worms, escorted by about twenty nobles, to take the Mainz road, through Oppenheim and Frankfurt on to Friedburg where Luther sent back the imperial herald. Through Grünberg and Hersfeld they journeyed, where Luther was entertained by the abbot and where he preached; thence to Berka and to Eisenach where the people received him and begged him to preach; and on to Möhra to his own folk, where they begged him to preach to them, which he did in the open air, there being no church in the village. It was after leaving Möhra that Luther was 'ambushed'; as he hurriedly grasped his Hebrew Old Testament and his Greek New Testament, he was unceremoniously hurried off through the forest on foot, and later set on a horse. At eleven o'clock at night

Luther and his captors rode over the clanking drawbridge of the Wartburg. Here he was received kindly and given two rooms, which he was ordered on no account to leave till his tonsure was overgrown and his beard complete. To clinch the anonymity he was introduced to the staff as Junker Georg, or, as we might put it, 'Sir George'.

The true story of Luther's disappearance was not known for a long time afterwards. Back in Worms the news was received with shock and apprehension, but when uncertainty rumoured itself into the certainty that his body had been found with a knife in its back, the atmosphere of the city was one of consternation and indignation. Eventually the ban was promulgated, threatening even every sympathizer with extermination. This firm development gave Aleander unconcealed delight, and when the same news reached the Pope, he celebrated it with a round of carnivals and comedies. Henry VIII wrote to the Archbishop of Mainz congratulating him on the overthrow of 'the rebel against Christ', but the Englishman, Tunstall, who attended the diet, reported back to his master Wolsey with sober realism that there were a hundred thousand Germans ready to lay down their lives for Luther. A letter of de Valdés, the Emperor's secretary, gives a still more discerning picture. He saw Worms not as an end but as a beginning. He knew the Germans were exasperated with Rome; he saw them openly ignoring the Emperor's decree and selling Luther's books and blamed the Pope for not acceding to the request for a general council and for preferring his own interests. He saw the Pope blindly insisting on the burning of Luther, and in his blindness failing to see Christendom being harried to destruction.

The forebodings of de Valdés were justified. Luther's books were burned in the Low Countries; Henry VIII burned them in England; they were burned in Scotland. But they prevailed. Once more the world was to hear the slow rending of the seamless robe of Christ, in a way more damaging than the tear of 1054 when East and West parted.

At Wittenberg the Reformation went on without Luther. Many tensions were to arise within this movement before long, some of them more serious than the tension between Wittenberg

and Rome; many antagonisms, many misunderstandings. But
Luther's purpose remained single: he sought to declare the full
meaning of the Gospel. What he had written and taught was 'for
the salvation of Christianity as a whole, for the benefit of the
entire German nation, for the extermination of dangerous abuses
and superstitions, and for the unburdening of all Christianity
from so many unceasing, innumerable, unchristian, and
damnable restrictions, hardships and blasphemies' (W. Br. II,
253 ff.).

At Worms he had shown his hand to Emperor and Pope, and
he was later to prove just as unyielding to the fervour of the
fanatics, the fury of the peasants, the theological indifferentism
of the humanists. He gave nothing away to Zürich or Rome; he
simply taught God as God had shown Himself in the Bible, and
preached Christ in whom God had declared His hand. It was not
that he was stubborn; he knew where he stood, and believed that
God had called him. He was no more determined or tenacious
than the gentle Jeremiah – and for the same reasons.

PART FOUR

THE CONSEQUENCES OF REFORMATION
1521–5

CHAPTER 16

LUTHER FACES THE PROBLEMS OF REFORMATION

WHEN the drawbridge of the Wartburg rattled behind Luther on that late evening of April 1521 the first half of his life was wound up. From now on he belonged to the evangelical cause he had fathered, and the world. He could not have known this as he was shown up to his study[1] with its tiny sleeping closet, for he could not possibly have imagined what the future had in store, or even if there was any future at all.

After the dramatic stand at Worms in 1521 interest in Luther tends to wane. There are three main reasons for this. First, many people think that by that time he had worked out the essentials of his theology and that after Worms there was little more of importance. Secondly, there is the feeling that after 1521 Luther was in the grip of circumstances over which he had no control and that therefore he gave no clear lead and his influence was no longer decisive. Thirdly, the events of 1525–46 lack the

---

1. Luther's study is in a splendid state of preservation. The wood-lined room, about twenty feet by thirteen feet, has lost its original stove, and his table has long since been cut to pieces by souvenir hunters. In its place stands a contemporary table from his uncle's house at Möhra, and on it a Luther Bible (1541), marked and underlined by Luther himself. The limed wooden walls have a myriad initials and signatures, many going back to the sixteenth century, with special bursts of initials dated 1617 and 1717, marking the homage of countless centenary pilgrims. The view from the window unfolds mile upon mile of dark Thuringian forests spreading over hills and mountains as far as the eye can see. Far down in a valley nestles the little town of Eisenach where Luther went to school and where he had lifelong friends. To visit the study is an awe-inspiring experience. The height, the beauty, the utter stillness make a very deep impression. Visitors noisily chattering through the staterooms, even through the chapel where Luther preached, are reduced to silence when they enter this gaunt room. Here a man meets history, for here a man talked with God and made history. The visitors always file off in whispers.

colour and drama which are the distinguishing features of the early years 1517–21.

All these opinions are true to some extent, but need considerable modification. As far as the first objection goes it may be freely admitted that Luther's theology was essentially complete by 1521. Yet that theology caused cataclysmic changes in Christendom, in the handling of which the hand and mind of Luther were determinative or influential. There was the reasoned and reasonable Catholic attack on his theology issuing from the university of Louvain and elsewhere. There was the aberration of the Enthusiasts and their bitter hostility to his reformed Catholicism. And then Erasmus issued his broadside on behalf of the humanists on the subject of free will. The last and perhaps gravest of them all was the association of evangelical theology with the tragedy of the Peasants' War. All these issues, and the part Luther played, are discussed in the next section. It was in reply to these problems that Luther wrote some of his finest works, for example, the reply to the Catholic attack from Louvain, and the reply to Erasmus. There is, in fact, a considerable amount of important theology which belongs to this period.

The second opinion, that in the period under review Luther had little or no control of events, may also be freely admitted. Yet what needs saying is what Luther had already said to Cajetan, and had stated at Worms. When asked to recant, he had argued that his individual retraction would achieve nothing, for the Reformation was a movement much larger than himself and were he to be destroyed the movement would go on and countless others would rise in his place.

The Reformation was larger than Luther as an individual; this was its strength. It was also wider than Luther in that there were associated with it reformatory movements other than spiritual; this was its weakness. Too many people found an interest in the Reformation which was little more than self-seeking, or at least self-interest: the nobility coveted the wealth and possessions of the Church without justification, the peasantry too often thought of the Reformation as a means of bettering their lot and bringing in social justice. Luther had no power over these vast amorphous social groupings beyond personal authority, and no sympathy with the covetous nobility though much sympathy with the oppressed peasantry, and when self-interest was excited, personal authority of this kind was simply howled down and derided. That did not make his views less true, any more than Christ's were less true on His rejection, for theological and spiritual authority can rest ultimately only on an appeal to the individual's intelligence and goodness. Moreover, it should be constantly kept in mind that the Emperor had outlawed Luther, and the Pope had excommunicated him. From 1521 onwards he had no rights outside Saxony and was not allowed to leave its confines. In the eyes of the Emperor, Luther did not exist; in the eyes of the Pope, he was outside the fold. Deprived of elementary human rights he could visit no university to dispute his theology, attend no ecumenical council to make his contribution. It was a cruel confinement to Luther personally and a disastrous impoverishment to the councils of the Church. The effect was to limit his authority from that of world-figure to that of a professor of theology and pastor of a small university town.

The third opinion, that the years 1525–46 lack the colour of the earlier years, may also be freely admitted, yet they do not lack interest or importance. It was during this time that the evangelical Church was founded and the entire pastoral system, Church worship and Church management established throughout the reformed areas. Liturgies were drawn up, catechisms composed, confessional statements compiled, new canon law established, university studies reorganized, social welfare and education re-ordered and arranged. These may not be spectacular activities, but they are mighty achievements and a real part of our Christian inheritance. It is good to remember, too, that it was at the parish level that most ordinary people would experience the Reformation; they would now see a minister and his wife and family at the manse; at church they would now hear the services in the vernacular and the Word of God preached; they would now have a village school for their children, and a parish chest for the poor and needy. This is a perspective of the Reformation not to be lost; we think too much of kings and popes, prelates and reformers, and tend to give too little thought to the farmers and weavers, their wives and children, the forgotten multitudes who have no memorial.

The importance of these years is underlined when it is remembered that it was during this time that the immense influences of Zwingli and Calvin developed, the former as a parallel movement of reform, the second as a sequel to Luther's movement. It is beyond the scope of this book to assess these Reformation movements. If the Zwinglian Reformation was independent of Luther's it certainly entered into continuous debate with it, particularly in the sacramentarian controversy: the Calvinist Reformation, different as it was, was yet born of Luther's protest.

Finally, it was during these years that the great attempts were made to reunite Christendom, when theologians of the stature of Melanchthon and Bucer on the Protestant side and Contarini and von Pflug on the Catholic side sought settlements to bring both sides together. They failed in the end, but we should recall how very nearly they succeeded at Ratisbon (1541). On all these grounds, these years deserve careful attention, not least in view of the recent deliberations of the Second Vatican Council.

We may ask, then: what were the guiding principles of the last twenty-five years of Luther's life? What were the themes that gave coherence and purpose to the years 1521–46?

In the foreground of all his activity there were the practical demands of his teaching and writing, together with all the other responsibilities that fall to a professor of theology in a university; and this at a time of inordinate expansion and activity when there were more students at Wittenberg than inhabitants of the town, and also when all problems were referred to Wittenberg for opinion or judgement. It is important to bear this fact in mind in estimating Luther: what St Paul described as that which cometh upon me daily, the care of all the churches. He never sat down to write a systematic *summa theologica*; but did every day's work as it came. Again, like St Paul. Consequently, the real Luther has to be mined from letters, lectures, books, polemical tracts and all kinds of occasional writings. This explains why it is so difficult to systematize Luther, and also why, when the generation that had known the reformer died, his influence and theological approach died too and the movement reverted to a new kind of Protestant scholasticism to meet the incursions from Rome in the form of the Counter-Reformation.

Although it must be remembered that Luther's first task was as professor of theology at Wittenberg, nevertheless we may also consider the broad lines on which he fulfilled his life as a reformer of the Church.

First, he sought to resolve all the problems that the Reformation occasioned on the principles of his established evangelical theology. These problems were many. There was the counter-attack of the Catholic theologians, Latomus, Eck, Emser and others. There was the devastating dissidence within the ranks of the evangelical movement led by his senior professor, Carlstadt, and carried to grave extremes by Müntzer and others. There was that awful hour when the humanists, led by Erasmus, pulled out of the Reformation and then opposed it, to be followed within the year by the disastrous Peasants' War. Finally, there was that disturbing disunity within the theological movement proper, when Zwingli took a more liberal line than Luther's reformed Catholic approach.

The second great principle of his work as a reformer was to organize a new pattern of Church life in those areas where Protestantism had taken hold. This was carried through slowly, even painfully, at parish level, by means of official visitations followed up by pastoral, educational and social reform. Luther had the assistance of his prince and the legal advisers of the court, considerable theological support from Spalatin, Melanchthon and evangelical ministers, and cooperation from leading laymen. The work covered the reformation of the liturgy and worship of the parish church, the pastoral ministry, the education of children up to university level, the care of the sick and poor. It was not the kind of reform that excites but rather that benefits posterity. The reformers met with appalling ignorance and the most intractable legal and other difficulties. It made immense demands on the spiritual, material and physical resources of the Wittenberg reformers, not least upon Luther himself.

A third great principle of Luther's later life's work was to seek to preserve the unity of Christendom on the threefold evangelical basis of scripture, patristic tradition and sound reason. Worms (1521) did not finally mark the division of Christendom; neither did Luther's burning of the papal bull a year earlier. Augsburg (1530) clarified the evangelical position but the door was still open. During the years from Worms to Ratisbon (1541) Melanchthon and Bucer laboured for the restoration of unity to Christendom on the basis of the recognition of evangelicalism within Catholicism. Luther remained critical all these years, even sceptical and aloof, for he knew what Charles V meant when he said he intended to 'settle the German question', and Luther had long lost faith in the papal curia. Yet he commissioned his young colleague Melanchthon to effect this reunion on the ground that the gentleness, courteousness and unimpeachable scholarship of Melanchthon might perhaps succeed, whereas his own fire and vigour and devastating humour might serve to open old wounds. Luther was always critical of these ecumenical activities, a feeling rendered unnecessarily painful by the fact of his exclusion from them on the grounds of the verdict of Worms, yet his whole bent was towards evangelizing the Catholicism which had given him birth and had ministered Christ to him.

The three principles just discussed are concerned with the practicalities of the Reformation. Are there any first principles of a theological kind to be discerned in and through these decisions and events? Two vital theological concerns engaged Luther's mind during these years and may be considered of prior importance. First, justification by faith alone; second, a doctrine of the Church. During the last twenty-five years of his life Luther sought to clarify these two basic principles in all he wrote and all he did. It could be said that he had two doctrines only, a doctrine of God and a doctrine of the Church: of God who had shown His heart and mind in Christ, and therefore of a people of God who had heard and heeded and who believed in Christ. When Luther said that justification by faith alone was the article by which the Church stood or fell, he brought into one formula these two guiding theological principles. These two principles[1] throw much light on the rich confusion

1. It is also of the greatest significance that these two doctrines have a prime place in the ecumenical debate today.

of actuality the tangled events of 1521–46 present to the inquirer.

As might be expected, at the Wartburg Luther at once set to work writing his books for the laity, to free them from the Roman yoke and to strengthen their spiritual life. Of special significance at this time are his great work against Latomus and his translation of the Bible, perhaps his greatest bequest to his country.

THE CATHOLIC ATTACK OF LATOMUS

The book *Against Latomus*, written in June 1521, is not generally accorded the importance it deserves. It is an answer to the attack on Luther's theology by the university of Louvain, and is a vigorous and learned polemic giving a very clear understanding of Luther's own theological position at this time.[1] As early as March 1520 Luther had answered a combined attack on his theology from the two universities of Cologne and Louvain. Louvain sought to press home their attack. They had long suspected that Erasmus was sympathetic to Luther and were anxious for him to clarify his position, either by coming out into the open against Luther in support of their attack, or at least by lending his name to the attack they intended to frame. Erasmus would do neither, but advised them to take the only appropriate course, open to every university, of writing a refutation of the Lutheran theology with a view to publication. They ought to have taken Erasmus's advice. Already one of their number, Jacobus Latomus, had conceived some such plan of attack by seeking to answer Luther's resolutions made at the Leipzig debate. By November 1519 Latomus, having attacked Erasmus as well as Mosellan, was planning a third book in defence of scholastic theology. Another colleague of Latomus, Turenholtius by name, was already engaged on a series of disputations with the Lutheran theology as the target. Erasmus knew what both of these men had in mind and accused them of not having sufficient courage to publish their views. Latomus accepted the challenge and went into print in May 1521.

1. See the translation with introduction in Library of Christian Classics, Vol. 16, pp. 308 ff.

This storm was already brewing as Luther set out for Worms, and he received a copy of the book at the Wartburg on 26 May 1521. Within one month Luther had framed his answer. In part one of his book Luther handles Latomus's attacks on him for his thesis that no man can in fact fulfil the commandments of God, as well as for his thesis that sin remains after baptism. Latomus had opposed Luther's opinion that confession had now become a tyrannical exaction. He had also attacked Luther's view that everything a man does is sin, even if he is a saint. In the second part, Luther develops his evangelical theology on the nature of sin and its cure. In part three, he discusses the authority of scripture and tradition with reference to Law and Gospel.

Meanwhile at Wittenberg the work went on without Luther, the university having increased its strength. John Bugenhagen, the celebrated humanist, had joined the staff, as also had John Agricola, and the learned Justus Jonas, all in addition to the old staff. There were many monks too who had taken upon themselves the task of popularizing this new theology; notable among them were the Franciscan Eberlin, the Augustinian Stifel and the Franciscan von Kettenbach. But through their writings ran the strong current of socialism, a movement Luther never fathered and which eventually was to damage irretrievably his religious and theological crusade.[1]

THE EXTREMIST ATTACK OF CARLSTADT

At Wittenberg, Carlstadt, the senior colleague of Luther's, remembered for his lamentable performance at Leipzig, now took the leadership in a way distinguished for its zeal, if not for its sense. He was aided and abetted by a fiery Augustinian monk, Gabriel Zwilling, who had a great reputation as a preacher. These men stepped forward as energetic and practical reformers to take over Luther's simpler and sounder method of preaching the Word and teaching biblical doctrine. They thought this method much too slow in yielding results. Carlstadt demanded the abolition of monasticism, the rewriting of the mass and its establishment on the lines of the original Last Supper, and the

1. See p. 236.

making of clerical marriage compulsory by law. Melanchthon, disquieted, sought Luther's advice. In the meantime one third of the monks at the Augustinian convent had left the monastery and this made it very difficult for the other two thirds. Luther gave advice and worked out his own views in two books *On the Abuse of Masses* and *On Monastic Vows*.

At this moment the Cardinal Archbishop of Mainz, who was short of money, decided to have an exhibition of relics at Halle to raise some funds. He claimed he had bones and whole corpses of saints, a piece of Isaac's body, some of the manna from the wilderness, portions of the burning bush of Moses, jars from the wedding of Cana complete with some of the wine, thorns from Christ's crown, one of the stones that killed Stephen, in all a total of 9,000 relics. Pious alms were invited, 'surpassing' indulgences promised, when he put them on display in September. At this time he saw fit to thrust a priest in prison for seeking permission to marry, and this in spite of his own notorious loose living. Luther wrote to the Archbishop in protest against his sheer knavery and trickery and corruption of the poor folk in pursuance of his own selfish and immoral ends. Before the bishops attacked honest priests who openly sought an honest marriage, they should put away their own mistresses. Luther demanded a proper answer within a fortnight, and threatened further action by publishing a pamphlet he had written about this scandal. Spalatin was as worried as Frederick about the outcome of such bold action, and the former kept Luther's writings undisclosed and undelivered in order to keep the peace.

But things at Wittenberg were disturbing Luther more and more, and frustrated by the impossible slowness of correspondence, not to mention the correspondence the court saw fit not to deliver, he secretly journeyed to Wittenberg as a knight with an attendant. He stayed three days, unknown to all save his close friends, and was deeply distressed to find that Spalatin, obviously trying to be loyal to Frederick, would neither look at nor discuss Luther's letters and pamphlets on the new indulgences started up again by the Archbishop of Mainz. Luther returned to the Wartburg disturbed and disconsolate but knowing that in God's good time he would one day, and perhaps soon, come out into the open again, and that in Wittenberg.

Luther learned two lessons on his secret visit to Wittenberg. He now clearly realized that Carlstadt saw the Reformation in a way fundamentally different from his own, and also that his friend at court, Spalatin, doubtless representing the mind of his prince, was very reserved in his support. Luther also realized that his prince wanted no change and that Carlstadt wanted everything changed. Both were mistaken. Luther sensed, and was later to learn clearly, that these two men represented two movements of thought within the Reformation with which he would always have to reckon. Yet he knew his hour was not yet come; in society he was but an outlaw, in the Church, an excommunicate. He had no choice but to wend his way back to the Wartburg and wait on God and events. He was utterly powerless to do anything, even to say anything. He was not supposed even to exist.

Luther saw the issue as one involving ideas, where the only weapons were words. He believed that once he had made the Gospel clear to men, the old mistaken practices such as the earning of merits or the repetition of masses, as well as all the accretions and innovations of current Catholic practice, would fall aside by the sheer weight of their falsity. He was not concerned about the reformation of the external order. In fact, he genuinely respected the traditions of church building, the minister's robes, the crucifix, the form of service. He sought only to make the Gospel ring out in the clear tones of Christ and His Apostles, within the historic Catholic tradition.

The evangelicals were like the early Christians who continued to attend synagogue and temple, who observed sabbath and circumcision, and hoped for the conversion of all Israel until Israel cast them out. They remained in communion with Mother Church; they attended mass and confession, genuflected to the consecrated elements, prayed their Ave Maria, went on pilgrimages to shrines. Bishops, monks and nuns were still everywhere to be seen. Everything looked much the same even though it was essentially different.

Luther at first contemplated no change. He had hoped for a

reformation of faith and doctrine in the Church without a division, and actually believed that the Church would thank him for raising the matter. It was borne in upon him eventually, first at Leipzig in 1519, finally at Worms in 1521, that the Church did not welcome his activity and sought not to hear him but to silence him. It was only then that he realized he would have to build a new structure on a new foundation. It was at this critical moment that the negative aspect of this reconstruction was violently taken over by the radicals and fanatics, men to whom Luther took on the role of the go-slow theologian, 'Dr Pussyfoot', 'the Armchair Theologian', as they described him. But Luther knew that a thing can be undone by being overdone. It is not always understood that Luther's worst enemy was not Catholicism but rather that wild left-wing radicalism identified with fanaticism and 'socialism'. Humanism came under the same condemnation in that its centre of gravity was with man rather than God, but it was at least tolerant and intellectual, never fanatical. Luther was painfully aware that to lose this battle, or even to compromise himself, was to lose the cause of the Reformation.

It was in his old university town of Erfurt, the town also of his monastery, that disturbances first broke out in June 1521, soon after his triumphal entry there on the way to Worms. Twelve hundred students, aided and abetted by ruffians and workmen, destroyed sixty priests' houses and drove the poor men away. Violence broke out frequently that summer. The monks left the monastery, scholars left the city. Erfurt never recovered its prestige and the university decayed. Luther saw in these deplorable events the hand of Satan.

Worse was to follow in Luther's own Wittenberg during his absence. He had said at Worms that the Reformation was a movement which did not belong to him personally, but that if he were taken away, other hands abler than his would carry it forward. In Wittenberg Carlstadt took over the leadership of the movement. In Luther's absence he wrote and preached against celibacy, monastic vows and the mass. At Christmas 1521 he changed the service of mass, abolished the elevation of the Host, distributed in both kinds of bread and wine, wore lay clothes to perform the ceremony, and with great publicity married a peasant girl some few days afterwards. He denounced images and pictures and stirred up the townsfolk to demolish and burn them. He opposed the baptism of infants, assailed the fasts, repudiated all his titles and dignities, ridiculed theological learning, and sought to turn the students to farming instead. He threw aside his priestly and academic robes and donned a peasant's smock, tossing his head in the airy clouds of communism and mysticism and appealing to his own inspiration.

This was disastrous. Not even Melanchthon knew where he was, or what the outcome of it all would be. Some thirty of the monks left the monastery in a very disorderly fashion in November 1521, and the remaining ten sought to regularize the whole matter with dignity and discipline on the advice of Luther. At the time of Carlstadt's performance at the mass, two fanatics, Nicolaus Storch and Marcus Stübner, were drawn to Wittenberg. They were joined by the theologian Martin Cellarius, who was to play a prominent role in the Peasants' War, and who had just come from Zwickau where he had stirred up much excitement. They boasted of direct revelation from God whereas Luther had humbly taught the submission of the faithful heart to the Word of God. Such theology would not satisfy these fiery enthusiasts. They claimed that they talked with God, that they knew the Holy Spirit direct. They spoke of the mystical abstraction of the human spirit from all things sensual until it was centred in God. These men merged into the activities of Carlstadt, now that the Catholic Luther was safely out of the way. The scholarly, disciplined and kindly Melanchthon grew more and more uneasy, and realized that he could never cope with violence of this abhorrent kind.

LUTHER RETURNS TO WITTENBERG

Early in March, Luther left for Wittenberg without waiting for permission. *En route*, at the inn in Borna, he met two students on their way to the theological faculty of Wittenberg. History records the charming intellectual and theological badinage at table when 'Sir George' discussed with the students Luther, the theologian, and the Faculty at Wittenberg. 'Sir George' solemnly sent his good wishes through the students to the Faculty at Wittenberg. History does not recall what the students said when they met the knight of the road again at the university of Wittenberg as Professor Luther!

At Wittenberg Luther preached a course of eight sermons extending over one week, and by sheer power, fervour and good sense prevailed. It was a critical moment in the history of Christianity. Were the sanity and sense of Luther to prevail, or the wild irrationalities of Carlstadt and his supporters? Order or confusion? Discipline under the Word of God or wild indiscipline and spiritual licence? Never has sober eloquence achieved more. He preached the Word of Truth, and without naming or instancing those in error, he demolished them utterly. No unkind word, no coarse personal allusion passed his lips. He handled the whole matter like a true pastor. The 'prophets' retired in confusion, Müntzer to come out in the open and later to stir up the disastrous Peasants' War of 1525, Carlstadt to take to the simple life of the country at first, and eventually, after many vicissitudes, to attain a chair at Basel.

Luther resumed his labours at Wittenberg at once, teaching in the university, preaching in the church (and in the region round about). In company with Melanchthon he revised his translation of the New Testament which gave rise to the complaint of his Roman Catholic opponent Cochlaeus that 'even shoemakers and women ... ventured to dispute, not only with Catholic laymen but even with masters and doctors of theology, about faith and the Gospel'. Directly the New Testament was finished Luther set his hand to the Old. He also sharpened his pen against Rome as well as clarifying his views on the relation of a Christian to the secular order and the responsibilities of secular government. He replied very firmly to Henry VIII, who had earned the coveted title of '*fidei defensor*' for attacking Luther's *Babylonish Captivity*. Henry was utterly flabbergasted to see his royal personage so rudely handled. Luther accused him of the pointless procedure of reiterating all the old dogmas of ecclesiastical authority without allowing them to be disputed. His most important work, however, was his treatise *On the Secular Power*.

The problem was provoked by the commands and threats of the Catholic princes who with ecclesiastical leaders were attempting to suppress evangelical theology, that is, Luther's writings, and in particular, his new translation of the Bible. Further, the enthusiasts were foolishly pressing to establish some kingdom of the Holy Spirit whose guidance was to be above and beyond all secular power, all spiritual power, and all common sense for that matter. And then there was the wrong-headed Romanist theology which set the civil government with its authorities beneath the so-called higher morality of the spiritual government and its authorities represented by the priestly office and monasticism. Luther restored the Pauline emphasis on the state as the minister of God doing God's work, a work that no other authority could do, which a Christian man might properly and lawfully engage in, and without which society would disintegrate. This civil and secular activity had legitimate use of force, restraint and punishment against all evil-doers. Luther raised the vocation of civil government (in the way he was to do for marriage too) in which and through which a man served God and his neighbours. But he was very careful to define and limit the authority of the state to the protection of what is external, that is, person and property only. He was utterly against the use of force or violence against the state; at the same time he would not permit a state or a ruler to invade the province of a man's soul and his relation to God. A man might never submit to any raiding of his papers, any snatching away by civil authorities of his Bible or books, even though he might never use violence in their defence.[1]

1. Eivind Berggrav, Bishop of Oslo, and the great leader of the Norwegian Church during the occupation by the Nazis, found Luther next only to the New Testament as the source of strength to resist an evil secular power. He described Luther as 'a magnificent weapon arsenal in the Church's fight against Nazism'. Of the quotations he turned against the Nazis two will suffice: 'Not one page, not one letter shall you let them have – against the wreck of eternal blessedness. He who does it delivers Christ into Herod's hands. For they act as Herod the murderer of Christ did. We shall submit to them running through the house and using violence, but we shall not agree with or assist them, or follow them or obey them with one finger or step. For such tyrants do not behave as the authorities should.' (W. A. 11, 267.) 'From ruling by hand they have made themselves rulers of the mouth! The worldly

At this point the political situation begins to play a more important part. The German nation as a people began to take a growing interest in the Reformation, and it was found more and more difficult to execute the papal bull and the Edict of Worms against Luther. The Emperor was fully occupied in Spain with an insurrection as well as the conquest of Mexico by Cortez and the war with France. The Turks had overrun Hungary and were dangerously close to Germany. And then Leo X had died in December 1521 and had been succeeded by Adrian VI, who was a striking contrast to his predecessors. A man of grave moral earnestness, unblemished character and of monastic piety, he entered Rome barefoot. He read mass at dawn every day, slept on a simple bed, ate frugal food and lived the life of a monk. But this same Adrian was a Dominican opposed to any doctrinal reformation. Further, he had advised Charles to take a firm line with Luther and while professor at Louvain had combined with Latomus [1] to refute the Lutheran theology. Adrian saw only the urgency of an ethical and moral reform, Luther a theological one which would result in a purified and true Church. It takes no stretch of imagination to know how the papal court received Adrian's parsimonious frugality and rigorously disciplined life: he was hated everywhere.

This was the background to the Diet of Nürnberg which met in March and November 1522. Adrian demanded the enforcement of the Edict of Worms against Luther, but almost gave away his case by decrying the scandals of the Church as strongly as Luther had already done. He castigated everybody: 'From the head the corruption has passed to the limbs, from the pope to the prelates. We have all departed; there is none that doeth good, no, not one.' He saw the rise of Protestantism as the punishment of wicked Catholicism, and promised to remedy the

---

masters want to rule the spiritual regime and govern the pulpit and Church, so that I shall be forced to preach what you, my Lordship, like to hear! No, rather the devil shall have my place and preach.' (E. A. 46, 186.) (See *Luther Speaks*, essays by Lutheran pastors, ed. Hans Ehrenberg, London, 1947, pp. 5–13).

1. See Library of Christian Classics, Vol. 16, p. 308, and this volume, p. 217.

evil, starting with the curia. He effected little, for he died too soon, in September 1523, rumour says of poison. Rome certainly rejoiced at his timely departure and saw to it that the next pope, Clement VII (1523–34), should restore the *status quo ante*.

At the diet the conduct of Frederick in permitting Lutheranism to grow was deplored, but Luther's handling of enthusiasm and radicalism at Wittenberg and elsewhere served to reassure many of the soundness of his position. Luther's books were openly printed and sold in the shops at Nürnberg, and Osiander preached freely. The diet in fact refused to execute the Edict of Worms and demanded a free ecumenical council within a year, repeating the charges of the German people, though commanding Luther to keep silence. Compromise though the Edict of Nürnberg was, it was yet a step forward for the Reformation cause, and marked clearly the beginning of German political emancipation from the papacy.

But a dark cloud was looming on the horizon. Clement VII very shrewdly pressed through the new Diet of Nürnberg in 1524 a resolution to execute the Edict of Worms. Archduke Ferdinand of Austria and Dukes William and Louis of Bavaria, together with twelve bishops from Southern Germany, formed a league at Ratisbon in July 1524 for the protection of Roman Catholicism from Reformation theology. The consequences were disastrous. Philip of Hesse and John of Saxony formed a counterleague at Torgau in 1526, though the Reformers disapproved of this action strongly and would have none of it. They wholly distrusted any alliance of religion and politics. This action at Ratisbon divided the German people into two camps, and the spiritual scars of the Schmalkaldic War and the Thirty Years' War may still be discerned in Germany today. When in 1525 the disastrous Peasants' War broke out, the cause of the Reformation suffered a check and misunderstandings from which it has never recovered.

But before we turn to the heartbreak of the Peasants' War we ought to look at Luther's brush with Henry VIII in the matter of the sacraments, and at his controversy with the mighty Erasmus on the bondage of the will and predestination, when Protestantism parted company with humanism.

THE CATHOLIC ATTACK OF HENRY VIII

Henry VIII had urged Charles V to use force to exterminate the Lutheran heresy and in 1521 had written a defence of the seven sacraments in answer to Luther's *Babylonian Captivity of the Church* which was an attack on the Roman sacramental theology. He dedicated the book to Pope Leo X. In it Luther was handled with the greatest contempt and treated as a blasphemer and agent of Satan. Henry reasserted Church authority against individual freedom and adhered to the dogma of transubstantiation. Clement VII saw the hand of the Holy Spirit in the work and promised indulgence to all who read it. He confirmed the title of *fidei defensor* given by his predecessor, a title our reigning monarch retains to this day (though in a very different sense, for the sovereign is sworn to protect and preserve the Church of England and the Church of Scotland, both reformed churches).

Luther treated the whole affair with scurrilous scorn. He abused the King's person mercilessly for the world to read, and dismissed his contemptible theology. Had Luther used at this hour the restraint and good sense he had so effectively displayed in settling the troubles of Wittenberg, there is no knowing what good might have ensued, for Henry was soon to want the support of Protestant Germany. Everyone regrets the abuse he poured on Henry, though most of it was deserved. It certainly did Luther more harm than Henry. When in September 1525 Luther on advice from courtiers apologized for his personal remarks and offered to withdraw them, publicly, though not his doctrine, Henry refused to accept, taking the apology for cowardice. Henry wanted neither his apology nor his heresy, and charged Luther with violating a nun consecrated to God and with leading other monks to their eternal perdition by his teaching. There was no putting the matter right now. The whole cause of the Reformation suffered a great blow from this controversy, and all the other correspondence it brought in its train. Luther again made his position clear, that he was withdrawing his discourtesies but not his doctrines.

People who seek to make capital of this issue and to use it against the Reformation, would do well to recall that none other than the saintly Cardinal Pole in his book *In Defence of Church Unity* (1536) abused Henry as violently as Luther did and much more sharply, although Henry was his king and benefactor and had given him no personal provocation for his attack. Luther was answering a gratuitous attack and though on this occasion he showed the fire of an aroused giant, he was nevertheless a man of great tenderness and generosity. It would go beyond our book to assert that the controversy wrecked any prospect of a rapprochement between the two nations. It certainly militated against this desirable prospect, and served to bring the theology of the Reformation into disrepute on grounds it never sought to defend.

THE HUMANIST ATTACK OF ERASMUS

The Anglican tends to be more sympathetic to Erasmus than he is to Luther, and has always shown interest in a reformation on Erasmian rather than Lutheran or Calvinist lines. He tends to be uneasy about the Reformation and its dogmatic theology and a little more at home with the Renascence and humanism. It is worth looking with some closeness at the separation of humanism from Protestantism, and in particular at the reasons why Erasmus eventually withdrew his support from the Reformation, even to the point of writing a book against Luther.

Erasmus was one of the most cultivated men of all time. Of quiet and reserved nature, he combined an intellect of the purest quality with a vivid imagination, an almost perfect memory, a robust and yet rapier-like wit, a sensitive and refined taste, a sincere and enlightened belief in Christ and Christianity, a hatred of humbug and a love of sincerity and truth. In his own field of classical and biblical learning he towered, a genius. The sovereign of intellectual Europe, he stands astride the middle ages and modern times. His mission was to revive classical and Christian antiquity and make it a reforming power within the Church. When he had done the former, he seemed incapable of forwarding the latter. It was not that his nerve failed him, but as he once said of himself, 'I haven't a drop of martyr's blood in my veins.' He could never have been a reformer in any sense of the word. He had a reformer's mind but none of the resolution and self-sacrifice reformation demands. He would not get involved. He once admitted when discussing this that if ever he had been put to the test he would have behaved like Peter and betrayed the cause. In his reply to Erasmus's attack on him Luther said, rather colourfully, that Erasmus had done what he could. He was like Moses who had led the children of Israel to the plains of Moab, but could not lead them into the Promised Land. This was to be the work of another Joshua. And that Joshua was Luther.

Erasmus did more than any of his contemporaries to forward the cause of the Reformation, on the one hand by his positive work in reviving classical, biblical and patristic studies and on the other by his negative work of exposing ecclesiastical abuses, the ignorance and bigotry of the monks and the intellectual obscurantism of the schoolmen. It would seem that when he had done this work he was uncertain or even afraid of pursuing it all to its outcome. By 1524 he seemed to withdraw and the rest of his life (to 1536) was conservative and reactionary. He was a reformer against the reformation, and tragically he lost the confidence and respect of both parties. History has always judged Erasmus kindly, and there is no reason to reverse this judgement. He was one of the men of transition, like Reuchlin or Staupitz, only bigger and weightier. He was the John Baptist of the new movement. Protestants owe him a great debt, not least for his edition of the Greek New Testament which both Luther and Tyndale used. He was never a Protestant and always showed a cautious scepticism of the movement. He disliked division, separatism and sectarianism, even enthusiasm, and never showed any love for the strong dogmatic and biblical theology of the reformers nor for their evangelical piety. He thought it a fatal error to leave the Catholic Church, and any reformation he ever sought was to be within Mother Church.

Erasmus was born in Rotterdam in 1466 or 1467, the illegitimate son of a Dutch priest and a physician's daughter. Educated at the Cathedral School of Utrecht and the classical academy at Deventer, he early showed himself a prodigy. When his mother died, his guardians misused the money entrusted to them for his care and education, and when the boy grew into a youth they solved their problem by forcing him into a monastery against his will. There he spent five years and learnt a detestation of monkery that never left him. Erasmus discarded the monastery as a prisoner does his prison garb, but Luther made of his monastic experience the raw material of a new life. Erasmus was delivered from this living hell by ordination, though he never had a cure of souls, and never took a wife. He led the life of a freelance *littérateur*, supported by his teaching and (especially later) by rich and influential friends. He liked England, which he twice visited in 1498–1500, and again in 1510. There he made friends with Thomas More, John Colet, John Fisher, Cardinal Wolsey and Archbishop Warham, and he was known to both Henry VII and Henry VIII. He graced the Lady Margaret Chair of Divinity at Cambridge, where his rooms at Queens' College are still in use. He travelled all over Europe and took a great liking to Italy. Finally he settled down in Basel in 1521, finding its intellectual and spiritual climate most agreeable.

Erasmus received adulation and homage from popes, kings and scholars. When he visited a city his visit took on the nature of a triumphal procession. His letters and books circulated everywhere in thousands. Julius II released him from his monastic vows, and Paul III actually offered him a cardinal's hat in 1536 for his attack on Luther, but he was not one to whom such things appealed and he now felt too old and frail to care. Such adulation might have gone to a lesser man's head, but it had little effect on Erasmus. Besides, he had many enemies in the world. There were Edward Lee and Cardinal Aleander, not to mention reactionary universities like Louvain as well as all the schoolmen and monks. When Basel accepted the Reformation in 1529, disconsolate and depressed, he removed to the Catholic city of Freiburg, where he lived for five years. Returning home to Holland via Basel he fell ill and died in 1536, genial and witty even on his death-bed. He died without a priest and without the Church's last rites and lies buried in the Protestant Cathedral at Basel.

Erasmus was not a theologian in the sense that Luther and Calvin were theologians. Neither was he a humanist of the frivolous and faithless kind that the Renascence threw up in Italy and France, men who poured ridicule on the Church. Erasmus was a much more serious man, concerned about the state of the Church and her future. He was a committed man, involved in the Church, a sincere and enlightened believer in Christianity like most of the English and German and other humanists of northern Europe. He never scoffed at religion, his ridicule was for pompous performers, the obscurantist theologians, the ignorant, irreligious monks. He gave himself and his genius to the service of religion. Oecolampadius, the Basel reformer, who was a colleague of Erasmus, said that he had learned from him that nothing but Christ had to be sought after in the study of scripture.

Positively, he sought to restore the Church to paths of biblical simplicity and spiritual purity, to reduce dogma to a minimum and to grant the greatest liberty of interpretation to the layman. He loathed the fruitless and worthless speculation of the schoolmen which raised questions nobody asked and gave answers nobody wanted. He hated the vices and follies of monks and clergy, but still more their crass ignorance and gross superstition. He criticized even the papacy for teaching things obviously contrary to the doctrines of Christ.

The weakness of Erasmus's theological vision lay in that his fine, upright character made him underestimate the slavery to sin which crippled lesser mortals, and therefore he never had the doctrine of God's Grace and Mercy which gripped an Augustine or a Luther or an Ignatius. Consequently, where Erasmus poured ridicule on the faults and foibles of his age, waxed eloquent in satire and sarcasm (sometimes almost profanity), Luther poured tears of sorrow and waxed eloquent with the mercy and power of the redemptive Word of God. Erasmus never diagnosed the problem, and his wit never cured it. It was at this point that he finally withdrew from the theological battle, making a Parthian shot (better, a volley!) at Luther in his diatribe on the freedom of the will. But even for this book he earned little thanks from Rome. They always spoke of him as having laid the egg that Luther hatched. Sometimes they called him *Errasmus* to show he was a man of errors, *Arasmus* because they believed him Arian and heretical, *Erasinus* because they thought him an ass. Paris condemned him, Louvain hated and opposed him. His books were burned in Spain and put on the Index at Rome.

To return to his part in the Reformation, and his attack on Luther in particular: as long as the idea of Reformation was in the air, Erasmus went along with it; as soon as Luther determinedly burned the papal bull and the decretals, Erasmus shrank back. Erasmus was for unity and peace, and dreaded a split in the Church. Luther would let nothing compromise the Gospel. It was in the matter of the Gospel that the two men parted company. Luther drew that distinction between the Law and the Gospel that characterizes the preaching of Christ and all the New Testament writers, particularly Paul. Basing his theology on the New Testament, he would allow no place for human merit, nor even man's freedom and ability to fulfil the moral demands of the New Testament or even the Old Testament. A man was justified by faith alone in Christ alone, and could never earn or deserve the grace or mercy of God in any degree. It was on this point that Luther graphically said of Erasmus that he had 'grabbed him by the throat', unlike all the other adversaries who never discerned the central theological concern of Luther but wasted everybody's time in discussing abuses and scandals. The central issue is one of grace. It is to know that in relation to God a man is nothing, has nothing and can effect nothing to make that relationship. All is of God, all is of grace – even a man's faith.

Erasmus had taken a favourable view of Luther's work at first and wanted him to be allowed freedom to express his views. He was critical of the procedure at Worms and very critical of the representatives from Rome called in to settle the Luther question, namely, Cajetan, von Miltitz, Aleander. (The last he described as a complete maniac and a bad man.) His worst fears were confirmed when Carlstadt played the fool at Wittenberg (1521), when Luther engaged in vulgar controversy with Henry VIII (1522), and when Ulrich von Hutten attacked him so bitterly. Still Erasmus counselled caution, gentleness, reformation and the calling of a general council.

Provoked by Hutten, goaded by Louvain and urged by Henry (and others at the English court), Erasmus eventually came out against the Reformation in September 1524, attacking Luther's doctrine of total depravity with his work on *The Freedom of the Will*. It was a clever move. It enabled him to attack Luther, show his own position, and win support. Luther thanked him for not wasting his time on paltry matters such as purgatory and the papacy, and for getting to grips with essentials. Erasmus defends the idea of the freedom of the will as an indispensable condition of any idea of moral responsibility. Without it the commands and requests of scripture are meaningless, as well as its exhortation to repentance and the promise of reward. There is a dash of Pelagius in Erasmus, though he certainly seeks to give the maximum glory to God and the minimum to man. He argues that the will must be exerted to the utmost, though without the grace of God such exertion will be ineffective. What would be the point of exhorting man to repentance if he was not free to heed or disregard? He also refers to the universalism of scripture with its promises that all men shall be saved. The work is courteous and respectful to Luther, yet its viewpoint, which is essentially Catholic, has its back to the direction in which the evangelical was looking. Erasmus never understood the evangelical theology – his very goodness, his decency, his intellect, his character, his refined taste, served to prevent the Gospel speaking to him. He hardly had need of the Gospel. He was blind to the Christian doctrine of salvation for he was not aware of anything to be saved from. The words to Nicodemus could have been spoken to him. 'Art thou the master of Christendom and knowest not these things?'

Luther's answer to Erasmus which appeared a year later in December 1525, *On the Bondage of the Will*, is widely considered his greatest theological work. Here he connects divine foreknowledge and predestination, and infers that everything happens by necessity and that there can be no freedom in the creature. The will has no freedom in its salvation, though of course it has absolute freedom in the non-soteriological affairs of life, whether to marry and whom, what to eat, what to wear, what to do, even whether to be a good member of society. The will is driven either by Satan or God. The exhortation in scripture to repentance and holy living are calls to convince us we can do neither, and are meant to convict us of our helplessness and hopelessness and to throw us on the mercy of God. It was Satan who persuaded man he was free to act and Moses who called him in his freedom to act, but the outcome of it all is to convince us that we cannot. Erasmus handled only part of the argument. God, of course, works in us, and of course, crowns the good and punishes the evil. But this is too superficial. What is the explanation of a God commanding a good we cannot do and prohibiting an evil we cannot avoid? The Augustinian view of the total depravity of man, that man in his totality – body, soul, mind – is a *fallen* creation, is the best empirical explanation of it all, and basically biblical. Man is corrupted, tainted, impure in all he thinks, says and does. It is this root conviction that makes men aware of the glorious dimension of the free unmerited grace of God who, while man was yet a sinner, sought him out for salvation and redemption and new life with him.

The reformers were not obsessed with sin; they treated it with the seriousness of Christ. They had realized that their own good works were getting them nowhere, and, when they were once aware of this and of the reason, they welcomed the Gospel as a prisoner the key of his cell, or a condemned man his reprieve. Such men remember their cell no more, nor their death warrant, but dwell wholly in their newly found freedom. This was how the reformers lived. That they were chosen and seemingly others were not was part of the inscrutable will of God. They knew they were chosen and that was all. They deplored intellectual speculation or explanation of the mysteries of God's workings. The reformers all taught this bondage of the will in all matters pertaining to salvation and righteousness. All that they now enjoyed was the direct gift of the grace of God, and on Him, not on themselves, they depended. They feared God and nobody and nothing else. Luther's theology in this respect is stronger than either Augustine's or Calvin's: he never retracted it. Melanchthon became synergistic, or rather Erasmian, on this point by modifying Luther's Augustinianism and allowing more place to man's efforts, but Luther never quarrelled with him about it, seeking always to refrain from speculation on the ways of God but growing certain of Christ's words, 'Ye have not chosen me but I have chosen you.' Rome, of course, respects Augustine, but has never adopted his views on total depravity and predestination. Protestantism, too, has tended to follow Melanchthon rather than Luther here.

Erasmus and Luther were totally estranged, and when the disastrous Peasants' War broke out at this time, Erasmus was confirmed in his worst apprehension. He hated controversy and argument, and sought for peace and good sense. He now regarded the Reformation as a calamity which harmed both the Church and letters. When he was summoned by the Emperor to Augsburg in 1530 to act as his adviser, Erasmus was bold enough to decline. He knew he could please neither side, so stayed away.

CHAPTER 17

THE PEASANTS' WAR

THE English, who arrived at the Reformation only after the Renascence, tend to support Erasmus when they consider Luther's theology, for they find the latter's dogmatic emphases on grace and the bondage of the will, on predestination and election, on salvation in Christ alone and not by works or merit, little to their taste. When they come to study the Peasants' War, under the influence of a long line of historians they are still less sympathetic towards Luther. They pull out the stock quotation 'to stab, kill and strangle' to settle the matter. No more is wanted or needed, Luther stands condemned out of his own mouth. This misunderstanding is no modern phenomenon. The peasants contemporary with Luther misunderstood him. His enemies misunderstood him. Many even of his friends misunderstood him. Luther lent himself to misunderstanding at this moment more than at any other time.

Let us try to look at the matter with fresh eyes. There had been many outbreaks of revolution by the peasants all over Germany before the Reformation – 1476, 1492, 1493, 1502, 1513 and especially that of 1514 in Württemberg. All had been quelled by brute force, and all had ended in disastrous failure – effecting nothing positive but bringing far worse suffering, injustice and oppression. The German peasants were justified in these rebellions, for they were little more than slaves. They were ground down by taxation, legal and illegal. The increase of wealth, luxury and pleasure following the discovering of America made their lives worse. There was a shortage of land owing to an increase in population; there was a shortage of money owing to the increased papal taxation which was draining the country of silver coinage. The peasants drew up secret trades unions. In Holland they called themselves the *Kaasbroeder* (cheese-brothers), in Germany the union of the *Bundschuh* (the peasants' lace-up shoe, indicative of his *tied* servitude as distinct from the buckled shoe of his overlord).

The Peasants' War was really a series of loosely coordinated risings such as had been occurring at intervals over half a century. They had many leaders, and though their cause was a general lack of rights and a common distress, they put forward varied programmes mainly concerned with individual liberties and not at all doctrinaire, though some based their appeal on Catholic, some on Zwinglian, some on Lutheran teaching, while in Thuringia the peasants accepted Müntzer's own revolutionary apocalyptic.

Englishmen will be familiar with the communist uprising of the peasants and villeins of 1381, under the leadership of Wat Tyler and John Ball, and its suppression, and will recall its fatal association with Wyclif's new evangelical preaching and the consequent disastrous purge from Oxford of all scholars and teachers associated with his doctrine.

The question that will be asked is how this was associated with the Reformation. The reformers attacked papal tyranny (which affected most Germans more as an economic or political scandal, though to the reformers it was a theological scandal which impaired the Gospel). They preached evangelical liberty, that is, supremacy of the Word of God and the common man's right to know it. They taught the priesthood of all believers. Such theological teaching stirred up great longings in the hearts and minds of men as well as a deeper discontent with their lot. The peasants' cause was just, their demands most moderate and fair. The tragic mistake they made was in identifying the religious cause of Luther with their own social and economic cause.

The Peasants' War was also closely related to the ecclesiastical radicalism which broke out at Wittenberg as a result of the fanaticism of Carlstadt (see page 218). Luther returned from the Wartburg and quelled these disturbances by the sheer weight of his sensible preaching. But the Wittenbergers were theologically aware in a way in which the peasants were not. The people at Wittenberg had responded to the moderation and sound teaching of Luther, rejecting Carlstadt and Müntzer outright, for they knew and trusted Luther, particularly after his stand at Worms. They accepted his authority.

Carlstadt remained in Wittenberg until 1523, when he retired to the parish of Orlamünde (near Jena), where he preached with considerable effect the destruction of all images and crucifixes. He further preached the total disregard of all civil, political and even spiritual authority, claiming the direct command of the Lord for his actions. He even went so far as to teach polygamy on true Old Testament lines, and by the same principle preached against all interest or usury as well as advocating the Jubilee return of land to its lawful holders. The poor people heard him gladly. He kept in touch with Thomas Müntzer, who was much more extreme than himself.

Thomas Müntzer, in whom the spirit of the Zwickau prophets seethed and boiled to bursting point, had been appointed pastor at Allstedt in 1523. In a lonely church tower, he claimed to hold secret intercourse with God and to be the recipient of super-natural revelations. He sought to establish a Kingdom of Saints and taught that all the ungodly, particularly rulers, should be killed and all altars and images burned and eradicated from his promised land. All property was to be held in common, and any prince or lord who refused to give up his land was to be beheaded or hanged. His aim was to build up a confederacy in which all his saints were enlisted and he kept in touch with them all by secret emissaries. Carlstadt's parishioners at Orlamünde, however, were rather cool about all this extreme teaching and talk of violence, though Müntzer had a great deal of support from the poor peasants who had nothing to lose but their poverty and servility, as they thought, and also from such men as Pfeiffer, the ex-monk. In 1524 Carlstadt was induced to return to Witten-berg, but he soon returned to his parish of Orlamünde.

Meanwhile, Luther was invited to declare his mind and he gave again his teaching as expressed in 1523 in his *On the Secular Power*. He sought to distinguish between spiritual and temporal government. The life of the soul in God, its reconciliation, its redemption, its relation to God and man had been fully and unmistakenly declared in the Bible. Nothing could alter this, and it was valid and effective for all men everywhere at all times. But

God had left it to man to develop the social, civic and political order according to his needs. This had never been the subject of revelation, and obviously never could be. The task of the state was to administer law in accordance with the laws that existed, and to make new ones when the need arose. In performing this task properly the state was the minister of God, whose role was to punish lawlessness and crime and to maintain a just, clean, proper, stable society. There was much in the Mosaic code that could be described as civil and external ordinances. These belonged to the development of Israel as a community and none of these ordinances or commands were any longer valid for a Christian, just as the ceremonial Law was no longer valid. Where moral commands were given in the Old Testament, these were always valid, and if there were good points in the Mosaic civil legislation, then German law should borrow and adapt these exactly as they had done in the case of Roman law.

Luther's views were always clear and consistent. His intention was to guard the civil power against an irregular assertion of religious, biblical and mystical authority, as he had sought to guard it against the overreaching aggression of the papal hierarchy. At the same time his intention was to defend the religious life of Christian men and women against the tyrannous encroachment of the papal hierarchy as well as to provide a clear relationship of the Christian to society and to secular authority as its seat of power. To Müntzer's reviling of his person, Luther never deigned to reply. To his threat that the spirit was soon to strike with the fist, Luther maintained that the Antichrist would be destroyed 'without hands'. If the rebels did use their fists, the prince should make it clear that force rested only with the secular arm, and that men who talked in this way should be asked to leave the country.

The cool common sense of Luther, and his unanswerable theological stand, served to provoke the fanatics rather than stabilize them. Müntzer wandered from place to place in Germany stirring up the poor peasants, and eventually returned to Mühlhausen from which town he had earlier been ejected by the magistrates. Luther warned the people of the dangers of Müntzer's doctrines and begged them to proceed cautiously. He went round preaching on this subject: at Weimar, at Jena, where he challenged Carlstadt as one of the 'new prophets', at Kahla, and at Orlamünde whence he was hounded out with vile execrations. The immediate outcome of this was that Carlstadt was deprived of his chair at Wittenberg and had to leave the country, and Luther re-formulated his views against Carlstadt and the whole movement towards the end of 1524 in his book *Against the Celestial Prophets*.

The storm broke earlier than expected. At Mühlhausen, Müntzer, with his fiery friend Pfeiffer, stirred up the folk to such an extent that the natural leaders withdrew in the face of mob law and new magistrates from the mob were set in office. People flocked in from the countryside. In southern Germany insurrections broke out like sores of a fever. The poorer masses of the towns, dispossessed and oppressed by the new power of capitalism, were quick to rebel against their masters and to side with the peasants. These men were revolutionaries who talked of a total reconstruction of society and the state. Had they had a Luther to lead them, or even a sane socialist, instead of mad pseudo-theological visionaries, they might have won through to a more stable society and have written the first chapters of the later trades union and socialist movement.

The rebellion began in the late summer of 1524 in the Black Forest and Hegau. It spread eastwards into Austria, westwards into Alsatia, northwards into Franconia, even as far as Thuringia. The rebels destroyed the palaces of the bishops and the castles of the nobility. They burned down monasteries and libraries and committed all sorts of outrages. At Rothenburg, Carlstadt prepared the way by inciting the people to destroy the images.

The demands of the peasants were drawn up in twelve articles, and very modest they were. It is vexing that this cause, which in purpose was so just, should in effect have been riddled with such an absurd semi-religious, semi-supernatural theory, and that it should have come to such an ignominious and shameful end; as a result, the movement towards social justice was actually retarded. But what was worse, from the point of view of our theme, the Reformation itself was irreparably damaged. The peasants professed that all their claims were Christian. Even this shows confusion of thinking. No *claims* of any sort can be Christian claims. Christianity can only give, serve, minister. Claims may be just, and therefore merit the support of all just men, Christian and otherwise. But it is disastrous to confuse the two.

The twelve articles were:

1. The right to elect their own pastor.
2. Freedom from the small tithe (but agreement to pay the grain tithe).
3. The abolition of bond-service since all men were redeemed by the love of Christ. They promised however to obey their lawful elected rulers in all things reasonable.
4. Freedom to hunt and fish.
5. A share in the forests for domestic fuel.
6. Restriction of compulsory service.
7. Payment for labour over and above the contract. (Payment for overtime, as we should now say.)
8. Reduction of rents.
9. Cessation of arbitrary punishments.
10. Restoration of the pastures and fields which had been taken from the communes.
11. Abolition of the right of heriot, by which widows and orphans were deprived of their inheritance. (Heriot meant originally restoration of weapons to the lord on decease of tenant.)
12. All these demands to be tested by scripture and if not in agreement therewith, to be withdrawn.

When the articles reached Luther at Wittenberg in April, he arraigned the peasants and exhorted the princes to moderation in his *Exhortation to Peace*. He criticized both the secular and spiritual princes for fleecing their poor subjects, and if God allowed the Devil to stir up these poor folk in tumult, it was not Luther's Gospel that was to blame but the sin of the princes. Gentleness and fairmindedness were to be the guide. To the peasants, though he realized that many were fighting for themselves under Gospel colours, he spoke as a friend and brother. He was aware that their godless overlords laid intolerable and unjust burdens upon them, but the Gospel had nothing to do with their demands and their conduct showed they had forgotten Christ and His ways. No badness of the authorities ever justified rebellion and violence on the part of the people. He warned them that if they persisted they would do more harm to the Gospel than the Pope and Emperor ever did. Finally he counselled that both sides, that is, a few nobles and a few councillors, should sit down and compose their differences, if not in a Christian spirit, then at least according to law and contract and arbitration. But he preached to deaf ears.

Müntzer[1] scorned Luther and the 'snare of a delusive peace', and increased his menacing sabre rattling. Events gained a frightening momentum. By this time the cruellest and bloodiest outrages were being inflicted by the roused peasants. Once committed to this course, they justified it, and were at first successful. Müntzer was now (1525) in Thuringia. Luther appeared in person among the population, imperilling life and limb to preach and exhort the peasants to sanity and sense, and the rulers to firmness – Stolberg, Nordhausen, Wallhausen, Weimar, Mansfeld all saw and heard him. At this tragic moment the old Elector lay dying, and summoned Luther to his bedside, only to die before Luther could reach him. As the conflict worsened, Luther saw that his reasoned appeal was unsuccessful and he now wrote his famous attack *Against the Murderous and Plundering Bands of Peasants*. Every man was to resist them 'as long as he could move a muscle'. Knowing the great numbers that had been dragooned into the devilish confederacy, he begged the nobility, 'Dear lords, help those people. Save them. Take pity on these poor men,' but as to the rest who persisted in their wicked out-

1. On a recent visit to East Germany (1965), the author found a considerable sympathy for Thomas Müntzer and a reappraisal of him as a socialist leader. This is doubtless officially inspired; nevertheless the views are not without foundation and need careful assessment. Müntzer has been judged harshly at the bar of history owing to the abysmal and catastrophic failure of his rebellion and owing to Luther's uncompromising criticism. It is only fair to point out that Müntzer was a theologian in his own right, a man of a remarkable mystical experience, a born leader of men and a socialist of uncommon vision. The communists are selective in their interpretation of Müntzer. We arer eady for a new judgement on him.

rages, the magistrates were to 'stab, kill and strangle' as they would a dog that had run mad. This statement shocked many of his contemporaries and is always used to blacken Luther. The words were harsh but he would never retract them.

Lacking military leadership, with no planned commissariat or even coherent strategy, the peasants roamed about plundering and robbing, living off the land. They never survived a pitched battle for more than a few minutes. So disaster overtook the Thuringian peasants at Frankenhausen on 15 June 1525, when the peasant army, led by Müntzer, was encircled by the combined forces of the Protestant Philip of Hesse and the Catholic Duke George of Saxony. Five thousand lay slain in the fields and in the streets. Three hundred were beheaded summarily before the courthouse in the market-place. Müntzer was captured, tortured and executed. Elsewhere in Alsace eighteen thousand had fallen the week before. In all, one hundred thousand souls perished in battle. Survivors were beheaded or mutilated; widows and orphans were left destitute, convents burnt, villages wiped out, cattle slain, implements destroyed.

The Peasants' War was an abysmal failure, and the victory of the princes an inglorious tale of merciless revenge. Margrave George of Brandenburg reminded his brother rather bitterly that unless he left some peasants behind, they would have nothing to live on. The conditions of the peasants were worsened, their grievances remained, the prospect of a remedy was indefinitely postponed.

But far worse than all this bitter and lamentable reaction was the injury done to the cause of reformation. The Romanists held Luther responsible for it all. Even Erasmus, who had always feared an outcome of this kind, attributed it to the violence of reformation thinking. The split of the nation was widened. The defeated peasantry were forced back into Romanism in Roman Catholic districts. The whole idea of social amelioration suffered such a painful shock that any subsequent attempt in that direction was suspect. Luther was far more clear-sighted and stood on such firm principles that from the very outset he waged total war against spiritualistic and anarchic radicalism, a war wherein he would use but one weapon and that was words. It was only at the eleventh hour when the peasantry were already engaged on brutal offensive action, and when Luther had already failed in his mission of reconciliation, that he counselled war to the death against persistent lawless devilry as the only effective course then open to bring the rebellion to an immediate end. For those led or dragged or dragooned into it, he counselled mercy, and when the rebellion was broken, clemency to all. It should be remembered he was as blunt and forthright to the princes and nobility as he was with the peasantry. What Luther saw at stake was the Gospel. Had it been identified with civil war and rebellion it might have been crushed, in Germany at least. The violence of his language is the measure of the issue that was at stake.

It was a dark hour in Luther's life. He showed the courage of his convictions, and although he was a man ready to admit his errors it is a stubborn fact that he would never admit to his dying day that he had been wrong in his attitude to the Peasants' War, even when pressed by friends who believed him mistaken. Had Luther withdrawn from the struggle after his preaching mission to conciliate both sides and bring them to the conference table had failed, and had he not written that final letter when he knew he had failed, history might have condemned him neither for his principles nor for his conduct. As it is he stands condemned by this final bitter and violent letter. Nevertheless, it is hard to see what other move he could have made when flouted by lawless and bloody rebellion, faced by men right in principle wrong in action. He could, of course, have said and done no more, and thereby in this respect have preserved his reputation. Not only could Luther never remain neutral but he saw further than his contemporaries. History has endorsed his opinions if not his conduct at this hour.

An important fact emerges from this tragedy. The Reformation movement was now no longer a spiritual and religious movement led by a competent theologian and supported by men and women seeking God. It was slowly but certainly being submerged under the contemporary political, social and cultural movements of the period, with the consequence that Luther's leadership in his own sector was dwarfed by the complexity and violence of the secular movements. These Luther had no power or authority to control.

Whatever view the reader comes to on the Peasants' War and Luther's part in it, to think of him as the 'man who let the peasants down' is to misjudge his role in society as well as to imply that the peasants were in the right. We should judge Luther by the known criteria of his expressed theological mission, even if we deem him wrong in the way he chose to uphold them at a particular point in history. Christ did not 'let the slaves down' when He did nothing to change their lot, any more than Paul 'let the natives down' when he did nothing about colonialism.

The Peasants' War marked the end of the destructive tendencies of the Reformation and the beginning of a period of reconstruction to the Religious Peace of Nürnberg in 1532.

CHAPTER 18

LUTHER'S MARRIAGE AND HOME LIFE

BUT before we leave this moment there is one quiet and lovely thing that belongs to the turmoil of these years – Luther's marriage. He had long taught that vows of lifelong celibacy were both unscriptural and unnatural, and most of the reformers and many priests and monks had seen the truth of his teaching and had in fact married. Many people wondered why Luther himself had never married and thought that his views were of questionable validity while he did not practise what he preached. But forty is not an easy age at which to marry. The normal time of youth and courtship was long over. He was a man who had worked himself to a state of ill-health for God and the Gospel, and heeded little the simple demands of the flesh such as sleep and food. Marriage had never arisen in his life as an issue on which to make a decision. As late as 1524, at the age of forty-one, he said that marriage was not for him. Daily he expected a sudden termination to his life, for he was a condemned heretic and outlaw. As the Reformation developed with all the bitterness of the opposition of the Pope, the Emperor and the Catholic princes, and with all the confusion and turmoil engendered by fanatics, radicals, enthusiasts and visionaries, there weighed heavily on him the care of all the churches. This has to be remembered when we see Luther a full-time university professor with a cure of souls and the 'manager' of the European Reformation. He once said that it would never be fair to ask a woman to share her life with such a man, and one moreover who had a price on his head.

But when the tumult and confusion were at their worst he very quietly married Katharina von Bora, a young woman of twenty-six years, without much beauty, but strong, healthy, frank and intelligent. A member of the lower nobility, she had been put into a convent as a girl, and some two years earlier had

had the sense to contrive an escape with seven other nuns. They appealed to Luther for protection, and help to rehabilitate themselves. It was during this sojourn that Luther and Katie decided on marriage. Even many of Luther's friends were shocked and shook their heads at the consequences of the great man Luther's 'lowering himself'. But he himself never saw his marriage in this way, and into those private and sacred chambers of a man's being one would not care to enter. He never discussed the matter but kept very quiet, saying very charmingly and characteristically, 'A man must ask God for counsel, and pray, and then act accordingly.' This describes his course of action precisely. It is noteworthy that (as his Master before him) he was accused as a gluttonous man and a wine-bibber (with little justification). Melanchthon, closer to him than any other man, used to marvel how the small amount of food he ate could keep so large a frame together, how he was often content to go a whole day on a herring and a piece of bread, and how he would often fast four whole days at a stretch. None ever sought to besmirch his name with unchastity.

In the family circle Luther behaved as the biggest child of all the children, full of fun and playfulness. On delicate matters such as marital relations, or on personal matters concerning public figures, particularly in the broad expanse of the supper table among friends, he occasionally expressed views which might shock modern ears trained to normal restraints and courtesies. But Luther, whenever he spoke, used words with a power and rugged humour that puts him in the company of men such as Socrates and Chaucer, Shakespeare and Dr Johnson, and his contemporaries found his expressions choice and memorable. He always spoke freely, and the words he chose have all the freshness of a newly turned sod. Critics have made too much of his alleged coarseness. He simply referred to natural things in the words men normally used, at a time when 'four-letter words' were the only words there were, and when polemical pamphleteering was somewhat unrestrained.

He once said, 'Next to God's Word there is no more precious treasure than holy matrimony. God's highest gift on earth is a pious, cheerful, God-fearing, home-keeping wife, with whom you may live peacefully, to whom you may entrust your goods and body and life.' He loved his Katie dearly, and wrote the most delightful and teasing letters to her when he was away from home. She was a good German housewife and managed a large household comprising several children, an aunt, a large number of boarding students and constant visitors. She was a devoted mother, a quality Luther valued. He said, 'All men are conceived, born and nursed by women. Thence come the little darlings, the highly prized heirs. This honour ought in all fairness to cover up all feminine weakness.'

Luther had six children: Hans (1526), Elizabeth (1527), Magdalena (1529), Martin (1531), Paul (1533), Margaret (1534). None achieved fame. Hans was a lawyer who attained a post with the government. Martin read theology but was too delicate to enter the ministry and died at the age of thirty-nine. Paul became physician to the Elector. Margaret married into the nobility, but Elizabeth died at the age of one and Magdalena, who was very beautiful and of whom Cranach left a fine painting, died at the age of fourteen. Luther, an affectionate father, suffered intensely at the death of his children. He wrote to a friend when baby Elizabeth died, 'My little daughter Elizabeth is dead. It is strange how sick at heart, how almost womanish, it has left me, so intensely do I grieve for her. I would never have believed that a father's heart could be so tender for his child. Pray to God for me.' The last words of Luther to his dying Magdalena, taken down by a member of the household, make moving reading. When they laid her in her coffin he peered in and said, 'Darling Lena, you will rise and shine like a star, yea like the sun. . . . In spirit I am happy, but the flesh sorrows and will not be comforted; the parting grieves me beyond measure. . . . I have sent a saint to heaven.' Confined to the Coburg in 1530, when the outcome of the Reformation was in the balance and Luther was excluded from the deliberations, when he had just learned that his beloved father had died asking why Martin was not with him at the end, and when he was suffering from considerable physical pain, he wrote the following tender letter to his four-year-old son. The sentiments are old-world, but they ring true.

To my dearly beloved son, Hans Luther, now at Wittenberg.

Grace and peace in Christ! My dearest son, I am glad to hear that you are doing well at your lessons and praying diligently. Continue so doing, my son, and make all the progress you can. When I return home I shall bring you a fine model of a fair.

I know of a most delightful garden where many children play. They wear little coats of gold and pick delicious apples from the trees, pears and cherries, golden and purple plums, while they sing and romp around happily. They also have handsome little ponies with golden reins and silver saddles. I asked the man who owns the garden whose children they were. He answered, 'They are the children who pray gladly, do their lessons, and are good.' Then said I, 'Dear friend, I also have a son called Hänschen Luther. May he not also come into the garden, and eat such lovely apples and pears, and ride such fine ponies, and play with these children?' The man answered, 'If he gladly prays, does his lessons, and is good, he, too, may come into the garden, Lippus[1] and Jost[2] as well. When they come along, they too shall have pipes and drums, lutes and all kinds of musical instruments. They too may dance, and shoot with the little crossbows.'

Then he showed me a smooth lawn in the garden prepared for dancing, where golden pipes, drums and fine silver crossbows were hanging from the trees. But it was still early, and the children had not yet had their meal. I could not wait for the dance to begin and said to the man, 'Dear friend, I will go at once and write to my beloved son Hans about this, so that he will pray diligently, learn his lessons well and be a good boy, and come into this garden. But he has an Aunt Lena. He will have to bring her along, too.' The man replied, 'Yes, of course. Go and write to him about these things.'

Therefore, my dear little son Hans, study and pray cheerfully, and tell Lippus and Jost to study and pray, too. Then you can all come along to the garden. Herewith, I commend you to the love of God. Greetings to Aunt Lena and give her a kiss from me.

Your dear father,

Martin Luther.

The Coburg, 19 June 1530 (W. Br. 5, Nr. 1595)

Luther celebrated the Church festivals with all the freshness and spontaneity of a child. The Germans like to think of him with lute in hand, his children scrambling on his ample knee for the

---

1. Philip Melanchthon, born 21 February 1525.
2. Justus Jonas, born 3 December 1525, playmates of Hans.

securest place nearest Daddy, all round the Christmas tree singing his own glorious carols. He gave to Christianity that peculiar
evangelical joy of Christmas, a Lutheran Christmas, the Holy
Night – so still, so joyful, with a mystery all its own. We English
may borrow the Christmas tree, bring in the *Adventskranz*, the
candle and the garland, but the genuine religious Lutheran
Christmas Eve must be experienced in a Lutheran home.

Luther began each day with his own private prayers, and then
joined the family to say the Ten Commandments, the Creed,
the Lord's prayer and a psalm. He retired at nine but rose early.
There is a delightful account of him at prayer when his faithful
scribe and companion Veit Dietrich overheard him praying at
the Coburg during those anxious days of the diet at Augsburg
in 1530:

No day passes that he does not give three hours to prayer, and those
the fittest for study. Once I happened to hear him. Good God! how
great a spirit, how great a faith, was in his very words! With such
reverence did he ask, as if he felt that he was speaking with God; with
such hope and faith, as with a Father and a Friend. 'I know,' he
said, 'that Thou art our Father and our God. I am certain, therefore,
that Thou art about to destroy the persecutors of Thy children. If
Thou doest not, then our danger is Thine too. This business is wholly
Thine, we come to it under compulsion: Thou, therefore, defend. . . .'
In almost these words I, standing afar off, heard him praying with a
clear voice. And my mind burned within me with a singular emotion
when he spoke in so friendly a manner, so weightily, so reverently, to
God.[1]

He used to say his prayers at an open window and talk to God
with as much ease and naturalness as to his dear Philip.

Luther lived a simple and disciplined life. He drank beer and
wine as everybody else did, but hated intemperance. Although he
suffered much painful illness in later life, he nevertheless had
robust strength. He was generously hospitable and always had
guests of one kind or another at table and beggars of one kind
or another at the door. Katie had to exercise some firmness in
the latter respect, for Luther had been known to give away the

1. Philip Schaff, *History of the Reformation*, Vols. 1, 2, New York, 1892,
p. 463.

coat on his back to a beggar; she realized that most of them were scroungers, not genuine souls in poverty and need, not, as we would call them, 'deserving' beggars. He liked music after dinner and played the lute himself. He sang well and composed many hymns. He also loved painting and poetry and the arts generally, and was in this respect quite dissimilar from the Puritans who banished the arts from Christianity. He was also a great lover of nature and a gardener by inclination. He loved watching the bees and listening to the birds. Every flower told him of the wonder and might of a gloriously wise God, and the rain of His mercy. Children he always thought lovely, in that they were so blessed in a simple trusting faith, and saw eternal life more clearly than adults. In his love of nature, and of people, and the simple natural earthy things of life he had much in common with his Master.

He showed rather a countryman's conservatism, and seemed to accept the idea of devils, hobgoblins, witches and all. It could be said, however, that these were simply convenient mythological names for his intense awareness of the objective, supernatural reality of evil, not dissimilar from our current use of pre-Copernican ideas like sunrise, or the common description of Hitler as demonic. Like Paul he wrestled not against flesh and blood but saw evil as an enemy of cosmic dimension, larger than man, or even the total of mankind. Every schoolboy knows of the legend of his throwing the inkpot at the apparition of the devil. But few remember he did the same when an apparition of Christ came to him. The latter was more deadly and deceiving than the former. He treated them both with short shrift and turned more deeply to *Die Schriften*. He considered all visions and apparitions whether they were of Christ, of angels, of the devil, as the supreme deception of Satan in his warfare against God's servants, and to be abhorred. God had once and for all given Christ, and left His people with the Bible through which he conveyed His ever-present Spirit. That was the pattern of God's handling of men and still is.

He was reluctant to accept the new cosmology of his near contemporary Copernicus. No doubt it was his devotion to the Bible that made him conservative on this score, for the reason he once gave was the naïve one that Joshua bade the sun stand still and not the earth! It was interesting at this point that though he had respect for astronomy, he ridiculed astrology, while the brilliant younger genius of Melanchthon gave credence to astrological predictions. Here again Luther's reason is illuminating. Again he turned to the Bible quoting the case of Esau and Jacob, born of the same parents, at the same time, under the same planets, yet wholly dissimilar.

All the reformers were very poor men. Luther never took payment for his books and lived a simple life free from avarice, the curse of the day. When his publishers offered him in royalties a yearly income far in excess of his salary he refused to take it on the grounds that he could not 'make money out of the gifts of God'. He received no fees from his students, and no salary as the town preacher. He was given gifts of wood and corn, occasionally of clothes, a keg of wine, some venison or game, and so he lived, cheerfully leaving everything in the hands of his great manager Katie, whom he often called 'Lord Katie'. His highest salary was three hundred guilders (fifteen pounds a year), but he had begun on a mere hundred guilders. Katie cultivated the garden, brought up six children, cared for students, guests and all the household, kept a fish-pond, and brewed fine home-made beer. She was a worker by nature. Once, after child-birth, when she was too weak to stand, she went round the house doing the necessary chores on her hands and knees. In his lifetime Luther willed all his property to her, so that she would never have to live on the children but would always be in a position to give to them and serve them rather than have to receive from them; all he wanted from his children was that they would honour her and obey her to the end.

It did not turn out after Luther's death as he had so carefully arranged. The disastrous Schmalkaldian War of 1547 drove the widowed Katie from her home. When she returned, the plague smote Wittenberg, and the university was moved to Torgau. She followed, but succumbed to consumption in poverty and affliction just before Christmas 1552 at the age of fifty-three. They were a sad seven years, bereft of her massive, mountainous Martin. When Luther ceased to push his burly figure through the streets of Wittenberg, Germany and the world knew that that void could never again be filled, but only Katie knew the extent of the wilderness which would one day consume her, alone and Martinless. But that story must wait till the end of the book.

In his early life Luther wore a lean and hungry look, and in the Cranach of 1520 we see him pale, haggard, intense, with eyes like gimlets. His enemies always remembered his eyes, as did the crowds that mobbed him at Worms when he flashed his glance over them. In later years he grew nice and *gemütlich*, the characteristic of the change from his early days of raw, disciplined, legalistic gloom to the expansive largeness of evangelical gladness of heart. He was of medium build with thick black curly hair and a strong open face. The picture I like best is that by Cranach done in 1525 when Luther was forty-two. He always stood like a man with feet firmly on the ground not easy to move. His voice was not strong but clear and sonorous. He was always neat in appearance, always modest, with a natural dignity in his deportment giving the impression of slightly leaning back with his face to God and heaven. He was uncomfortable when his students showed him deference by standing up as he entered the classroom, and wanted Melanchthon to give up this old-fashioned custom. Whenever they did so, he once said, he muttered a prayer to keep him humble, and wanted even to return home without reading his lecture.

He objected strongly to the idea of a *Lutheran* church, or to his followers calling themselves *Lutherans*.[1] He begged them to call themselves simply Christians. He hated parties and divisions.

1. Luther's views in this respect were signally disregarded owing to a combination of historic factors. In the early stages the reforming movement fathered by Luther was stigmatized as 'the Lutheran sect', and therefore the evangelical reforming movement began to be described as 'Lutheranism'. The Catholic princes under Charles exerted political pressure which ended in war, and the Counter-Reformation theological pressure which ended in anathematization. These factors made what was really a reforming movement within Catholicism into an outside anathematized movement that went anti-Catholic. There was also the factor common to all revivals after the death of their leader, the institutionalizing of them. All these helped to harden Luther's reform movement into Lutheranism, even Lutheran scholasticism, in spite of Luther's warning, and in spite of Luther's theology.

Let the papists be called after the Pope, he said; there was a seemliness about this, for they were not content with Christ's doctrine but wanted it improved by the Pope's. 'I neither am nor wish to be the master of any one. I and mine will contend for the sole and whole doctrine of Christ, who is our sole master.'

PART FIVE

THE PEASANTS' WAR
TO THE RELIGIOUS PEACE OF
NÜRNBERG 1525–32

CHAPTER 19

SAXONY

LUTHER'S call for reformation had not occasioned a unanimous response from Christendom. After the tragedy of the Peasants' War of 1525 several discordant movements crystallized out, some theological, some moral, some social and political. All of these were associated with the Reformation in one way or another, but they were not motivated by the theological concerns of Luther and his supporters. Consequently, particularly since Worms had condemned him to spend the rest of his life within the confines of Saxony, Luther's responsibilities lay now in the reconstruction and reorganization of the Church in that area, a remote backwater of Europe. There are in fact two issues to be disentangled: Luther's reconstructive work in Saxony, and the contemporary discordant movements that had followed his stand at Worms.

These heterogeneous movements involved the princes, the scholars, the nobility, the peasants, the fanatics, to confine our-selves only to the main groups. The Catholic princes (among them Henry VIII) had themselves now taken an initiative in remedying some of the glaring abuses and scandals. This move-ment was not theological reform in any sense of the words. It was actually opposed to Luther's cause. Scholars, notably Erasmus, and some of those in England had declared themselves against the Reformation. The nobility to whom Luther had so hopefully appealed in those stirring days of 1520 were now alienated owing to the disaster of the Peasants' War following that fatal and foolish rebellion of von Sickingen against the Archbishop of Trier in 1522.[1] The nobility in many areas were

1. Sickingen was a type of German Robin Hood resolved to champion the poor and the oppressed against their spiritual and temporal overlords, as well as to maintain the role of the knights in German society. He admired Luther and made attempts before and after Worms to be Luther's self-appointed 'protector'. Luther would never let his cause be identified with this kind of

now compelling the peasants into the Catholic fold on pain of deprivation of human rights. The fanatics were a growing danger. They attacked all and any doctrine of the sacraments, opposed orthodox Trinitarian theology, took a wrong-headed fanatical view of scripture and the inspiration of the Holy Spirit, and were determined to wreck any movement towards unity on a basis of reformed Catholicism. And further, even among the theologians themselves, disagreement was emerging. Luther's firm stand on the Real Presence which he defended against Carlstadt (though rejecting the current Catholic view of transubstantiation) was soon to have very serious theological opposition from Zwingli, even from Bucer and Oecolampadius, and later Calvin. The theological divisions among the reformers themselves served more than anything else to retard the pure and vigorous growth of the Reformation, and engendered some bitterness in the otherwise cheerful and robust Luther.

But the new situation was not without relief. There was a clear territory in which the cause had won unqualified victory, and here a new system and constitution for the revived conception of a classical Church could be well and truly laid. John, the new Elector of Saxony, showed (unlike his brother) a clear desire to establish a renewed Evangelical Church in his domains. Prussia had already gone through a total reform. Philip of Hesse (born 1505), though but a slight twenty years of age, had shown a resolute hand against Sickingen as well as against the peasants, and had learned a deep love of evangelical theology, perhaps largely through Melanchthon. His bigoted father-in-law, Duke George, sought in vain to disenchant him. By 1526 there existed between Philip and John the League of Torgau which the princes of Brunswick-Lüneburg, Anhalt and Mecklenburg and the town of Magdeburg joined. This cooperation of the territorial princes made it possible (as Paul had secured from Rome) for the evangelical cause to be established firmly both in idea and in

---

movement. When Sickingen focused his attack on the prince bishop of Trier many of the victims of his depredations took the opportunity to rid themselves of him and he died of wounds besieged in his own castle. This indiscreet and foolish leadership of the lesser nobility lost a valuable lay potential to the cause of the Reformation.

constitution, in prescribed areas, in spite of the hostility of the Catholic princes and that of the Emperor. (A further benefit of this was to keep the young Church free from the incursions of fanatics.)

In the matter of liturgical reform it was the extremists, Carlstadt, Müntzer and Zwilling, who had seized the initiative, not Luther, who had shown himself reluctant to move in this direction. In fact, on his return from the Wartburg he lived in the monastery, wore the monk's habit, and celebrated the mass. It was only when he was approached by the parish of Leisnig on the matter of a parish chest and was further invited to advise on worship that he wrote his *Concerning the Ordering of Divine Worship* (1523). In this tract he argued that the liturgy had been debased in the first place in that the centrality of the Word had been lost; secondly, that fables and legends had crept in in its place; and thirdly, that worship was now considered a meritorious work. His first principle of daily worship was the reading and exposition of the Bible, to last about one half hour and to be followed by prayers and thanksgiving, using Psalms and good antiphons; the whole not to take longer than one hour. This service was to take place every morning and evening at the parish church, but only on Sunday could the whole community be expected to attend. He advised the dropping of the daily mass and the abolition of most festivals and thought that the legends of the saints and the stories of the Cross needed pruning and purifying.

If Luther's controlling principle in every liturgy was the centrality of the Word, his second was to seek renewal not invention, the perpetuation of the true and not its abrogation. His conservative approach sought for simplicity and doctrinal purity, with intelligent and reverent participation by the congregation in every action. After the sketchy plan just outlined he drew up his *Formula of the Mass* for Wittenberg (1523). Here he reformed in two directions – holding to all that was divine, setting aside all that was human.

We assert, it is not now, nor has it ever been, in our mind to abolish entirely the whole formal cultus of God, but to cleanse that which is in use, which has been vitiated by most abominable additions, and to point out a pious use.

In this work he shows the New Testament origins of the mass, and explains how it had developed from the Last Supper by the introduction of prayers, Psalms, kyries, the epistle, the Gospel, the gloria, creed and sanctus. These Luther considered as legitimate liturgical developments within ancient Catholic tradition in the context of which he refers to Cyprian and Athanasius. Luther saw the fatal corruption not in these developments but in the introduction of the Canon and the making of the mass into a priestly monopoly, aggravated by its association with money and masses for the dead, and all that long uncontrolled development of candles, images and idolatrous practices.

He then outlined the shape of a reformed mass:

Introit
Kyrie (Lord have mercy upon us)
Gloria
Salutation
Collect of the day
Epistle
Gradual
Gospel
Nicene Creed
Sermon
(Offertory abrogated)
Preface
(The Canon abrogated)
Consecration
Lord's Prayer
Communion
Agnus Dei (O Lamb of God, that takest away the sins of the world, have mercy upon us)
Alleluia
Blessing

Most liturgiologists are of the opinion that this was Luther's best liturgical work. It bears a striking resemblance to many reformed Holy Communion services, not least the Anglican.

Giving way to external demand, Luther wrote his *German*

Mass (1526), a folk mass in German idiom and in the vernacular, though interestingly enough, he was never wholly in favour of the mass in the vernacular. He also feared the petrifying of the reforming movement into any kind of rigid uniformity, and was always most concerned to allow for the greatest liberty possible. He did not think in terms of a mere translation of a Latin liturgy reformed, but rather of a fresh creation in German thought and music for use on Sundays, while on weekdays the Latin mass was to continue. Some Lutherans have seen in this vernacular German mass Luther's greatest liturgical achievement, but he himself regarded it only as a simple service for the uneducated laity, a judgement the best liturgiologists share. In fact, in an interesting preface to the service he discusses the nature of worship and classifies it in three categories: the reformed Latin mass; the German mass; and finally the house congregation, where the truly evangelical assemble for Bible-reading, prayer, the celebration of the sacraments, and to determine the pastoral responsibilities to the parish. It is certain from a study of the document that his heart lay in this simple house church rather than anywhere else, anxious though he was to reform Catholic tradition and practice. But the first essential, Luther believed, was less the reform of the liturgy than the provision of a good simple catechism for the people of God. This he provided.

With the exception of the *Kyrie*,[1] the German mass was in the vernacular with a German idiom of music and language. Its shape was:

> Hymn or Psalm
> Kyrie (threefold not ninefold)
> Collect
> Epistle
> Hymn
> Gospel
> Creed
> Sermon on the Gospel
> Paraphrase of Lord's Prayer
> Blessing of bread and administration

1. The *Kyrie* (Lord, have mercy upon us) is still sung in Greek in German churches to this day.

(Priest facing the people as at Last Supper)
German sanctus and elevation
Blessing of cup and its administration
Hymns
Agnus Dei
Collect and benediction

At this time Luther also wrote books for the pastors on the practice of confession, marriage and baptism: a Litany, an Ordinal and about twenty-four hymns; as well as rewriting the baptismal service (1523, 1526).

There grew the necessity for some system of Church organization and some planned reconstruction in the whole area where so many were totally evangelical. But Luther knew that among the country folk there were many who, though they liked the new teaching more than the old ways, had neither an understanding of, nor total commitment to, the cause. They were little more than spectators. Many of the clergy were no better and were still obscurantist and incompetent, ready to trim their sails to any wind. Many nobles, supported by priests who depended on their patronage, were opposed to the new ideas. Moreover, there was some financial anxiety for the movement, since the payments for private masses had dried up and many of the nobility had secularized Church property.

Luther faced an acute problem here. He wanted to establish Church principles based on his elementary evangelical principles of justification by faith and the priesthood of all believers, but knew in his inner heart how few there were who were ready for this. Worse, if such a Church were to be established, what was to become of the vast numbers outside this fellowship who would be left without preachers, their children unbaptized, and without Christian education? When Philip of Hesse convoked a synod at Homberg in October 1526 to establish such a reconstruction, Luther took the view that the people were not ready for it. Further, he still stuck to the views expressed in 1520 in his *Address to the Christian Nobility* that the civil authorities were obliged to prohibit any oppression of sound doctrine, and should be concerned to maintain the establishment and preservation of the Church and therefore give proper support to the Reformation.

In this frame of mind he turned to his own Elector. Now that the university had been reorganized and the regulation of public worship completed, there remained two things for the Elector to do: to reorganize parish life, and to overhaul his civil administration. Parishes should be allowed to have an evangelical preacher and should subscribe for his maintenance, the necessities of which Luther defined. Ministers, incompetent to preach owing to age or ignorance, being otherwise of pious life, should be instructed to read the Gospel and one of Luther's homilies. The Elector was willing, but the task was immense. Spalatin helped to see the work through in two districts, and for the rest, the Elector issued general instructions. Further, the civil administration was inspected and its cooperation with the cause of evangelical theology set on the same basis in law.

But in the larger world of the Empire the situation changed adversely for the cause of evangelical theology. Charles finally defeated Francis, and in January 1526 victor and vanquished both vowed to take up arms to drive out the Turk, and also to expel the Lutheran and all other heresies. Certain princes in Germany received an admonition to confer and act. In face of this the evangelicals formed the League of Torgau. The Pope, with this golden opportunity of cleansing Christendom, responded by absolving Francis from his solemn oath, in order to conclude a warlike alliance against Charles, of whose power he was very much afraid. This agreement enjoyed the spiritual misnomer of the 'Holy Alliance'. But meanwhile the Turks were on the move, and so it happened that at the Diet of Speier in 1526 what was to have been the final execution of the Edict of Worms resolved itself into the Imperial recess, whereby it was declared that until the General Council was convoked each state was 'to live, rule and bear itself as it thought it could answer to God and the Emperor'.

In his concern for life at the parish level, Luther, although he despaired of ever doing much with the peasants, showed a very deep concern for their children. He begged the Elector to take his obligations seriously and compel towns and villages to provide a school and a parson just as they were compelled to maintain roads and bridges, believing that if this were not done they would bring up a breed of savages. He showed concern for the monasteries and convents, and now that the papal yoke had been removed, besought the Elector as the only constitutional power available to take over legal responsibility for their regularization and administration. Luther severely deplored the prospect, which he now foresaw, of the misappropriation of Church lands and property by courtiers and others, for they had all been dedicated to the service of God in the first instance and this intention should be respected in perpetuity. The Elector responded and the work was set under way at a conference (February 1527) attended by Chancellor Brück, Luther and others. Visitors were there appointed to make a formal visitation and to report.

In the midst of these negotiations Luther was struck by a painful attack of the stone, an illness that was to cause him much suffering before he died. In June of the previous year (1526), joy had come to his home with the birth of Hans, his first-born son, and he was seen taking his share in the housework and doing a lot of gardening. The winter illness, which nearly proved fatal, was followed by another serious illness in July, and by now he was suffering much bodily pain as well as spiritual and nervous anxiety for the cause that had been put in his hand. As he lay stricken he asked for his wife and son, comforted them, and bequeathed them all that he had, a few silver goblets which the university had presented him with on his marriage. When he recovered he said the spiritual paroxysm had been worse to bear than the physical pain and threatened death. The illness dogged his steps in spite of his persevering with his work. At this moment the plague attacked Wittenberg and the university was moved to Jena, but Luther remained, for he thought the people, as well as the students who had remained behind, now needed him more than ever. He was going through intense spiritual anguish and bodily travail. A friend and pastor, Leonard Kaiser, had been burnt alive in Bavaria for adhering to the cause, and another minister, Winkler, cited by the Archbishop of Cologne for distributing the communion in two kinds, though released, had been murdered by unknown hands on his return from the inquiry. Erasmus had renewed his attacks on the evangelical cause, while Zwingli, Oecolampadius and others were opposing Luther's conservative sacramental theology. The plague struck his own household and those of the university circle. Katie lay in confinement. Little Hans fell grievously ill. Luther's letters show the enormous burden of all this on the body and spirit of the man, but a robust and rugged humour breaks out. He felt intensely this weight of the wrath of God. In a letter to his friend Jonas, he wrote: 'Pope, Emperor, princes, bishops, and all the world hate me, and as if that were not enough, my brethren too [Zwingli, Oecolampadius and Erasmus] must needs afflict me.' He felt too his sins, the threat of death, Satan and all his legions raging unceasingly against him and asked what would happen if Christ were to forsake him. Luther took all these experiences into his own being, interpreting them as the Wrath of God to make him humbler and more receptive to His mercy.

The New Year brought an improvement and the return of his friends. His great hymn 'Ein' feste Burg ist unser Gott' (A safe stronghold our God is still) was born of all this sorrow, and became the battle-hymn of Protestantism. Melanchthon returned to his visitational labours and to the drawing up of articles and instructions for the common man in the churches of the electorate, a document published in March 1528. Luther wrote a preface to the report in which he said this course of action had to be carried out by the Elector, since the bishops were wholly faithless to their duty, the Elector being, as he called him, an 'emergency bishop' (*Nothbischof*). The work was speeded up in the summer when commissions were appointed to cover the whole of the electorate, each commission to consist of a theologian, a lawyer, state officials and laymen. Luther had the responsibility of the Wittenberg commission, and in addition at this time the pastorate of Wittenberg in the absence of Bugenhagen – a task requiring three or four sermons a week. He was again suffering from headaches at this time. One marvels that he did not drop down dead from overwork!

The visitations produced the information Luther expected. Things were encouraging in the Wittenberg vicinity, but in the country there was still much to be desired. One priest near Torgau could not repeat the Lord's Prayer or the creed, but did a brisk business as an exorcist! Others had to be ejected for immorality, drunkenness, irregular marriages, and prevented from keeping public houses and doing other jobs. Poverty and destitution were rife, but what grieved Luther most was the gross ignorance of the people even in the towns, and the dearth of schools everywhere.

There is pleasant evidence of Luther's easy and free mixing with the people with all his irrepressible boisterousness and energy. For the clergy who needed help in their preaching his friends had now made available publications of his sermons for all the Sundays of the year. He sensed the urgency of teaching the young, and earnestly set to work to do what he had long wanted to do – to write a 'rough, simple good Catechism' for the German people. This he completed in 1529, and followed it immediately by a shorter and simpler text for children called the Little Catechism.[1] Luther's concern should not be underestimated. He was consumed by the 'wretched and lamentable state of spiritual destitution' which he had uncovered in his visitations. The simple folk knew no Christian doctrine at all, and the priests were unable to enlighten them. Everywhere he saw ignorance and darkness, sheep without shepherds. The Little Catechism was meant for the clergy to help them to provide simple directions for daily prayer, texts for the home, guidance for living. He exhorted the clergy to teach their folk. But especially interesting was the emphasis placed on the responsibility of the head of the family for the teaching of his children and household, for helping them to pray, and for inculcating in them thankful hearts. A sense of responsibility is characteristic even today of the Good 'Lutheran' father, just as it is of the good Jewish father.

The Great Catechism, or rather the German Catechism, to give it its oldest name, appeared in the spring of 1529 at the same time as the Short Catechism. The latter was not a shortened form of the former but had its own nature and purpose. The Short Catechism may be described as the 'iron ration' for Everyman: the Great Catechism was a pattern for the pastor of what

1. Translations of both catechisms in *Luther's Primary Works*, ed. Henry Wace and C. A. Buchheim, London, 1896, pp. 1–156.

he should teach and preach, and rose out of the desperate situation disclosed by the visitations in Saxony.

The pattern of the two was:

Great Catechism	Short Catechism
I. The Ten Commandments	I. The Ten Commandments
II. The Creed	II. The Creed
III. The Lord's Prayer	III. The Lord's Prayer
IV. Baptism	IV. Baptism
Holy Communion	V. Confession
Confession	VI. Holy Communion
	Appendix I. Daily Prayer
	Benedicite
	Grace at meals
	Appendix II. Lectionary of Texts for the guidance of:
	Bishops, pastors, and preachers
	Responsibilities of laity to clergy
	Rulers
	Married people
	Family relationships
	Servants and workers
	Masters and mistresses
	Young People
	Widows
	All men

Both works show Luther at his best. Free of all polemic and controversy, they state in the simplest language the essentials of the Christian faith. The Commandments are perfectly related one to another, and all grounded in the first. In the Creed Luther shows that man meets God only as he accepts Him in the unfolding of the biblical story of salvation, and thereby and in no other way, knows God, Father, Son and Holy Spirit. The Church he explains as that divine fellowship in the Holy Spirit where the pure Word is preached and where men meet in faith and hope. In the Lord's Prayer Luther shows the Christian man in his frailty and finitude wholly dependent on God whose promises never fail, whose grace redeems man to all eternity. In the fourth part, the Great Catechism explains the sacraments of baptism and holy communion, followed by an instruction in confession, while the Short Catechism adds two appendixes, one of prayers and the second of biblical texts for simple guidance in Christian life.

It should not be thought that the Great Catechism is for children. It is a weighty document of some one hundred and fifty pages, simply expressed, but packed with mature theology in non-technical language. Luther once said that it was, with the *De Servo Arbitrio*, his best work, and that he read it daily. The Catechisms were based on Luther's preaching at the time, and have an impressive evangelical appeal and an unerring pastoral touch.

CHAPTER 20

THE SACRAMENTARIAN CONTROVERSY

THEOLOGICAL DIFFERENCES BETWEEN LUTHER AND ZWINGLI

THE differences between the Reformers received their bitterest expression in the matter of their eucharistic theology. Zwingli would in no way support any doctrine of a real presence. He rejected outright the Roman doctrine of transubstantiation and with it Luther's view of the 'real presence' which he saw as a conservative compromise with the medieval position. By the sacrament, Zwingli understood quite simply a spiritual feeding of the faithful, who by partaking in faith heard the Word of God and received the Holy Spirit. "The flesh profiteth nothing,' he used to emphasize. Luther's doctrine of the real presence meant that a believer was in communion with his Saviour and was a partaker of the forgiveness and salvation offered by Christ. Zwingli's idea of God prevented his taking this view: God was sovereign and supreme, and Christ's body was in heaven at the right hand of God. Luther's theology here is almost Eutychian in its Christology: in non-technical language he almost allows the divine and the human to interpenetrate; he thought of Christ as everywhere present in the sacrament with his human trans-figured body. In a sense Zwingli's Christology is 'Nestorian' in this matter; in non-technical language he was reluctant to take this same idea of the union of the two 'natures' in the conse-crated elements. To Zwingli, Christ was available everywhere by faith and did not 'require' the sacrament to make that real. Zwingli unyieldingly refused to objectify Christ. To him the faithful commemorated that death and pledged themselves in faith; the sacrament was a symbol of a pledge. To Luther's in-sistence on the words 'This is my body', Zwingli said that the word 'is' meant 'represents'. (In the sense, presumably, in which Christ said, 'I am the door.')

Luther saw Zwingli as a 'fanatic' and because of his interest in politics and socialism identified him with enthusiasts and fanatics such as Carlstadt and Müntzer. This accusation of fanaticism was only partly true, for there was more to Zwingli than radical fanaticism. He was indeed a man of sober intelligence and behaved much better than Luther in controversy. But others besides Zwingli, even among his friends, were giving Luther much concern on this matter, and he sensed in them a carnal, speculative, revolutionary, radical mind which would not let well alone, and accept the simple words of Jesus, 'This is my body,' and 'This is my blood,' at their face value, but must speculate and theorize on their meaning. To Luther these words were those of the Lord Himself at the close of his final work for man's redemption. He resented the insolence of anyone's discussing them.

A spate of books broke out on the subject, and Zwingli wrote several articles to Luther whom he quite simply put under the same condemnation as the Pope. Although more moderate and courteous than Luther, there was always about his writings a certain self-assurance. His language was by no means beyond reproach and he ought never to have dragged into the dispute questions such as Luther's conduct in the Peasants' War. It was a great pity that when at last Luther and Zwingli met each other they did so as foes.

This difference was not merely a theological squabble. The divergence was as deep as the controversy between Luther and Erasmus, with whom Luther associated Zwingli. It involved a doctrine of God, different Christological emphases, different religious values, different ideas of worship. It was a different interpretation of God's work in Christ. The Church had always preserved the idea of the union of the two natures of Christ, each retaining the attributes and qualities peculiar to itself. Luther seemed to seek to intensify the reality of the Divine Nature in the man Jesus which had stooped to wear our humanity. As the Son of God He had died for us and as the Son of Man He had risen for us, and was now at the right hand of God, limited to neither place nor time, everywhere yet nowhere. Zwingli, like Erasmus in this, emphasized the humanity of Jesus (though not questioning his divinity). He kept separate what Luther thought of as a single reality, though at the same time Luther tended to emphasize the reality of the divinity by a very sensitive stress on the humanity, the helpless babe at the breast, the broken man on the cross.

Luther finally wrote to Zwingli his *Confession Concerning the Lord's Supper* in 1528, a calm and collected statement. He courteously let Zwingli have the last word. At this time the plague was in Wittenberg; Luther was ill; the Catholic princes were organizing themselves; the Anabaptists and fanatics were active again; and the whole situation was making tremendous demands of Luther. He wanted to be done with controversy and to get on with his proper work.

POLITICAL DIFFERENCES

The theological differences had deep political ramifications. The eucharistic controversy caused great injury to the political integration of the Protestant cause as well as to its spiritual unity. The Elector of Saxony and Philip of Hesse were very apprehensive of the strength of the Roman party at the Diet of Speier (1529) and formed a secret alliance with the cities of Nürnberg, Ulm, Strassburg and St Gall for mutual protection. When the Emperor made peace with both France and the Pope, he determined to exterminate the Lutheran heresy at the Diet of Augsburg to be held in 1530. It is interesting to notice that at this time theological and religious questions seemed more determinative for the life of Europe than political ones.

Luther and Melanchthon wholly disapproved of any political alliance to buttress the Reformation. They believed that the truth of the Gospel would prevail of itself: it had been established without arms and would maintain itself without arms. Further, they could never sanction any rebellion against the Emperor as emperor. When Luther learned of the agreement at Speier, he successfully persuaded the Elector to annul it.

Zwingli sought a Protestant alliance betwen Zürich, Hesse, Strassburg, France, Venice and Denmark. His vigorous practical Christianity appealed to Philip of Hesse. Not only was Luther hostile to Zwingli's religious-cum-political settlement *per se*, but he also thought it would alienate the Emperor and involve Protestantism in unnecessary complications and misunderstandings. He was very concerned at this time about the activity of the Turks, whose depredations he saw as a divine punishment of a corrupt Christendom. In any case he had expressed his views on Zwingli and his supporters in no uncertain terms, and this made the idea of a colloquy foolish.

Nevertheless it was pressure from the young Philip of Hesse, who was personally sympathetic to Zwingli's views, which eventually brought about a colloquy of the theologians in October 1529. Zwingli took with him the Strassburg theologians, Bucer, Hedio and Sturm.

THE MARBURG COLLOQUY

Luther now faced his third great public appearance. At Leipzig in 1519 he had faced Eck and wrested from the struggle emancipation from papal and conciliar infallibility and freedom for his theology. At Worms in 1521 he had stood before the Emperor and defended biblical theology, the liberty of conscience and the authority of reason. At Marburg in 1529 he was now to defend a doctrine which he believed was central to the Catholic faith against his fellow reformers.

The proceedings began on 1 October 1529. The Landgrave put the 'lions' (Luther and Oecolampadius) in one room and the 'lambs' (Zwingli and Melanchthon) in another. The lions had a rough time; the lambs found much in common; but certainly the Wittenbergers realized the basic theological soundness of their fellow reformers. The main conference began the next day. On the Wittenberg side Luther and Melanchthon were supported by Jonas, Cruciger, Myconius, Osiander, Agricola and Brentius; on the Swiss side Zwingli and Oecolampadius were supported by Bucer and Hedio. Luther, Melanchthon, Zwingli and Oecolampadius sat at the same table. The Landgrave sat aside, the keenest listener of all. They were a very formidable crowd indeed. There were many guests, both scholars and noblemen, but still more were refused admission, among those

Carlstadt, who at this time was a penniless wanderer forced to sell his Hebrew Bible for bread.

In the debate little that was new arose. Luther stood firm on the plain meaning of the words 'This is my body', Zwingli on its spiritual, figurative meaning. Luther felt that no agreement could come out of such a basic difference, though Zwingli earnestly desired friendship with the Wittenbergers. Towards the end of the conference the horrible disease called the English sweat broke out and the delegates wanted to return home. The Landgrave made frantic efforts to bring the reformers together. Zwingli believed that differences existed only in what he described as non-essentials, and such differences should not be allowed to destroy the unity of Protestantism, for they were united in essentials. Luther took the view that the corporal presence of Christ in the sacrament was no 'non-essential' and he could never free his mind from the prejudice that Zwingli's liberalism was only indifference to truth decked out in fine feathers. Melanchthon was very quiet all the time and left Luther to do all the arguing. He was much more eirenically disposed by temperament, but all the evidence shows his complete sympathy with Luther. Luther refused the right hand of fellowship to Zwingli, an act which brought tears to Zwingli's eyes. This was not a mere refusal of normal Christian charity and courtesy, but rather a refusal to make doctrinal identification. Finally Luther yielded to the Landgrave's request to draw up a common confession in German. This consisted of fifteen articles expressing the evangelical doctrines on the Trinity, Christ's person, His death and resurrection, original sin, the work of the Holy Spirit and the sacraments. To fourteen of the fifteen the Swiss assented. Even on the sacraments there was considerable unity. Only the matter of the corporal presence and oral manducation were left in dispute:

In the matter of the fifteenth article we all believe with regard to the Supper of our dear Lord Jesus Christ that it ought to be celebrated in both kinds according to the institution of Christ; also, that the mass is not a work by which a man obtains grace for another, either dead or alive. Further, that the sacrament of the altar is a sacrament of the true body and blood of Jesus Christ, and that the spiritual manducation of this body and blood is specially necessary to every true Christian.

In like manner, as to the use of the sacrament, we are agreed that it was given by Almighty God just as His Word was, and was ordained that weak consciences might be moved to faith through the work of the Holy Spirit. And although at the present time we are not of the same mind on the question whether the real body and blood of Christ are corporally present in the bread and wine, yet both parties shall regard each other in Christian charity in so far as their consciences can ever permit, and both parties will earnestly implore Almighty God that He will strengthen us in the right understanding through His Spirit. Amen.

The articles were signed and at once printed and circulated. On 5 October the delegates all shook hands, a handshake of friendship though not of brotherhood.

The outcome was regrettable. The conference very nearly succeeded and went much better than Luther ever expected. No charges of heresy were made on either side, no anathemas hurled across the table. Luther found the Swiss more acceptable than he expected. Many observers, noting with approval a friendlier relationship develop between Luther and Zwingli the more they saw of each other, began to speak of a real possibility of agreement. It is interesting to note that the Swiss carried the laymen along with them in their arguments. There was a direct simplicity and common sense about Zwingli's arguments which invited acceptance, but a touch of Catholic scholasticism about Luther's which aroused suspicions, certainly reservations. It is not otherwise today.

The matter did not end at Marburg. Indefatigably, even if unsuccessfully, Bucer worked in season and out of season to heal the breach between the German and Swiss Reformation, even taking the English Reformation into his purview. But Luther's mind had long been made up, and subsequent events, particularly the civil war in which Zwingli met his untimely end only two years after the colloquy, served only to strengthen Luther's convictions and prejudices. When the conference was over Luther confided in Melanchthon that he thought the Lord's Supper had received a disproportionate emphasis in Reformation theology, and that after his death the responsibility would devolve on the younger Melanchthon of restoring peace to the Church – a hope that remained unfulfilled.

In spite of Bucer's commendable efforts to promote and preserve peace and unity among Protestants the Sacramentarian
controversy was foolishly opened up and unnecessarily aggravated by Swenkfeld in 1544, when considerable damage was done
by false rumours that Luther was coming round to the Reformed
view after all. At that time Luther lay gravely ill in agony and
pain, knowing that he had but a short time to live. Enangered, he
drew up a *Short Confession* to make clear where he stood once
and for all and to state his case against the Swiss. It was the work
of a man painfully aware of the nearness of his death and feeling
that he might never be given the opportunity of expressing
himself again, and the strong language met with Melanchthon's
disapproval. Luther charged the Zwinglians with enthusiasm,
socialism, radicalism and liberalism, all of which he viewed with
the profoundest mistrust as inimical to true reformation, which
he believed should rise from within the Church not from without. He thought the Zwinglians indifferent to Catholic redemptive theology with an impoverished doctrine of Christ, the
Church and the Sacraments, without true evangelical faith.[1]
Luther believed that theological indifferentism, intellectual
radicalism and what he called fanaticism (enthusiasm and
radical socialism) were more inimical to evangelical theology
than reactionary Catholicism. The intensity of this conviction is
illustrated by his graphic remark that he would rather drink
blood with the papists than mere wine with the Zwinglians.

*

In a book on the birth of Protestantism it is germane to compare
the views of Luther, Zwingli and Calvin on the Eucharist. Negatively, they all rejected the doctrine of transubstantiation, the
mass as a sacrifice, and the withdrawal of the chalice from the
laity. Positively, they all taught the divine institution of the
Lord's Supper, the spiritual real presence of Christ in it, its
commemoration of Christ's atoning sacrifice, its centrality in the
Christian liturgy, and the grace attached to a proper partaking of

---

1. It is interesting to record that Luther approved of Calvin's doctrine of
the Eucharist as expressed in (1) *The Institutes*, (2) in his masterly *Reply to
Cardinal Sadoleto* (1539), and (3) in his *Supper of the Lord* (1541).

it. They differed on three issues. First, the mode of Christ's presence: whether it was a bodily presence in the elements, or a spiritual presence discerned by faith; secondly, and closely related, how the believer partook of the body and blood, that is, by eating, or receiving in the heart by faith. Thirdly, whether, therefore, everybody who received the elements partook of the body and blood of Christ, or only believing souls.

As agreed earlier in the chapter Luther taught a real, corporal presence of the very body and blood of Christ 'in with and under' the elements, and that all alike, believers and unbelievers, actually partook of both substances. He supported his views on three grounds. One, the plain meaning of the words of institution; two, a belief in the ubiquity of Christ's body (stronger in Lutheranism than in Luther); three, the Catholic tradition. On the first, modern exegetes would permit the figurative exegesis of Zwingli rather than the literal one of Luther. Secondly, the idea of the ubiquity of Christ's body is scriptural though the word is not. Christ did say 'Lo! I am with you always even to the end of the world,' and, 'Wherever two or three are gathered in my name, there am I in the midst of them.' Luther always thought of this ubiquity in the sense of a dynamic presence, and likened it to the sun shining everywhere, or a voice heard by countless people, or an eye seeing several things at once. Thirdly, he was right in maintaining that Christendom had always held a firm confidence in a sacramental presence. It is difficult not to come to the conclusion that he was holding on to truths that Zwingli seemed prepared to jettison. If with Melanchthon he hoped for a healing of the break with Rome there might be even an additional reason for his conservatism. Luther's view is pious and mystical, even profound, Zwingli's rather matter of fact.

To Zwingli the sacrament was only a seal or confirmation of what the believer was already aware. He held the spiritual presence of Christ (a truth later critics often obscure), but denied the corporal eating and drinking, teaching a spiritual participation in faith. The Zwinglian view can be traced quite clearly in the Church today among liberal Protestants, but on the whole liberalism tends to dispel the spiritual significance of the eucharist undoubtedly held by Zwingli. Zwingli's sacramental theology has suffered much dilution in liberal Protestantism of the twentieth century.

Calvin, coming a generation later, and in whose theology Zwingli's finds its fruition, brought his glorious genius to bear on the problem and indeed on the whole range of evangelical theology. His position on the matter of the eucharist was midway between those of Luther and Zwingli. Sharing Luther's deep spiritual approach, he nevertheless understood the force of Zwingli's realism. He accepted Zwingli's view of the symbolism of the words of institution; he rejected the corporal presence as well as the Lutheran idea of ubiquity. But he held the real presence as well as the spiritual participation of Christ's body and blood by faith, and with them the benefit of His atoning death and the virtue of His immortal life. He spoke of the real presence in terms of the way one experiences light or warmth. The sacrament to him united the crucified Christ in the believer's heart, and gave the believing man the redemptive work of Christ and the victorious assurance of that work at one and the same time. He restored, too, the vital primitive emphasis on the activity of the Holy Spirit, and saw His office as that of uniting the glorified body of Christ with the believing communicant.

The cleavage between Luther and the Swiss was deeper than a mere difference of sacramental theology. Luther could never find in the Swiss the characteristics of his own deep evangelical theology: humility before God, conviction of sin, faith born of God's redemptive mercy. In the colloquy Luther had said to Zwingli, 'You have a different spirit from ours.' How different may be discerned in some words of Luther's farewell sermon:

To the world I may be pious and do everything I ought – to God it is nothing but pure sin. And since you are a sinner and remain one, your conscience condemns you and confronts you with God's wrath and punishment so that you cannot see any mercy. Therefore prove for yourself whether it takes so little effort to believe in the forgiveness of sins, as unexperienced spirits suppose. It may be quickly assented to and put into words. But to make it habit and nature, so that one's conscience is calm and fixed upon it, that is beyond human ability.

CHAPTER 21

THE SECESSION OF PROTESTANTISM
(SPEIER, 1526, 1529)

As time wore on it appeared to most people that the Edict of
Worms of 1521 against Luther was not going to be enforced, and
when the evangelical princes, supported by the imperial cities,
protested at Speier in 1526 in profession of their faith, and when
the Roman party yielded owing to the threat of the Turk as well
as the quarrel of the Pope with the Emperor, the Reformation
made a real advance. The Diet came to the unanimous conclusion that pending the settlement of the Church question by a
properly instituted international council 'every State shall so
live, rule and believe as it may hope and trust to answer before
God and his imperial majesty.' This the Protestants interpreted
as an act of toleration. Both Philip of Hesse and the Elector of
Saxony interpreted it as meaning far more than it said, while
even Luther took it as a kind of acquittal. This view became
established, particularly as in the course of time the long-hoped-
for council seemed indefinitely postponed. But in actual fact the
resolution was simply an armistice and not a treaty. Never for a
moment had it entered the head of Charles V to grant the Protestants any toleration or even to show them any moderation.

At all events the exercise of territorial sovereignty and the
establishment of separate State Churches dates from Speier, on
the principle of *cujus regio ejus religio*. Every Protestant sovereign
claimed and exercised the *jus reformandi religionem* and settled
the Church question as he thought fit. Saxony, Hesse, Prussia,
Anhalt, Lüneberg, East Friesland, Schleswig-Holstein, Silesia,
and the cities of Nürnberg, Augsburg, Frankfurt, Ulm, Strassburg, Bremen, Hamburg, Lübeck supported the Reformation.
On the other hand the Dukes of Bavaria, the house of Austria
and the Emperor never accepted this state of affairs. The division
was firm and each side intolerant of the other. Protestantism had

to fight for the right to be tolerated at a very high price. Victory was eventually conceded at Augsburg in 1555, after Luther's death, and finally guaranteed only as late as the Treaty of Westphalia in 1648.

Charles V had not shown his hand at Speier. Earlier in the year he had cleverly defeated Francis I at Pavia in February 1526, the engagement which first showed the superiority of small fire-arms over hand-to-hand fighting. The French army was destroyed, Francis was captured, and all the illustrious generals taken prisoner or killed. Decisive terms were imposed on Francis, but Charles showed some moderation in not following up his extraordinary victory and in not seizing the theological initiative in Germany. Francis never meant to honour the treaty and in this he was supported by the Pope, who formed a league with him and with the northern Italian duchies against the Emperor. The Pope paid dearly for this deceit and intrigue. The imperial troops marched on Rome and sacked the Eternal City in May 1527. The soldiers plundered treasuries, libraries, churches and palaces, dishonoured sacred tombs, committed outrages on defenceless priests, monks and nuns, exceeding the worst of the barbarian invasions. Never had Rome suffered such indignity. The sacking was a crime against civilization, humanity and religion. Luther saw it as a grim punishment for the unforgivable worldliness and secularization of the papacy. Melanchthon reacted with great magnanimity. In addressing the students at Wittenberg he spoke of it as a calamity that had happened less to the Pope and more to Rome, the mother of civilization. He acquitted the Emperor and blamed the robber hordes of soldiers. But Charles did not break with Rome, and in the treaty concluded in November referred to his intended extirpation of the Lutheran heresy. In the spring of 1528 the Emperor sent an ambassador to Germany to arouse interest in this cause.

These political and military hostilities between the Emperor and the Pope favoured the free development of the Reformation, but war panic was raised by an unprincipled scoundrel named Otto von Pack. He approached Philip of Hesse with forged documents (for which he was paid very handsomely), which purported to prove that a league of Catholic princes, spiritual and temporal, had convened at Breslau in May 1527 in order to exterminate Protestantism.

A counter-league was hastily formed and extensive military preparations undertaken, an action which obviously put the Protestant princes in the undesirable position of aggressors. Luther opposed the idea of a war, and feared that a civil war among the princes would be a disaster worse than the Peasants' War. Melanchthon saw the whole affair as a damnable provocative forgery and his gentle soul was both mortified and horrified at the conduct of the princes. It is a wan reflection to think of these quiet theologians in the confines of Wittenberg showing time and again a political sagacity and common sense far in advance of their rulers.

The Emperor summoned a diet to meet at Speier again in February 1529 to secure the unity and sole supremacy of the Catholic Church and to find a policy against the Turk. Since the autumn of 1528 Luther had been writing his book *On the War against the Turks*, in which he explained that though the sword had nothing to do with the Gospel it was the responsibility of the Emperor to protect Christendom against its attacker and for the Germans to do all they could to support this cause. At the diet, however, the real interest was directed towards the internal affairs of the Church. The Catholic dignitaries appeared in full force, hopeful of permanent victory over the Reformation. The Catholic Estates succeeded in pushing through an article which in effect was most deleterious to the cause of the Reformation and neutralized the decisions of the former diet of 1526. It declared that those states which had held to the Edict of Worms should continue to impose its execution on their subjects, but that the other states which had not should abstain from any innovations. Further, the celebration of the mass was not to be obstructed. Also, no member of one state could be protected against another state. This decision meant that the Reformation could never spread and would be cut out in many places where it had already established itself; that mass could be imposed again in evangelical territory; and power given to Catholic lay lords to coerce local clergy. This was the occasion on which the Lutheran members of the diet entered their famous 'Protest', and thereby gave the name 'Protestant' to the world. They refused to accept this decision and denied the power of the diet to annul the work of a previous diet except by unanimous consent, but the Catholics would not accept their objection. Philip and the Landgrave sought some secret effective alliance with sympathizers, but again Luther would never sanction the sword being drawn in the interests of the Gospel. He sought only to rely on God and to persuade his followers to do likewise. As for his enemies, he wished to persuade the Emperor that the sole concern of the evangelicals was for the truth of the Gospel and the removal of all the abuses every decent man sought to remove; and to show that the evangelicals had always resisted fanaticism and iconoclasm and had been loyal upholders of law and authority. It was at this time that Philip was pressing for an alliance with the Swiss, to which neither Luther nor Melanchthon gave any support. The outcome was the Marburg Colloquy just described.

Luther's protest at Worms in the interests of the Word of God and the responsibility of individual judgement had now grown into the Protest of Speier of 1529, undertaken by princes and cities determined to uphold scripture and conscience. It is important to see that the protest was not merely a negative one against error and tyranny and popery, but a positive assertion of freedom for the authority of the Word of God and of the conscience. One meaning of the word 'protest' is 'bearing witness' and this should be remembered for a true picture of the Reformation. The Reformation is seen all too often as a negative protest against Rome, but thoughtful people will realize that the positive pressure of *all* reformers was to let the Gospel be proclaimed in all its purity and power. Any opposition they had to Rome lay in that she refused to grant this freedom and demanded the control or at least the interpretation of the Gospel. Luther had nothing against Rome itself, nor even against the Pope as senior bishop of Christendom.

Meanwhile the Pope and Emperor were again reconciled, for their breach was temporary and political rather than permanent and religious. In November 1527 the Emperor had concluded an agreement whereby the Pope was reinstated on promise of convening a council. This agreement was crystallized eventually in June 1529 when the Pope acknowledged the Emperor's sovereignty in Italy and the Emperor guaranteed to the Pope his temporal possessions. The Emperor was crowned in Bologna in February 1530 with the crown of Charlemagne as the temporal head of Western Christendom. Within a few weeks he crossed the Alps on his way to the Diet of Augsburg which was convened to decide the fate of Lutheranism in Germany.

CHAPTER 22

DIET AND CONFESSION OF AUGSBURG
(1530)

CHARLES convoked a diet, using the kindest and most conciliatory tones in his proclamation. But he never meant that the diet should be a means of coming to an agreement between the opposing parties but rather that the Protestants should accept the terms dictated by himself and the papacy. He hoped thereby to heal all internal dissension. In fact Protestantism was now facing a perilous situation in spite of Luther's quiet confidence in the Emperor. Let us recall the facts: the Diet of Speier had forbidden further progress of the Reformation; Luther was still under the papal and imperial ban announced at Worms; Charles and the Pope had patched up their differences and Charles had been crowned Emperor; the Protestants had failed to unite; further, the Turk was astir, and was even at the gates of Vienna. The Catholics went to Augsburg for the dual purpose of defeating the Protestants as the enemies of the Church once and for all, and of mustering forces to defeat the Turk, the enemy of the Holy Roman Empire. The Protestant minority also had a dual purpose: to defend the Gospel against the Roman church, and Christian society against the Turk. The Emperor, though he stood by the Pope and his earlier Edict of Worms, nevertheless treated the Lutherans with courtesy and consideration. Luther and Melanchthon gave him praise which he hardly deserved. Neither side would let the Swiss or the Strassburgers partake in any way.

The Saxon Elector summoned his Wittenberg theologians to prepare a confession of faith and to meet him at Torgau. There with a few noblemen he met them and journeyed to Augsburg leaving Luther at Coburg. Luther earnestly desired permission of the Elector to partake in the Diet of Augsburg, but the refusal was adamant.

Here Luther stayed, once more an honourable prisoner in a great castle. The parallel between his stay in the Wartburg after Worms in 1521 and his stay in the 'kingdom of birds' in Coburg during the Diet of Augsburg in 1530 lay in his occupation – translating the Bible and writing letters. He was still under the anathema of the Pope as well as the ban of the Emperor and could not appear outside the confines of Saxony. But he was much too valuable to leave in Wittenberg, so his prince set him in his own watch-tower within his own boundaries near enough to be approached for advice. Of this Luther gave with his wonted large-hearted liberality.

But he again suffered serious illness while he was at Coburg. His much-loved father died at this time. Unable to reach him, Luther suffered intense grief and was left stricken and heart-broken. He found some solace in work. When his books arrived he resumed his translation of the Bible, working on the Prophets and the Psalms, just as he had done nine years earlier in the Wartburg. He wrote a fine book to the clergy assembled at the diet warning them of the scandals from which the Church was suffering and begging them to exercise sense and care how they resolved the matter, asking them but to leave the Gospel free. He also wrote tracts about the Romish abuses. At every step both the Elector and Melanchthon consulted him. He approved of Melanchthon's work, though he would have expressed himself much more strongly. The only point on which Luther could never tolerate compromise was doctrine and this accounts for his so-called intolerance or his 'scholasticism'.

In all these communications his inextinguishable faith and invincible confidence burn and shine. His doctrine was God's and his Gospel Christ's; neither God nor Christ would ever betray him or let him down. Luther wrote and talked as a man whose cause could never fail. There is about him at this hour that disconcerting certainty of the Johannine Christ. He marvelled at the concern of many of the princes and theologians lest the Reformation fail, and once described himself as a detached observer watching a cause that could only prosper. One learns a great deal from Luther at the Coburg, now in his forty-sixth year, in the full flower of his maturity, confident in his cause, certain of his calling. He wrote his words of strength to Chancellor Brück, to Melanchthon, to the Elector, to the world; even to his little child Hans he wrote the most beautiful letters.[1]

At one point in the negotiations Melanchthon came near to retraction but Luther reacted with courage and energy. 'I will not budge an inch,' Luther protested. 'Let the Emperor do what he can.' He feared Melanchthon was about to surrender and wrote:

You worry yourself sick because you cannot grasp how or where the matter will end. But if you could grasp it, I would have nothing to do with this cause, much less be its leader. God has put the matter in so homely a word that it does not exist in your vocabulary or wisdom, namely, faith. That is where all things which cannot be seen or grasped have been put (Hebrews xi, 1). . . . He who does not like it can lump it. If Moses had insisted on understanding how he was to escape from Pharaoh's army, Israel might still be in Egypt today. May God increase your faith and ours. If we have that, what can Satan and the whole world do to us?

Such faith could move mountains.

It is his unconquerable faith nourished by a pure fear of God and an unaffected love of Christ that shine from that great height at Coburg at this time. He had brought into being a fresh flowering of the ancient Catholic Church and had given it, because of the hostility of its parent, a fresh theology, a new grammar of theology, a form of worship and government, a life no longer dependent on his own personal labours.

At the diet the Emperor's first task was to secure support against the Turk, but the evangelicals insisted on the priority of the Church question. The Emperor gave them four days to prepare a confession, which was read in German at the diet on 25 June. Charles, whose German was weaker even than his theology, fell asleep, but most participants gave it their rapt attention for its whole two hours. The Catholics were surprised at its moderation. The Bishop of Augsburg described it as 'the pure truth', and the Duke of Bavaria complained to Eck most discerningly, if not devastatingly, that as far as he could judge

1. See p. 249.

the issue the evangelicals were within the scriptures and the Catholics without. At considerable risk to their crowns seven princes signed the document: the Elector of Saxony, Philip of Hesse, George of Brandenburg, Duke Ernest of Lüneburg, Duke John Frederick of Saxony, Duke Francis of Lüneburg, Prince Wolfgang of Anhalt, together with officials representing Nürnberg and Reutlingen. These brave confessors weakened their cause by refusing to allow the other four free cities, Strassburg, Lindau, Constance and Memmingen, to sign, on the grounds of Zwinglian sympathies.

The Confession had been mainly the work of Melanchthon. Luther could never have been so gentle and conciliatory as Melanchthon was, but the latter had all along hoped to conciliate the papists and keep the peace of the Church. He humbled himself before the papists in a vain attempt to secure this. When the Romanists were talking of putting Wittenberg under the ban, bringing the Inquisition into Germany, and exterminating Protestantism with fire and sword, Melanchthon's gentleness and concessive genius were of no avail. Rome would accept submission only. Melanchthon was shocked to find out the guile and malice in the breasts of the papist theologians, and he earned a great deal of odium from the vigorous Protestants for 'letting the side down'. But his stalwart friend Luther stuck by him.

The Roman theologians produced a refutation of the Lutheran Confession, but it was declined by Charles as being too long and too bitter and actually went through five revisions before the Emperor would accept it. A small committee of theologians of both parties was formed in the hope of reaching some agreement, but though Melanchthon made concession after concession he found the Romanists insisting on an infallible Church, the sacrifice of the mass, a sacerdotal priesthood. They even insisted on clerical celibacy, communion in one kind, and the restoration of all Church property. Luther wrote from the Coburg, though suffering from very grave illness, urging both prince and theologian to stand firm and never yield the freedom to preach the Gospel. He thought papal absolutism would have to go before there could be any unity of doctrine.

On 22 September the Emperor ordered the recess of the Diet.

The Protestants had been heard and refuted; they had been given conferences to reach some agreement. He now granted them until 15 April 1531 for consideration of his terms, ordering no innovation to be made, no attacks on Catholic faith and worship, and assistance to be given him against the Anabaptists. He promised a general council within a year to settle ecclesiastical grievances. The Protestants rejected the recess. Luther interpreted this decision as a reaffirmation of Worms, and wrote a spirited attack against the recess early in 1531. There is evidence that even the Catholics were not altogether satisfied.

The Lutheran princes formed in December 1530 a defensive alliance at Schmalkald, named the Schmalkaldian League. They sought to protect themselves against the impending lawsuits to recover Church property and were prepared to resist by force of arms if necessary. The theologians were once more opposed to taking up arms against the Emperor. The outcome of all this was the tragic Schmalkaldian War just after Luther's death. But, in the meantime, political unity was created by the threat of Suleiman II, who with a newly mustered army of three hundred thousand Turks was again threatening Christendom. The Emperor convened a Diet at Regensburg in April 1532, later moved to Nürnberg, and there in July 1532 concluded a temporary truce and undertook vigorous and successful measures against the Turk. The victorious Emperor went to Rome to urge the Pope to convene a council, but the Pope continued to play delaying tactics. Luther showed a statesmanlike support for this truce though he has earned much criticism both from contemporaries and successors for failing to support the full principle of evangelical freedom for all. He was largely instrumental in staving off a war in Germany.

The Confession of Augsburg was the first evangelical confession and is the most famous, though in the way it was conceived, written and modified by Melanchthon it was more essentially a classical apology similar to the 'Apologies' of the ante-Nicene age than a confession as such. It was an explanation and a statement of the Lutheran theology as opposed to the Roman theology, expressed in dispassionate and non-polemical terms. It was conciliatory, eirenic, comprehensive, Catholic, churchly and conservative. Luther (as well as the theologians at Augsburg) was perfectly aware that Melanchthon was seeking to emphasize the common ground between the two parties at the risk even of allowing certain points of Lutheran doctrine to go unmentioned or modified.

Melanchthon has received much criticism from historians for showing himself prepared to go to such lengths to mollify the papists, for his constant modification of his original statement, and for his unbending opposition to the Swiss view. But Melanchthon knew that this was the last historic moment when evangelical theology might be contained within Catholicism. He wore himself out to attain this end, stayed up all hours, and nearly wrecked his health. Had the other side shown one half of Melanchthon's conciliation and Christ-like gentleness the whole history of divided Christendom would have been a brighter and braver story. When all is said, his greatest critic, Luther himself, wholly approved of Melanchthon's work, though well aware that he had 'danced a few light steps' over the difficulties.

If any man could have effected the rapprochement, that man was Melanchthon; he did not set out to attempt a final infallible standard, only an eirenic, dispassionate statement of the Lutheran position to which Rome might agree as a *modus vivendi*, a formula of concord rather than discord. For instance, the Confession makes no mention of the Protestant principle of the supremacy of scripture, nor of the Catholic abuses and innovations such as indulgences, purgatory, the supremacy of the papacy; it blunts the doctrine of justification by faith. It failed in its immediate objective but attained an abiding place in Protestantism; it even had an influence on the Thirty-nine Articles.

The historical origins of the document can be found in the Articles of Marburg of 1529 when the Wittenberg and Swiss theologians tried unsuccessfully to come to an agreement. This document was modified and expanded immediately afterwards by Luther in the Articles of Schwabach. He inserted his doctrine of the real presence into this document which was adopted by the princes. A third contributory document was the Torgau Articles drawn up against Roman abuses by the Wittenberg theologians at the command of the Elector in March 1530.

Part One of the Augsburg Confession defined the following points of doctrine:

1. God: the Nicene doctrine
2. Original sin
3. Christ's Divine–Human personality
4. Justification by Faith (not Faith *alone* as a concession to Rome)
5. The Ministry of Word and Sacrament
6. Christian obedience
7. and 8. The Church
9. Baptism
10. Supper of the Lord
11. Confession to be retained
12. Penance, an evangelical interpretation
13. The use of the sacrament as a means to increase faith
14. Ordination, as essential to the ministry
15. The retention of ecclesiastical rites not offensive to the Gospel
16. Civil government
17. The return of Christ
18. The bondage of the Will and the necessity of grace
19. The cause of sin
20. Faith and works
21. Worship of saints and the sole mediatorship of Christ

Melanchthon actually concluded this Apology by stating that the Lutherans held no doctrine contrary to the scriptures, contrary to the Catholic Church, contrary even to the Roman Church as far as was known from the fathers. He disavowed the charge of heresy, and expressed the belief that the differences were attributable to certain traditions and ceremonies of doubtful origin which had been allowed to creep in.

Part Two of the Confession discusses those abuses of Rome the Reformers found most objectionable:

22. The withdrawal of the cup from the laity
23. The celibacy of the clergy
24. The sacrifice of the Mass
25. Compulsory auricular confession
26. Fasts and feasts
27. Monastic vows
28. The secular power of bishops

Article 28 does not receive the attention its importance deserves. It teaches that ecclesiastical and civil powers should not be confounded. The former exists to preach the Gospel and administer the sacraments. The second, on the other hand, has nothing to do with the Gospel, and does not exist to protect the mind, but the body, against injury. The article favours the restoration of episcopal jurisdiction in its proper field of spiritual and ecclesiastical authority, and the delimitation of the secular arm. Critics of Lutheranism who reiterate the charge of selling out to the princes disregard this evidence.

In conclusion the confession loads the sin of schism squarely on the shoulders of Rome if it refuses to let the Gospel be freely taught and these obvious abuses removed.[1]

The Augsburg Confession had one or two interesting sequels. The Emperor ordered his theologians to draw up a Confutation, a task in which some of Luther's bitterest opponents were involved, for example, Eck and Cochlaeus, though the Emperor made the express command that its tone be moderate. The Confutation follows the lines of the Confession. It approves eighteen of the Lutheran points: article 4 on justification is allowed; article 10 on the Lord's Supper is approved, provided the Lutherans grant the whole Christ in either element; article 7 on the Church is rejected, along with article 20 on faith and works and article 21 on the worship of saints. The second part of the Confession dealing with abuses is rejected outright, though the existence of abuses (especially among the clergy) is admitted and

1. Rome has virtually conceded this in recent years. The Roman Catholic theologian of Tübingen, Professor Hans Küng, in his book *The Council and Reunion* (Sheed and Ward, 1961), actually accepts this statement, and even writes of Rome's taking some responsibility for a share in the sin of schism. At a higher level Pope John XXIII said in those memorable words to the Protestant observers at the Council, 'We do not intend to conduct a trial of the past; we do not intend to prove who was right and who was wrong. The blame is on both sides. All we want is to say: "Let us come together. Let us make an end of our divisions"' – words endorsed on a similar occasion by his worthy successor, Pope Paul VI, 'If we are in any way to blame for that separation we humbly beg God's forgiveness and ask pardon too of our brethren who feel themselves to have been injured by us. For our part, we willingly forgive the injuries which the Catholic Church has suffered, and forget the grief endured during the long series of dissensions and separations.'

a reformation of discipline promised at the next general council. The document deploys a few biblical and patristic quotations but they are ill-selected. Rome had no answer worthy of the Wittenberg theologians. Melanchthon wrote an immediate reply to the Confutation but it was declined by the Diet. Rome still has the test in front of her of offering a respectable answer to the Lutheran protest.

The contents both of the Confession and the Confutation were not fully known for some years because their publication was prohibited. Men had to rely on the notes and memories of participants. Melanchthon set to work indefatigably, even on the homeward-bound cart, to write an Apology to his Confession. This document showed still more strikingly the theological unworthiness of the Confutation. Seven times longer than the Confession, it is written in a fine bold literary style with a sure theological tread. Melanchthon handles the papists with a firmer hand. As a permanent expression of a *regula veritatis* it is limited by its occasionally outmoded exegesis, and what was very common in those days, certain errors in patristic quotations. But it gave great support to the Reformation in its day especially among scholars. Its chief value is historical in that it shows Melanchthon's own interpretation of the Confession. It was not signed by the Lutheran princes present at Augsburg, being written after they had dispersed, but it was signed by the theologians at Schmalkald (1537) and finally embodied in the Formula of Concord (1580). Like the *Confessio* the *Apologia* has gone through many transformations and emendations.[1]

It will be recalled that many reforming theologians were excluded from Marburg. At Augsburg the position was worse, for both the Swiss and Strassburg theologians were pointedly disallowed. After their exclusion from Augsburg, Bucer, Hedio and Capito presented their views too in the name of the four cities of Strassburg, Constance, Memmingen and Lindau (called the Tetrapolitan Confession) still in the hope of finding unity. Their Confession was perforce very hastily drawn up, and presented three days after Zwingli presented his. It was received

1. See *Die Bekenntnisschriften der evangelisch-Lutherische Kirche*, 4th edn (revised), Göttingen, 1959, pp. 141 ff.

most ungraciously and not allowed to be read at the Diet. The Roman theologians made a very unfair confutation of it and would not deign even to give the Strassburgers a copy of their answer.

The Tetrapolitan Confession is rather similar to the Lutheran but more strongly Protestant. It takes a much stronger line on the sole authority of scripture, and states a more distinctively evangelical doctrine of justification and a more definite view on the abolition of images. Bucer tried to combine the Lutheran and Zwinglian view of Holy Communion, a task very dear to his heart since the collapse at Marburg. He stuck to this role to the end. The Tetrapolitan Confession fulfilled itself in Calvinism eventually. The four cities joined the Schmalkald League later and signed the Lutheran Confession.

As for Zwingli, he, too, in great haste and without being able to consult the others, produced his own Confession for the judgement of the whole Church of Christ. This was treated with all the contempt and contumely Eck could muster. He was calculatingly insulting to the reformer, and would not let the document be considered. Yet when one reads Zwingli's document with its sheer sense and soundness, its genuine simplicity and integrity, its dignity and its courtesy, it makes the heart bleed to consider that responsible men could react in this way.

In his confession Zwingli attested his orthodoxy according to the creeds. He taught free and unmerited grace perceived and received by faith alone, as well as the doctrine of the visible and invisible Church. Purgatory was rejected. On original sin and the sacraments he made a clear departure even from Luther's views, not to mention Rome's. He rejected completely the association of himself with the Anabaptists and finally appealed to all in the interests of truth and of the contemporary situation to heed his words. Both Rome and Luther were wrong to reject Zwingli at this hour outright and unheard.

PART SIX

POLITICAL AND ECCLESIASTICAL DEVELOPMENTS
1532–46

CHAPTER 23

POLITICAL PROTECTION OF THE REFORMATION

JOHN FREDERICK the Magnanimous succeeded his father John as Elector in 1532. He was utterly evangelical, pious and godly by nature, and did all he could as a ruler to further the Reformation. A very gracious wife, Princess Sybil, supported him, and she showed a particularly warm friendship to Luther and his family. Some very fine correspondence exists between Princess Sybil and Luther.

Luther was now to enjoy a measure of political stability, a background to his work for which he had always longed. This new situation changed very much the pattern of his life-work. He seems less the dominant European figure and much more the quiet professor of theology, teaching, writing, thinking, to whom accrued the additional burdens of a parish parson in Wittenberg and the wider demands of adviser to the Reformed Church of Saxony (and farther afield when demanded). By now the hard pattern of a Protestantism that would not yield and a Catholicism that would not change was emerging in Europe.

In his teaching ministry Luther turned to expounding Galatians, and made of it his finest exposition of what it meant to be justified by faith in Christ only:[1]

One article, the only solid rock rules in my heart, namely, faith in Christ; out of which, through which, and to which all my theological opinions ebb and flow, day and night.

[1]. James Clarke have republished a fine sixteenth-century translation of this work which Philip Watson revised and completed by inserting a few controversial anti-Zwinglian omissions (left out in the sixteenth-century translation in the interests of unity and peace) and by writing an introduction to the completed work (*Martin Luther: Commentary on the Epistle to the Galatians*, Middleton translation revised by Philip Watson, Edinburgh, 1953).

He pursued, too, his great life work of translating the Bible. He had completed the prophets now, a labour which exhausted him, and had turned to the Apocrypha. The completed translation finally appeared in 1534. The immensity of this task and the perfection of the result, through tumult and tribulation, trials and temptations, not least much grave illness, must be one of the greatest human achievements of all time. He was also to be found preaching regularly in the parish pulpit.

With regard to the wider needs of the Church, the Elector pursued reform in his province, positively by visitations, seeking to maintain a disciplined and decent Church life for lay and cleric alike, negatively by seeking to abolish gross sin and to root out persistent superstition and witchcraft. One sometimes senses in Luther the faith that once the evangelical trumpet had blown loud and clear all the walls of sin and ignorance would fall. In principle he was right, but in actuality many people continued to hold to their old ways rather than meet the new situation created by the Reformation.

Luther showed at this time a marked concern for the sophisticated immorality of the nobility and the coarse vulgarity of the peasants, and expressed himself in the clearest and strongest terms. Drunkenness, particularly, caused him much distress, and this was a fault, almost the only fault, of his good Elector. Luther had much to dishearten him. His strength was his weakness. He had little or no faith in rules, discipline and regulation, but total faith in preaching the Word and leaving all to God. It was not the first time that the world proved unworthy of the man God sent it. The seed was good but much was lost on shallow, stony, weedy ground.

As for the political situation, Anhalt now openly joined the evangelical cause. Under pressure from the Emperor the Pope was eventually prevailed upon to send a nuncio to the German princes to explore the possibility of the now oft-promised but long-delayed free general council. Luther took it all as just talk, 'muttering in the dark' he called it, but in his desire to keep the door open, though with little hope in his heart, he answered courteously, even if briefly.

These years, 1532 to Luther's death in 1546, are difficult to disentangle in their intricacy. Secular historians tend to trace the meaning in the social and political events whilst under-estimating the theological. This does not imply that secular events are less important than religious, but it is to say that the sixteenth century was an age which was theologically aware in a way that the twentieth is not. In the sixteenth century almost all men, Protestant and Catholic, desired a reformation of the Church. Men thought theologically at that time in a way modern man can scarcely imagine. It was only the papal Curia that opposed the reformation in any shape or form.

There were two main opinions on how that reformation should proceed. One idea was that the Church should once more be restored to her pristine splendour, retaining all the characteristics of her sacerdotal priesthood under the papacy, though disposing of abuses and discredited practices. The other was that the Church had to go through a theological revivification on the lines of the cardinal reformed evangelical doctrines of the priesthood of all believers, justification by faith, supremacy of God's Word under the authority of the New Testament, retaining the organic structure of traditional Catholicism but freeing it from all its sacerdotalism and secularism as well as its unwarrantable accretions and developments.

As far as our study is concerned, Charles V was the type of the former and Luther the latter. Charles wanted to preserve the medieval structure of the Church and maintain the Church monolithic and entire. Luther wanted to preserve the theological entirety of a Catholic Church, but was utterly free of any idea of imposing any structure or any organization on any Church anywhere, provided she held the full Gospel. Charles was prepared to accept changes in usage, even in doctrines if shown necessary, provided, as he expressed it, 'the seamless robe' was not torn. True, he postponed time and again the settlement of the Church question owing to external pressures, but he never intended and would never have consented to the granting of any separate existence to the Lutheran Churches of Germany. If by compromise or any other means the Lutherans refused to be induced back to the fold, Charles's intention was to 'compel them to come in'.

Philip of Hesse showed a thoroughgoing acceptance of the Lutheran reformation, but he had an implacable hatred of the Hapsburgs and of their dominance in Germany. The Dukes of Bavaria on the other hand were convinced papists, but they too hated the Austrian house. The German religious settlement was made impossible to Charles not only because of his *a priori* idea of a monolithic settlement, but because of a deep resentment held equally by both religious sides against his dynastic aggrandizement and the extension of his power in Germany in any way. Further, there was the continuous conflict between the Pope and Charles, giving the paradoxical situation in which the Pope, though hostile to Charles, was yet essential to him for his purposes.

For these and other reasons, not to mention his own theological convictions, Luther pursued his own course, council or no. Hostility to Rome was marked in his writings. His work *On Private Masses* stems from this time. In it he shows that the idea of a private mass and the idea of the sacrifice of Christ's body are an utter perversion. He contrasts the mass priest with his sacrifice on the one hand, and the great evangelical doctrine of the priesthood of all believers, with its preacher called to the Word of God, on the other.

CHAPTER 24

ATTEMPTS AT THE REUNION OF CHRISTENDOM

AT this juncture Erasmus sought to restore unity in the Church by urging the abolition of abuses and the submission to authority in current theological disputes. Luther argued that this would only have the effect of strengthening the papists, and asked the direct question – what is a man to do who finds the papist doctrines contrary to scripture? Should he obey the Pope? Erasmus sought mutual concessions but in fact advocated unilateral submission. According to Luther, the evangelicals were not in need of such admonition. They had always shown themselves prepared to submit to anything, as long as the Gospel did not suffer. Luther thought Erasmus but a sceptic and an Epicurean, wanting peace at any price. At the same time a fresh though smaller quarrel broke out with Duke George who had expelled from their homeland some seventy or eighty families of evangelical sympathies. Luther wrote letters of kindly encouragement to these families. He continued unyielding in matters of faith and the Gospel whether it was local or national. He still showed a remarkable loyalty to his 'dear good Emperor', and showed a sturdy disapproval of the Pope's planning and scheming against the Emperor as well as Francis's ill-will and double-dealing.

Early in 1534 Philip of Hesse took it upon himself to oust King Ferdinand from Württemberg and restore the land to the banished Duke Ulrich, its rightful owner. Ulrich had been deprived of his territory in 1519 by the Swabian League and had been living in exile ever since. It will be recalled that he had attended the Colloquy at Marburg as Philip's guest and shared the theological views of Philip. In the event Philip experienced no difficulty in driving Ferdinand out and restoring Ulrich, for the Bavarian Catholics had a strong desire to weaken the

Austrian house and remained neutral. Both Luther and his Elector disliked this fishing in troubled waters and would never consent to using force to further the Gospel. At the Peace of Cadan (1534), Philip secured a public undertaking from Ferdinand that he would never again drag a Protestant through the courts of the *Reichskammergericht* in a religious cause. This was a most valuable concession to the reformed cause. Since the Diet of Nürnberg, Catholic powers had been proceeding against the Protestants through these courts to secure repossession or indemnity of schools, property, land, etc., where the territory had gone over to the evangelical cause. Had this process continued, Protestantism would have suffered much material loss and therefore effectiveness. In return the Protestants recognized Ferdinand as King of the Romans. Two other important changes were effected by the Peace: the hostile Swabian League was dissolved and the immediate reformation of Württemberg secured. This was the effect of increasing the formidableness of the Schmalkald League. Luther was quite astonished to witness the beneficial effects of Philip's action, namely, the speedy restoration of peace and the territorial spread of Reformation ideas, though he never modified his principle of using tongue and pen, but not the sword, in God's kingdom.

The moment seemed opportune for Bucer to renew his unifyng policies. Luther still remained rather aloof. Although he had liked Zwingli much more after he had met him face to face, he never changed his mind on his theology. He always saw it as of the same *tendency* as that of the humanists and socialists, the fanatics and Anabaptists, all of whom he put under the same condemnation. Luther abstained from entering into any controversy, yet at the same time was stiffly embattled against making any facile agreement lest error should thereby creep in. The world does not always see Luther in this role of guardian of the faith but is apt to dismiss his concern as a further example of his obstinacy. Luther always remained suspicious in this matter, even when advocated by a Bucer. He had now seen the fulfilment of his worst fears when the Anabaptists had wrested the rule of Münster. Claiming to be the spiritual and intellectual élite of the new dispensation in Christendom, they established their coarse, fanatical, communist kingdom of the saints, a nightmarish rule broken the next year by imperial forces. As a result, all Protestantism was excluded from Münster when she reverted to episcopal rule. To this day the marks of this folly are still to be seen in the streets and churches of this old cathedral city. What was once a Reformation stronghold is today the most Catholic of German cities.

Bucer remained undeterred. He sought a public acknowledgement and expression of doctrinal unity of the kind Luther had already effected with the South Germans. He laboured to convince the Swiss that they were taking too rigorous a view of Luther's doctrine. The Swiss, however, proved to be as touchy as Luther. Bucer tried to convince Philip that unity of doctrine already existed among the evangelicals to quite a considerable extent, and that all that the Swiss were holding out against was any idea of a bodily eating of the flesh of Christ. He explained to Philip that all that Luther wanted was sacramental unity, and that the whole conflict was a matter of words. Thus heartened, Philip approached Luther, whom he found cordial and sympathetic. It is true Luther very much desired a solid, combined, well-established front to combat the arrogance of the papists, yet he never let that influence his sincere, scholarly concern lest that unity be built on a rotten foundation. A conference between Bucer and Melanchthon, therefore, was arranged to take place at Kassel on 27 December 1534, to which Luther sent his tract, *Consideration, whether Unity is Possible or Not*. Here Luther discussed the idea of unity on the basis of the Augsburg Confession and counselled time for reflection. This was certainly an advance. The ecumenical movement today needs a Bucer. How easily one could imagine him leading hopeful delegations in New Delhi or Rome, Toronto or Amsterdam, or as an observer, at the Second Vatican Council!

The new Pope, Paul III (1534–49), seemed anxious to hold a Council, and to this end he sent Cardinal Vergerius to Germany. The Elector consulted Luther at this point, but Luther expressed some doubt about the sincerity of the overtures. Vergerius visited Archbishop Albrecht at Halle whence he proceeded to Wittenberg on 6 November 1535. He invited Luther to dinner,

an invitation which was declined, though another, with Bugenhagen, the town parson, to breakfast the next morning was
accepted. Vergerius was anxious to sound Luther in the hope
that the latter would not hinder his plans.

Luther did not prove very amenable. He asserted that the
papists were not sincere about the Council, and that even if it did
come about, all that they would want to discuss would be monks'
cowls, tonsures, diets and all the rest. At this remark a legate was
heard to whisper to one of his staff, 'He has hit the nail on the
head!' Luther went on to say with some bluntness and some
truth that it was not the evangelicals who were in need of a
Council, for they were utterly sure of the truth of their doctrine
based as it was on God's Word; he could understand why the
papists felt that need, led astray as they were in their theology
under a papal tyranny. Nevertheless, Luther agreed to attend
any Council called at any place at any time. There was a lot of
good humour at the meeting, with not a little intellectual fencing.
The proceedings give a clear impression of Vergerius's theological uncertainty in the presence of the reformers. Some ten
years later he was converted to evangelical theology.

All this needs setting within the political framework of events.
The Emperor was fighting in North Africa. Francis I was raising
claims on Italian territory. Relations between Austria and Bavaria
were strained. Ferdinand seemed to be developing more respect
for the Lutheran position. Sensing this more favourable climate,
the Schmalkaldic League resolved to invite other states to join
them in a meeting at Schmalkald in December 1535. Francis,
with a cool and calculating eye on his Italian campaign, professed to seek the advice of Luther and Melanchthon with a view
to bringing in reformations in the Church of France. This
delighted Melanchthon in his innocence, but Luther saw through
him, as did his Elector. England, too, made overtures, sending
the idealist, Robert Barnes, among others. Although Luther
entertained dear Barnes, teasing him and pulling his leg for his
combination of deep evangelical theology with his political
naïveté, he yet felt a little more hope for England than he did for
France, because he believed that neither Henry nor the English
theologians would ever return to Rome. Yet he knew how

utterly non-evangelical Henry really was and did not believe that very much would come of the negotiations. At dinner he often teased 'Saint Robert' (as he called him), saying he would be better advised to go home than to stay on hopefully in Wittenberg for nothing. When at this time Henry executed Anne Boleyn, his second wife, a sinister light was shed on the whole affair.[1]

Nevertheless, the total effect of the events described in the last three paragraphs gave Luther some gratification for the progress so far achieved, sufficient to make him propose a conference on unity at Eisenach for May of the next year. The invitation was readily accepted by the South Germans who passed on the invitation to the Swiss, though Bullinger, Zwingli's successor, courteously declined. Unfortunately, Luther fell ill at the time and was too sick to travel to Eisenach. The delegates responded by changing their rendezvous to Wittenberg.

Luther saw Bucer and Capito privately. His feelings were that he would rather leave things as they were than make a union that was unreal. He expressed some anxiety about safeguarding his high doctrine of the sacrament, but Bucer reassured him that they were all at one with Luther on this. When Bucer came to show Luther the document Bullinger had given him Luther demurred on one or two points, but it was clear that there was a real desire for unity on all sides. An Apology was drawn up and signed together with the Augsburg Confession, but Luther insisted that the document should be published only when all the interested parties had had time to study it, and further, had shown their concurrence. He moved cautiously but was sincerely desirous of some union among evangelicals before he was taken from the scene. He actually wrote to this effect to the burgomaster of Basel, who returned a very kindly letter. The Swiss found themselves unable to agree to the German formulation, but they expressed a genuine and unfeigned delight at the progress so far made and an earnest hope for real unity. Bucer was asked by the Swiss to continue his good offices to this effect. The

1. Barnes returned to England to meet a new political situation, where Henry had no longer need of German allies. Without trial Henry summarily sent the saintly Barnes to the stake at Smithfield on 30 July 1540, a deed which gave Luther much distress that one 'who had eaten bread at his table' should meet this fate.

importance of this conference was that it marked unity among German Protestants.

Within a few days of the Wittenberg agreement the Pope announced his intention of holding a Council in Mantua the following year. He made his purpose clear, namely, to extirpate the Lutheran heresy. Luther made his intention of going to defend his cause equally clear, but his Elector was implacably opposed to the idea from the outset. He asked Luther to furnish him with a list of articles of faith he would want discussed at a Council. Luther insisted on justification by faith in Christ alone in the first instance. He condemned the mass as an idolatrous practice and destructive of the evangelical doctrine of justification in Christ. He further expressed his views on the papacy, a matter on which he had kept silent at Augsburg. He argued that the Pope was not the Head of Christendom by divine right but in fact the Antichrist who set himself up against Christ. John Frederick (Luther's prince) was anxious for his theologians to come to a common mind and suggested a consultation at Schmalkald at which an imperial envoy and a papal nuncio attended. Most tragically Luther was seized with an excruciating attack of the stone from which agony none of his physicians knew how to deliver him. He was given up for dead, but a measure of life returned to the pain-racked, care-worn body, and with great difficulty he was taken back to Wittenberg on a cart. Even at this hour the indefatigable Bucer, during a temporary lull in the agony, pursued negotiations with him, but Luther warned against compromising theological truth for the sake merely of unity. He begged everybody to build on proper foundations.

Meanwhile his friends pursued their course at Schmalkald and came to the decision that they should decline the Pope's invitation to the Council on the grounds that it was not adequate to the demands of the situation, for which nothing less than a free general Council on German and not Italian territory would be appropriate. They did not therefore carry the discussion of Luther's theological points any farther, but Melanchthon wrote a statement against the authority and divine right of the papacy. The evangelical decision certainly eased the position of the Pope.

Before they wound up the conference at Schmalkald, the Wittenberg Concord of the previous year was approved and submitted to the various princes and cities for ratification. Towards the Swiss, Luther maintained the same firm line shown in his letter to Meyer, though he wrote very friendly letters to the Swiss cities as well as to Bullinger, to whom he clarified his view on the real presence in contradistinction to the Swiss view of the spiritual presence. Bullinger dismissed the difference, but though Luther held to it as a vital point he yet refused to discuss it further, in the belief that discussion would not serve to promote unity and understanding.

At this time Luther also made friendly relations with the Moravians, whose deep biblical theology and sanctity of life impressed him. These qualities he missed very sorely in his fellow-Germans. Nevertheless, there is a deep difference between Luther and the Moravians. They lacked Luther's majestic redemptive theology and his doctrine of justification by faith alone. They rather took the medieval line, and thought of righteousness as something attained or worked for, and not as a consequence of faith. Their priests were celibates and their morals, undoubtedly high, were those of monks shunning the world rather than converted men in the world. They strongly resisted any doctrine of transubstantiation, and would not concede even Luther's doctrine of the real presence. They were in fact Wyclifites and read his works. They were great reformers. Nevertheless, what distinguished Luther from Wyclif and therefore from the Moravians was his central doctrine of justification by faith alone. For a time, just after his stay in the Wartburg, there seemed promise of some rapprochement, but hopes foundered on the rock of the sacrament. The Moravian view was essentially Calvinist. Yet at the time of Schmalkald, when Bucer was active in the cause of ecumenical unity and the Moravian leader John Augusta was seeking an alliance with Luther, the effect of these two movements was to bring Luther to a more conciliatory and respectful view of the Brethren.

Luther was now ageing. His heavy responsibilities had taken severe toll of his health and vigour. It was not all news of peace and reconciliation. The Elector was now anxious after Luther's grave illness at Schmalkald to do all he could to spare the warrior reformer and so sought to reduce his commitments at the university, and graciously increased his emoluments (Melanchthon's too) by one hundred gulden. It was at this time that Luther began his famous course of lectures on Genesis where he mined the pure gold of evangelical theology for nine years, until a year before his death. He continued his regular preaching, on weekdays as well as Sundays, on the Gospels of Matthew and John. He also revised, with the help of his Wittenberg colleagues, his translation of the Bible from 1539–41. The rest of his activity was bound up with work for the coming Council. In this connexion he wrote in 1539 his well-known book *On Councils and Churches* in which he made a vigorous defence of the Church as the world-wide community of faithful men and not an assemblage of cardinals, priests, and monks under the pope.

We need to remind ourselves that Luther held no official status of any kind in the government of his Church. He gave his views and advice freely and was naturally consulted on matters of morals and general guidance. He had the strongest feelings on social and moral virtue; to him a converted man was bound to show Christian morality, and where this was lacking, he saw theological failure. His feelings against usury and avarice in any shape or form were strong. In this he was in agreement with medieval moral theology. He felt deeply for his German people with their gluttony and gambling, their drunkenness and unchastity; their looseness and immorality caused him the deepest pain. He always showed, too, an old-fashioned concern for the honourable behaviour of servants and workmen to their masters on the one hand, and on the other, that justice and consideration should be accorded by overlords to their subjects. It was this latter concern that brought about the final break with his Archbishop in the Schönitz affair.

Albrecht had treated Luther with respect while Luther responded by not showing any public hostility. The Archbishop had a steward named Schönitz who had not only forwarded large sums of money to him for legitimate and illegitimate purposes, but had even gone to the extent of letting him have his own money. Albrecht, owing to his dissolute life, was now seriously embarrassed financially. The estates refused to help further until a full account was rendered of where the money was going. To save his reputation he basely turned on Schönitz, who had always helped him, and ordered his arrest and imprisonment. Schönitz languished in gaol for a year, but the imperial court found in his favour. In spite of this, and in spite of frantic appeals for a proper trial before the law, he was tortured cruelly until a confession was wrung out of him. He was summarily hanged and his body left to swing for two years till it finally disintegrated under the beaks of birds and the tooth of a winter's gale. Meanwhile the Archbishop had seized all his property.

Justices remonstrated with the Archbishop in vain. Relatives begged for the small solace of proclaiming the innocence of Schönitz and redeeming the only thing left him, his reputation. Luther was drawn into the affair when a friend confided that action was being planned against him for having supported the steward's just cause. Luther at once wrote to the Archbishop and expressed his mind as only Luther could. He called him a murderer, who for his wicked squandering of Church monies in furtherance of his own dissolute ends deserved to hang on a gallows ten times higher than Schönitz'. Certain high authorities and relatives of Albrecht tried to put the whole ghastly affair in a better light, but when one of them had the audacity to attempt this at no other place than Wittenberg, Luther openly came out and gave both Albrecht and his sycophant a verbal flogging of the highest order. He added a few home truths on where in fact the money was going, and why Albrecht needed 'special princely protection', a protection other men neither enjoyed nor needed. Albrecht was speechless before the righteous indignation of Luther and their relationship came to an end.

There were internal troubles in the Church too, not only in society at large. It was basic to Luther's theology that if faith and doctrine were sound, then the fruits of morality were secure and prolific. This he always impressed on his followers. He was, therefore, much troubled and distressed when wrongs and scandals kept breaking out within the Church. He grew increasingly concerned to preserve doctrinal unity among the reformers. Agricola, now back in Wittenberg, was teaching an antinomian theology cultivated by some of his own eccentricities. Luther knew, as Agricola did not, that not to measure and appreciate the full power and authority of the Law as part of the Gospel as well as for its abiding intrinsic moral sanction was to lose the full power of the Gospel as Luther understood and preached it. Luther was reluctant to come out against an old friend, but in the end he was compelled to state his mind on the matter again. Agricola recanted, later relapsed, then went to Berlin, finally to recant while there once more. The friendship was broken and never mended again. It is a delicate balance, this living relationship of Law and Gospel. Some men hold to Law and lose the Gospel; some grow intoxicated with the Gospel and disparage the Law; but the Gospel is organically related to the Law both historically and existentially, and both Gospel and Law suffer if these living tissues are torn asunder.

Further, no less a person than Melanchthon laid himself open to a charge of deviationism, if that is not too strong a word. He had always been more concerned about the break-up of Catholic unity than Luther had, and already at Marburg in 1529 and Augsburg in 1530 had clearly shown how far he would go to meet Rome. He was prepared to lose the Swiss altogether, if unity with Rome could be kept. But it was more than a matter of expediency, for Melanchthon's ideas had begun to alter slightly. He came to believe that some element of human choice should be allowed for in the central doctrine of justification by faith alone. Further, he had changed his thinking somewhat in the matter of the sacrament. He thought that Luther was wrong to insist on the real bodily presence, for this insistence had never been the mark of historic Catholicism, not even of Augustine. Melanchthon sought to be less rigid in these matters than Luther, indeed than many of the Lutherans, but Luther never challenged him on them. On personal grounds he had a deep affection for Melanchthon and an enormous respect for his academic weight and spiritual integrity, and doubtless these feelings restrained the older man. Besides, at this moment his main concern was the same as Melanchthon's – to reconcile the difference and preserve peace.

When at Schmalkald the Protestants had rejected the Emperor's offer of a Council, there was wide expectation that Charles would take action against them. The Emperor's vice-chancellor sought to bring some united opposition to bear against the Schmalkaldic allies and actually enrolled Austria, Bavaria, Duke George of Saxony and Duke Henry of Bruns-wick. Charles, however, stood on uncertain ground. He had no confidence in Francis and what he would do. Luther hardly deigned to notice their activity and counselled loyalty to the Emperor. The Emperor showed himself wiser than his advisers and sent a legate on a peace-making venture who negotiated in Frankfurt in 1539 the cessation of those iniquitous law-suits which the Catholics insisted on bringing against the Protestants in the imperial chamber.

Suddenly Luther's implacable foe Duke George died, and his dominion passed to his brother Henry, a convinced evangelical. At once the Reformation was introduced throughout the duchy. On Whitsunday, 24 May 1539, Luther had the moving experience of preaching at Henry's accession in the very place at Leipzig where twenty years earlier he had disputed with Eck in the presence of Duke George and where in fact he had made his first public defence of the Reformation. At this time the Elector-ate of Brandenburg went over to the Reformation, too. Then the Emperor called a meeting at Speier to end 'all the wearisome dissension in a Christian manner', a meeting actually held in Hagenau in June 1540 owing to the plague.

Favourable as these developments were, the cause of Protest-antism was about to suffer a deadly wound from the hand of one of its most ardent champions. At the early age of nineteen, Philip of Hesse had married a daughter of the Catholic prince, Duke George of Saxony. The early marriage turned out to be a failure owing, as Philip expressed it, to his wife's infirmities and her unamiability. He had found a mistress (even mistresses?), a practice condoned in the nobility in those days, but his strong evangelical theology caused grave disquiet in his heart to such an extent that he felt unable to approach the Lord's Table while he was living in sin. He had been to communion only once during the last fifteen years. Of course, the answer was obvious – repent of his sin and make his peace with God. But Philip wanted both God and his sin, and like countless others was finding no man can make terms with God. At this time he met a lady whom he really loved, and he saw the possibility of a true and full Christian marriage. The mother of the lady was worldly-wise, and refused to let her daughter become involved save in proper and decent marriage; nor would she let Philip court her on any other terms. Philip had to come to her as a free man and offer pure marriage – no concubinage nor privy 'arrangements' were going to satisfy her. Desire clouded Philip's mind, and he conceived the idea of a 'second marriage', in line with the current Anabaptist argument that the Old Testament permitted polygamy and that the New Testament had never explicitly condemned it.

Philip pleaded his plight to Bucer. He argued that as things were he was quite unable to do his work properly, and added ruefully that everybody was quite happy for him to continue in his present state of sin but that nobody would help him to a proper marriage. He argued, too, that there were historical precedents for double marriage, and that scripture was on his side. Bucer agreed to do what he could and took his case to Luther and Melanchthon.

The Wittenbergers told him in no uncertain terms that Philip's 'arguments' were specious, that in the first place both the Old Testament and the New Testament taught lifelong marriage, and that in the second place marriage would not 'settle' his problem of incontinence, which was a grave sin, no matter how the world regarded it. They conceded that exceptional circumstances could conceivably arise where a dispensation might meet the situation, but they did not say that Philip's case merited such a grave course of action. They begged Philip to reconsider the whole matter in the light of their views. But the fatal concession was made, that in the event of Philip's still being unable to resolve the matter, they would be prepared to grant the dispensation, provided that the matter be considered personal and private to Philip and that it be not permitted to hurt or scandalize others. This was a disastrous and ill-considered concession destined to wreak mischief most merciless on the evangelical cause. The only practical way to deal with the situation was by the Catholic method of annulment or the later Protestant method of divorce. Luther, owing to his principles, could grant neither, and therefore found himself compelled to agree to this secret and foolish compromise. John Frederick, showing his usual robust sound sense, reacted like the simple layman he was, and refused to be associated with the affair from the start. The mother of the lady had all she wanted, and at once informed the world of the 'approval' of the 'marriage' by the Wittenberg 'authorities'. This put the whole thing in another light, respectable to her, damning to the theologians. Even Philip was foolish enough not to preserve secrecy in some fond hope of persuading the world and himself that he had done the right thing. When the affair leaked out, the evangelicals were as scandalized as the papists, who not unnaturally made great capital of the scandal, and still do. It was all a disastrous mistake. Luther, for his part, withdrew his support and Melanchthon did likewise. Melanchthon was trapped into a position of compromise on a later occasion when he was thrust into company with the personalities concerned. He then made the discovery, as painful as it was ignominious, that the alleged 'necessity' in connexion with this unknown young lady was in no way as necessitous as he had been led to believe.

The whole affair was a grave set-back to the evangelicals, more grave than we shall ever know. The only explanation of this lamentable tale must lie in the first instance in the way the original 'necessity' was expressed to the Wittenberg theologians, details of which are not known. It is inconceivable that men of the age and judgement of Melanchthon and Luther could have taken such a step lightly, though it must be admitted that John Frederick saw through the whole scheme and would have none of it. Luther, bound hand and foot by his refusal to accept either annulment or divorce, had insisted that the arrangement be considered as secret and personal as between a penitent and his father confessor, but, as penitential practice, that would be countenanced by no school. He had further insisted that in his eyes the second marriage was not marriage but concubinage, and that is how it would have to be regarded at the bar of the law as well as at the bar of public opinion. He counselled Philip to parry all inquiries as best he could and to discuss the affair with nobody. Nevertheless, when all is said that can be said in defence of the Wittenberg theologians, it was a grave error of judgement, as events were soon to prove.

Meanwhile it had been decided at Hagenau to call a further meeting at Worms later in the year, when competent and peaceably-minded theologians were to represent both sides. On the way to Hagenau Melanchthon collapsed at Weimar. The Hesse affair had filled him with worry and remorse, and had brought on great illness of body and mind. He was ready to give in and had accepted his imminent death. There is a moving account of how Luther at a session of prayer at his sick friend's bedside earnestly implored the Almighty with the necessity of saving Melanchthon for His cause, and when the patient feebly responded to Luther's intensity of prayer by opening an eye to show signs of life, Luther with a bowl of food in his hand threatened him with excommunication if he continued refusing the food. He recovered! Meanwhile at Worms the proceedings were kept open and extended to the Diet of Ratisbon (1541).

At this time Luther produced his remarkable book *Against Hans Wurst*, in which he showed his old severity and violence. Duke Henry, a zealous Catholic, whose religious loyalties did nothing to allay his infamy, coarseness and ill-repute, had taken it upon himself to attack the evangelical lay readers as well as Luther. He used in his argument the name 'Hans Wurst', a German slang expression which may be translated literally as 'Jack Sausage', and means, among other things, a fool playing the part of a wise man. Luther replied in the same tone. He exposed the gross sexual immorality of Duke Henry and his utter lawlessness, but at the same time vindicated the evangelical cause in condemning popery. Serious illness now struck Luther again, and he lay in dire pain of body with excruciating pains in the head marked by a copious discharge of pus from the ear.

When the theologians eventually met the following year at Ratisbon (1541) hopes of reunion ran higher than they ever had. In the first place the participants were men who were both theologically and spiritually adequate to the demands of the hour. On the Catholic side distinguished theologians of proved ability with a known concern for truth, reform and unity sat at the table. There was the kind and scholarly Julius von Pflug, supported by the earnest reformer Gropper of Köln as well as by Contarini, a man of known evangelical convictions. On the Protestant side there were the trusty and eirenical Melanchthon, and the man above all others with a Europe-wide reputation for ecumenical thinking, the patient, understanding, scholarly Bucer. In the second place the conference launched into matters of faith at once, and left aside the relatively external matters of order. They tackled the central doctrines of salvation, sin and grace, as well as the divisive doctrine of justification in Christ alone apart from works. The Romans moved a long way towards the evangelical theology. Never had the sides been closer, never have they since been nearer. Luther remained oddly aloof, critical, even suspicious of the text the theologians evolved. He thought too much concession had been made to faith in works, a doctrine with which Melanchthon had earlier shown a little sympathy. Luther also felt the whole report of the proceedings was just a patched-up affair, a suspicion much strengthened when he found the signature of his old enemy John Eck at the bottom. Yet even this statement, obviously a most desirable advance, proved to be more than the Catholic provinces would accept, and the conference broke down on its failure to reach agreement on the doctrine of transubstantiation. Luther's fears were justified.

Those of the evangelicals most desirous of unity sent a deputation to Luther with two requests: that he would use his influence to bring about some permanent validity to the agreement God had so mercifully granted them in the earlier formula at Regensburg; and that he would make some temporary workable compromise with respect to those points where no agreement had as yet been reached. Luther concurred, on two conditions: provided the Protestants were allowed to continue to preach those articles of salvation on which mutual agreement had so far been reached; and provided they were allowed to continue to further those articles upon which no agreement had been reached. The Emperor saw matters differently. He was prepared to permit the former, subject to a later decision of a General Council, but was not prepared to permit the latter. Further, the Catholic estates were uncompromisingly opposed to the whole scheme. Luther knew all along that the difference between the two sides was a matter of right doctrine, and that unless the Catholics were prepared to change in the direction of an evangelical and biblical theology, there was no hope of any reunion of Christendom. This point was to be the nearest Catholics and Protestants were ever to approach, and though the Protestants eventually gained something in the religious peace of Nürnberg, in the matter of unity the Diet was regrettably ineffective. One thing at least stands clear. There could be reunion only on doctrinal grounds and none other, a judgement which holds good for our own day as well as Luther's.

Doubtless Charles's leniency and toleration were partially induced by fear of the Turk, a fear shared just as intensely by Luther. It says a good deal for him that, though aware of the Emperor's implacable opposition to the evangelical cause, and of his determination to stamp out the heresy before he died, never at one moment did Luther fail in his duty to support his Emperor, and in this grave hour he urged all men to do likewise in the struggle against the Turk.

Despite the Emperor's continued opposition to the cause of the Reformation, it continued to spread. When the new movement captured Halle, a favourite seat of Cardinal Albrecht, it was particularly gratifying to the reformers, for it was the Cardinal's own continued irresponsibility and immorality that had occasioned the change. In 1541, owing to his extravagant and licentious living, Albrecht had again run himself into vast debts, and he was compelled to call on the inhabitants for the enormous sum of twenty-two thousand gulden. They responded by stipulating their terms, namely, the appointment of an evangelical pastor. The cardinal had no choice but to surrender what was in fact his spiritual office, a galling humiliation. At once Wittenberg supplied the man, the learned and godly Justus Jonas, and immediately two other churches successfully demanded the same. It gave Luther a grim satisfaction that 'the wicked old rogue' who had begun all the trouble with his scandalous traffic in indulgences had to submit to the demands of plain lay folk to be given a godly pastor. Yet, this same 'wicked old rogue' actually had the audacity to collect his precious relics and take them to his own capital, Mainz, where he peddled his wares with the announcement that the collection was now bigger and better than before. Three tongues of flame were preserved from the burning bush and a small piece of the left horn of Moses (*sic!*). To visit the relics and leave a gulden guaranteed a remission of ten years for any sin whatsoever. Such prostitution of the Gospel twenty-five years after Luther's protest was indefensible. Albrecht made no answer to a polemical sarcastic broadsheet issued by Luther on the occasion. There was none to make.

An event happened at this juncture which occasioned very real anxiety in the minds of most moderate evangelicals, and has certainly been a major factor since in preventing any reunion of the Church. The Bishop of Naumburg died. The chapter, whose responsibility it was to provide a successor, elected a thoroughly acceptable person, the saintly and scholarly von Pflug, who had so nobly sought theological unity at Hagenau, Regensburg and at other times. Most regrettably the chapter had acted without any reference to their ruler, John Frederick, on the grounds that he had no legal standing in the matter, having already seceded from Rome. But John Frederick was having none of this talk and reacted very strongly indeed. The Duke was not only determined on an evangelical bishop but also was determined to have his own way as head of state. Both the Wittenberg theologians and his own chancellor advised caution in order to avoid a precedent being established which could cause and continue disruption. Chancellor Brück took the view that it was one thing to handle the monks and priests firmly, but it was a different matter in the case of bishops and bound to cause schism. The Chancellor and the theologians were right, particularly in this test case when the nominee of the Catholics was a good and godly man. They advised a compromise, the aristocratic George of Anhalt, who would of course have been acceptable to the Catholic party too and would have prevented any unnecessary difficulties about invalid consecration. John Frederick was adamant, and determined on Nicholas von Amsdorf, a good enough man, and being unmarried and of noble blood, less unacceptable than others. He was presented in January 1542.

Everybody knows the Catholic view on this matter of episcopal consecration, that the authority is transmitted by anointing and laying on of hands in a long unbroken line from the apostles. At least in an external way the evangelicals were in a position to preserve this in the negative sense of not allowing the succession to be broken, for the old Catholic bishops of Prussia had gone over to the Reformation in their entirety. It might have been better had the evangelicals taken the view that there was no need to break this tradition unnecessarily, better that is for subsequent Church relations, for though the consecrated and subsequent ordinations of evangelicals would always have been open to a charge of irregularity, they would not have been open to the charge of invalidity. The evangelicals were theologically firm and resolute. To them apostolic succession spelt only a matter of succession in sound evangelical apostolic theology. To demur to tradition and custom was to allow historical and geographical issues to blur the clear light of New Testament teaching for human and sentimental reasons. They took the view that it was ancient Catholic practice for the sovereign to nominate in conference with the leaders of the Church, and for the whole assembled laity to signify their concurrence by a loud unanimous 'Amen!' When Luther therefore consecrated Amsdorf in this very way in the traditions and practice of catholicity, the apostolic succession as the Catholics understood it was broken, but in the eyes of the evangelicals a purer doctrine of apostolic succession was restored to Christendom.[1]

Another dark cloud loomed over the Wittenberg sky. In the

1. An anomalous position has arisen in reformed Christianity today, where for example in Sweden the apostolic succession was 'preserved' but in Denmark 'lost', that is, in the sense argued above. Certain high Anglicans, for instance, are prepared to accept the orders of the Swedish clergy, but not those of the Danish clergy, though Swedes themselves accept those of the Danes on sound evangelical theological principles and reject the high Anglican 'argument' which accepts Swedish orders while rejecting Danish. Nevertheless, it may still be regretted that this departure was made at Naumburg at the cost of Catholic practice. An Anglican may be forgiven for wishing that both Catholic practice and evangelical theology had been preserved in the one settlement!

midst of the acrimonious resentments occasioned by the 'irregular' consecration at Naumburg, a war threatened to break out between two evangelical princes, who were also cousins, John Frederick and Maurice of Saxony. It was all over a sordid matter of taxation. But a tragic conflict was averted by the energy and thought of Luther, aided by the readiness and effectiveness of the alert Philip of Hesse. How thin and superficial religious principles often turn out under the hammer blows of self-interest or even worldly considerations! That God could be so unreal and faith so ineffective in the lives of evangelical men gave Luther much distress of mind.

Luther was very troubled about the state of religion and morals at every level of society in Germany at this time. He was deeply aware of the feeble root that evangelical religion had taken in the hearts, not only of the nobility, but in particular of the peasants and workers. In spite of continuous and clear preaching and instruction from their teachers and preachers the people showed little change in their lives and their morals. In his consuming faith in God and the Gospel Luther had expected a cataclysmic change in the Church and in society, when once the true Gospel was made known again. He found churchmen, princes, and common folk concerned not about the Gospel but for themselves and their place in the scheme of things. He began to dread the future, particularly now that he was ageing and knew that in his state of health the end could come at any time. There is, however, an important element in his thought here, not easily understood by contemporary man. To say that Luther believed that when once the Gospel was preached the power of God would be shown in salvation does not mean that he had some naïve belief in progress and was deceived in his judgements, but rather that Luther was talking only of the power of God and of his faith in God. He never had any hope whatever in progress as such, nor faith in the development and future of his cause. He was wholly eschatological here in the full New Testament sense of the word, and waited every day for the good hand of God to bring the whole sad story to an end. As far as the world was concerned he had long reached the conclusion that the nobility were no better than vicious parasites seeking to grab Church lands, Church property, Church money for their own ends, prepared even to wage war if it would serve their own interests. He found the peasants and workers no better, and began to think of them as drunken sots little better than the pigs in their sties. Luther had no faith whatever in man or in society. He was simply a religious man waiting on God, holding a responsible chair of theology and helping his Church as God demanded, suffering from no illusions, hoping only to be faithful to the end.

Meanwhile, the geographical area of the Reformation was extending and had now reached and included the territory of Brunswick. John Frederick and Philip of Hesse had taken the field against Duke Henry of Brunswick, who was threatening the evangelical stronghold of the old Kaiserstadt of Goslar in the Harz. With lightning rapidity they routed Henry, who fled the territory. The population begged the allies to establish the evangelical faith in the duchy and this was done. Further, Maurice of Saxony, another vigorous and muscular evangelical, extended the Reformation to the bishopric of Merseburg, fortunately without bloodshed. As a consequence of this quiet victory George of Anhalt (the man Luther had nominated for Naumburg in the consecration crisis) was consecrated to the bishopric in 1545 by Luther.

There is still more to recount. In Köln, the Archbishop and Elector, Hermann von Wied,[1] resolved to introduce the Reformation to Köln, though the good man's efforts were soon to be defeated. At the same time, too, the Bishop of Münster began to attempt some reformation. All this gladdened Luther's heart. Still more, the Emperor, somewhat harassed by the French, showed some graciousness to his German Protestants at the Diet of Speier in 1544. He promised a proper council on German

1. Hermann has a special interest for the Englishman. For some time he had been leaning towards the Reformation. He had been seeking a Christian reformation of doctrine, liturgy and the cure of souls, and pending a council sought to effect changes in these directions in his own archdiocese. To this end he consulted Osiander, Melanchthon and Bucer. The outcome was the publication of his famous *Consultation* in 1543, a document which was to have much influence on the *English Book of Common Prayer*. He was bitterly opposed, excommunicated in 1546 and deprived in 1547. He died five years later.

soil with the added firm prospect of a further diet to discuss the religious question. He asked the estates to start preparing a general scheme which could bring about a Christian reformation but at the same time preserve Christian unity. Both Albrecht and the Pope reacted violently against these proposals. Albrecht had had all he could stand of the Reformation, and saw quite clearly that it was so strong in Germany that a Council on German soil would mean victory for the evangelicals and therefore an open schism in the Church. The Pope was furious with Charles and would not even countenance the idea that 'mere laymen' could judge these holy matters.

Charles's motives were not altogether pure in this matter. He wanted to stabilize his political position, from this stability to call the Council, and then to move finally to impose a Catholic unity on the Protestants. He realized that Protestantism was now in a position to become the religion of Germany and even saw this as likely. That possibility might have been realized had the German laity, upper and lower classes, had one part of the courage and faith of Luther. He reproached his folk more severely than he did his opponents – the peasants were castigated for their indifference, their stupidity and their coarse selfishness; the burghers for their luxury and worldly values; all his countrymen for their drunkenness, gluttony, immorality and indifferentism. It pained Luther to witness these things where the gracious mercy of God had been freely proclaimed in His Gospel. Even his students came under the lash of his tongue for living like swine and indulging in loose sexual activity. He saw (as Calvin later saw and effected at much cost) the need of Church discipline. He found the courtiers violent, greedy and vulgar, preying like vultures on the spoils of the Reformation. He thought it impossible for a Christian man to govern as a true Christian at all. He developed a violent antipathy to lawyers sticking to outmoded canon law in defence of arranged and clandestine marriages and sought a fine evangelical freedom for young people to contract Christian marriage openly and in the face of the community. He saw a grim future for his beloved fatherland, and for the Christians within it a bitter testing and severe sifting by suffering under calamity.

At this moment, owing to the mischievous revival of the 1529 controversy,[1] the peace and equilibrium which was believed to have been established between Luther and the Swiss theologians broke down, and Luther, very ill and desperately frustrated, took his old line of condemning the Sacramentarians outright as seditious blasphemers and of brooking no fellowship with them whatever. This angered the Zwinglians, who rose to the defence of their beloved master. Rumour was rife and mischief-makers busy. It was rumoured that theological changes had set in at Wittenberg where Luther had ceased to elevate the Host, a practice he had never altered. It was rumoured that he was about to attack Melanchthon and Bucer for their liberalizing work at Köln, but all we can find in this respect is his warm-hearted, self-effacing support of Melanchthon and a cheerful reference to Bucer as a chatterbox (doubtless correct, for he was a great talker).

There was another shadow at this time, Luther's polemics against the Jews. It was alleged that the Jews in certain parts, Moravia in particular, were seducing Christians from the Gospel back to Judaism, and were saying insulting and blasphemous things against Christ. This latter stirred Luther to the depths. The world might say what it liked about him and he could never be roused to reply, but to attack his theology, to criticize the Gospel, or cast aspersions on his Lord and Master Christ was to invite all the invective of his fiery pen. He made some unpleasant remarks about the Jews always being connected with usury, and declared that if they would not do an honest hard day's work like any other German they should be chased out of the country. Luther's attack was primarily theological rather than anti-Semitic, but he was not beyond criticism at this point.

All the time he laboured continually at his *magnum opus*, the translation of the Bible, improving each edition. With the help of the amanuenses, Roth and Cruciger, he also worked on his earlier sermons, with a view to bequeathing them to posterity.

1. See p. 269.

CHAPTER 25

THE DEATH OF LUTHER

BEFORE describing Luther's end it may not be inappropriate to sketch an estimate of him as a person. So far we have seen him the earnest student giving himself up to God by becoming a monk. We saw the conscientious monk called to the chair of theology in the new University of Wittenberg. We saw how his studies inexorably drove him to his new evangelical theology which in turn involved him in the indulgences scandal. We saw him defend his cause before the sympathetic criticism of his fellow-monks at Heidelberg, as well as before the hostile attack of John Eck at Leipzig. We saw him brooding, as he sat on the cart on the journey home from Leipzig, over the abysmal breach that was opening. With clear-sightedness he addressed a book to the German nobility explaining his cause and their responsibility; with courage he addressed a book to the Roman theologians, showing the theological plight of Christendom and the evangelical remedy; with kindness he wrote a book appealing to the man in the street and showing the content and nature of the evangelical theology. We saw him cross his Rubicon as he solemnly and quietly burned in public the hated canon law and with it the Pope's bull of excommunication. We saw him face the Emperor at Worms, quiet and unostentatious, yet unflinching. The enthusiasts, the radicals, the socialists, the peasants; Henry VIII, Erasmus, hostile Roman theologians, Zwingli; all these people and causes had to be met and answered, including the immense nexus of problems of maintaining some unity among the protestants and a possible *modus vivendi* with Rome.

A modern person will find it difficult to realize that Luther did all he did and said all he said in immediate and direct response to the challenge of every situation rather than from any set purpose or plan. He never sought to control, guide, organize or manage things. In his view, events were all in the hands of

God, and the important thing for him was to be found waiting on God so that he was ready to do or say anything God called or demanded of him in the event. His view of 'the hour' or 'the time' or 'the occasion' was part of his general view of the sovereignty of God and of man as a fellow-worker with God. To Luther man could not determine the moment for an action since everything happened according to God's will. At that hour when *God* willed the action to be effected the man of faith received from Him a divine freedom and a divine power to carry through the God-demanded action successfully against all opposition. It is a gross travesty to think of Luther as the Germanic Hercules; he knew himself as a frail human being made strong by God for *His* work at *His* hour. That is why he knew he could never fail, and why all that met him knew they had met a man who knew he could not fail because God could not. For the total picture of Luther there is a vast wealth of rich human material. He freely expressed his thoughts and feelings, almost always with an irrespressible wit and humour, almost always in a quaint, earthy metaphor. Everybody remembered what he said and the way he said it, as the thousands of pages of his *Table Talk* testify, full of wit and wisdom, recalled and written down for all time by those who shared his intellectual and domestic hospitality. A full picture of Luther must include his teaching in the university and preaching at the church (sometimes three or four times in the week and always carefully prepared); Luther with his wife, his children and his friends; Luther struggling with many illnesses; Luther falling on his bed exhausted, too tired to say his prayers. We grow accustomed to the idea of this great Colossus striding across the world's stage, but it is good to see Luther at table; Luther working in his study, dreading Katie's efforts at 'tidying up the mess' and utterly at home in what appeared to her a chaos of books and papers undusted; Luther with his children on his knee after dinner singing in a fine tenor voice to his own accompaniment on his lute; Luther longing to get out of his study and do some work in the garden to smell again the earth and hear the birds singing; Luther with his devoted dog Tölpel[1] wrapped in a

1. Approximate translation 'Rascal'.

mysterious understanding and affection one to another; in short, Luther the man.

He often theologized, sometimes moralized over his children and their little ways. As he looked at Martin, his heart full of love, he realized all it must have meant when Abraham set out to sacrifice his only son Isaac. When nursing the baby Paul he soiled his lap. Luther staggered the guests by grimly remarking as he handed over the child to Katie that that was exactly the way we all treated God our Father; He reached out to us in love, we soiled Him and His world. When another was yelling, and disturbing the household, Luther demanded what cause the child had given him to love him, how he had deserved to be his heir; not only no awareness nor gratitude but also filling the house with howls! As we have seen, on one occasion he was so angry with one of his sons that he refused to speak to him for three whole days, and made the shattering remark, 'I would rather have a dead son than a disobedient one.'

In addition to his six children Luther also brought up eleven orphans and nieces. He had as well in his house a handful of students who helped in the home for their keep, and with poor relatives, needy priests and frequent distinguished visitors, it was certainly a large household for Katie to manage. A contemporary described the home as 'inhabited by a miscellaneous and promiscuous crowd of youths, students, girls, widows, old maids and children, and very unrestful'. There is interesting evidence of distinguished visitors being strongly advised to decline Luther's hospitality as far as staying with him was concerned and to seek a quiet room and a bed elsewhere.

Among the guests some dozen or so kept notebook and pencil in their pocket to jot down every scrap of wit and wisdom that fell from Luther's lips. Melanchthon, the soul of dignity and decency, deplored all this. Over the years these scribes compiled volume after volume of Luther's talk, now graced with the name *Table Talk*. The remarks are often quoted nowadays, but careful students should remember that they were spoken over a glass of wine or beer, and not only are they rather private but also they are often highly coloured and have passed through many hands. No comment at table is accepted by a Luther scholar as authentic unless there is corroboration for its substance in Luther's writings. This is not to say they were not said, and said in a form very near to what is recorded, for many of the sayings crop up in similar forms at different times at different hands: it is only to say that they can be no more than corroborative evidence. These scribes were most assiduous. Once as Luther was retiring to bed a messenger arrived at the house from a pastor's widow asking him to find her a husband. Luther demurred; he could not help in a matter of this kind, and as the messenger left he mumbled something about taking him for a matrimonial agency. He then looked over his shoulder at the scribe watching and listening, and said, 'I suppose you'll note all that down, too, you old rogue.' When Katie laughingly commented on all the young men having notebooks at table assiduously copying down every word, saying in her homely frugal way that they were being taught without payment, Luther replied he had taught and preached for nothing all his life and did not mean to start charging now. These comments ranged over the whole of Luther's world. Most valuable of all are his *obiter dicta* on theology and religion, and the religious events and personalities of his day; but hardly less interesting are his views on politics and peasants, poets and princes, even his own hearth and home, his own field and farm. He had a large and luxurious humour, fresh, natural, unrestrained and earthy.

And so we reach the closing years of Luther's life. The Emperor's mind was now increasingly given to the Church question which he wanted to settle before he died. The Pope was increasingly embarrassed in his efforts to stave off a Council. Eventually, under pressure, it was called for March 1545 at Trent. The Emperor had temporarily freed his hands from the Turks by buying them off with an eighteen-month truce, a contract Luther scathingly criticized on the grounds that it was paid for by the gold wrung from innocent folk by indulgences and other nefarious practices, and intended not to bribe the Turk but fight him.

Meanwhile, as a consequence of the Diet of Speier, 1544,[1] Elector John had commissioned his theologians to prepare a

1. See p. 318.

scheme of reformation. This was to be the last great document of peace designed to bring together the two sides. It put forward the great principles of an evangelical Church, and on the practical side took the moderate line that if the Catholic bishops would concede evangelical theology and fulfil the proper duties of their office in accepting and preaching the Gospel, the Protestants in their turn would concede them canonical obedience. No mention was made of the Pope or the papacy. No mention was made of the evangelical doctrine of holy communion nor criticism of the Romish doctrine of the mass. Critics were disquieted by the moderation and evasiveness of the document, and traced the absence of Luther's hand. Nevertheless, his signature was appended.

To the detriment of the proceedings some very ugly information leaked out. By far the worst was a letter from the Pope to the Emperor after the decisions of Speier, in which he expressed most indignant objections at the audacity of the Emperor even in considering the possibility of recognizing the evangelical cause at any conference at all. Luther refused to believe the authenticity of the document and, when the Elector reassured him it was no forgery, Luther reacted very violently against such deceit and trickery in a matter which involved the fate of the world and the truth of the Gospel. He knew the sands were running out, and that if this failed the last chance of restoring peace to Christendom in his lifetime had gone. He wrote against this double dealing a violent anti-papal document, the fiercest and foulest he had ever penned. History always remembers this against Luther, but the facts and circumstances of the case modify harsh judgements. He said in this document that he was not surprised that the idea of a free council was abhorrent to the Pope. In any event the Pope had arrogated to himself beforehand the right to alter any decision such a general council felt moved to make. This made the whole idea of a free general council utter nonsense. The Pope had deliberately tricked the Emperor in these proceedings. He alleged great concern 'for his son the Emperor' and was in honour bound to admonish him. Luther then directed a very pointed and personal remark. He asked about the Pope's real son, a bastard, whom the Pope was then seeking to enrich with the Church's money. Charles had been tricked for twenty-four years in his plans to secure peace and unity in the German Fatherland as well as a Christian council for Christendom, and seeing this had failed was now working for a national council. 'Whose sin was it?' Luther demanded. Luther questioned now whether in fact the Pope was the head of Christendom. He questioned too the Pope's right to remain above all conciliar judgement, and raised the matter of his being judged and deposed by Christendom. He also resented his temporal claims over Germany, and the arrogant boast of having brought the empire to Germany. The Pope, he argued, lived only to plunder the empire with his idolatry and his secularism. He had never 'made' the Emperor by his anointing and coronation: the Emperor was elected by the Electors; the Pope merely confirmed and blessed their decision. This meant in effect that the evangelicals accepted neither his temporal nor his spiritual authority. Luther thought this devilish popery the supreme evil on earth.

The Protestants could take no part in the Council when it was eventually convened at Trent. But it was equally hard for either the Emperor or the Pope to concede a free general council. In the first place because it meant some sort of recognition of the Protestants. In the second place, the Catholics would have been confronted with a new idea of authority: they would have found it settled not in the Pope but in scripture, even the whole matter of the authority of tradition questioned, and certainly the decrees of earlier councils scrutinized. The only concession allowed to the evangelicals was that by the Emperor who agreed to hold a religious national conference at Regensburg in January 1546. He also informed the Pope that he was not ready to make war on the Protestants for at least another year.

It takes little imagination to envisage the sore dismay of the evangelicals in this position, men to whom God and their religion meant all. The cold calculating cynicism of the Emperor, biding his time, the double-dealing irreligion of the Pope, playing his cards to win the game, religious war impending, their theological champion nearing his end. Who could tell what might happen? The Council opened in December 1545 without the

Protestants. The opportunity was lost and has not presented itself again these four hundred years. Perhaps the Second Vatican Council marks a new beginning?

There were other anxieties and troubles burdening Luther. A fresh rupture with the Swiss theologians opened out. In 1545 Bullinger addressed himself to Luther on the subject of his Short Catechism. It was a clever reply, but Calvin criticized it, quite properly, as dwelling too much on Luther's personal faults and making no fresh theological contribution to the debate. Nevertheless, Melanchthon remained very friendly towards the Swiss, a friendliness with which Luther never saw fit to upbraid him. But when Louvain engaged on a fresh attack against Luther, he clearly showed his opinion of the Zwinglian theology by stating that in his view if anybody denied the bodily reception of the true body of Christ they made themselves into heretics and schismatics of the Christian Church. Even when war was threatening Luther felt unable to win a tactical advantage at the risk of theological truth. This is not always remembered of him. At any rate, his Catholic theology cost him the support of the Swiss, for they remained outside the Schmalkaldic League.

Another great burden and sorrow to Luther, almost a mystery to him, was to find the evangelical theology resisted and attacked. He had long ago answered all the arguments of his enemies and detractors but they were still being put forward. Perhaps Luther never understood why the patent evangelical truths did not carry the day once they had been stated and argued, though he often recalled the world had always so reacted in the face of the prophets and the apostles, even of Christ. When he saw this human resistance to the Gospel, the parlous condition of the empire with the Turk standing over it, scimitar drawn, the very internal spiritual and secular weakness of society without true justice, without sound government, without even any proper administration, an empire that was no empire, he truly believed the end was in sight. He saw the last day of the empire at hand, and its day of salvation approaching. Four centuries later it is hard to imagine that Luther, that immense dynamo of activity, actually awaited the end of the world, the break-up of rotten governments with the concomitant collapse of an immoral Church, and Christ coming to wind up events. Yet perhaps this was the strongest element in his thinking at that hour.

Another thorn in the flesh of the ageing Luther was the spiritual condition of Wittenberg and its university. It galled him with increasing bitterness of soul that Wittenberg, the cradle of the Reformation, the place where he had devoted his whole life to the evangelical cause, should bear such meagre fruits of spirituality and morality. Catholic opponents were always quick to criticize the evangelicals for alleged lawlessness and licentiousness, and any evidence of this was all too readily used by them against the Reformation. On one occasion when reprimanding two nephews for giving an example that would bring discredit on the reformed theology Luther complained that they were letting him down as well as the cause, and they ought not to give this offence and provide a weapon for the enemy. He wrote to them very expressively, if not very delicately, saying, 'If I break wind in Wittenberg, they smell it at Rome.' Calvin, too, was to go through this same spiritual distress on behalf of his townsmen. In a similar situation he was appalled at the immorality of Geneva and, so strict was his discipline, he was compelled to leave the city. Religion and morality were related in the minds of the reformers as cause to effect. Luther hated drunkenness and gluttony, intemperance and luxury; he criticized the provocativeness of the ladies' *décolletage*; the vulgarity and rioting in the streets; the loose women hanging round students' quarters; the dishonesty and sharp practice of trade and usury; the weakness of civil authority. All this meant to him how thinly true theology had penetrated, how little changed the human heart, for all the torrents of the Gospel that had flowed through Wittenberg. He sensed that his life had been largely spent to no purpose, and he knew too well that he had no longer the sheer physical energy and strength needed to deal with these miscreants and give to Wittenberg the fresh start it needed.

We must recall that Luther was bearing this 'care of all the Churches' at a time when he was suffering intensely from stones in his bladder, when, to use his own words, death would have been an acceptable release had not God willed otherwise. Everyone knows of the intense agony of this ailment, then unrelievable, but we may add to this his other frailties – failing sight, blindness in one eye, general weakness, creeping old age – to know what it cost him to persevere.

At this juncture Luther was persuaded to take a business journey to Leipzig and Zeitz with his old friend Cruciger to give him a break and a change of scene. He entered into it and enjoyed meeting all his old friends once more, talking with them, eating with them, reminiscing with them, laughing with them. The trip did him much good, though he was persecuted mercilessly by the stone, an old enemy who had now achieved the reality of a proper name, the Tormentor. He was much distressed to learn that fresh riotings and tumults had broken out at Wittenberg. In a letter to Katie he said he would willingly leave the place for good and go and live on her farm in the country if the Elector would only allow him his teaching salary for the few months of his life that were remaining to him. This pathetic letter frightened them all at Wittenberg. The university sent Melanchthon, Bugenhagen, the mayor of Wittenberg and the Elector's physician post-haste to give what solace they could to the suffering reformer. He recovered somewhat to preach a few sermons, not a little heartened to learn that firmer measures had been taken in Wittenberg to quell its unruliness.

On returning to Wittenberg he started lecturing again and completed at long last his lectures on Genesis on 17 November with these words:

This is the beloved Genesis; God grant that after me it may be better done. I can do no more. I am weak. Pray God that he may grant me a good and happy end.

They were the last lectures he was ever to give.

In the autumn of this year, a quarrel arose between two brothers, the Counts of Mansfeld, chiefly over the matter of patronage. This was hardly a matter worthy of the attention of the ageing reformer but it was his home town; these men were his original lay lords, and they were utterly unable to reconcile their differences. He set out with Melanchthon and Jonas only to find the counts were called to the wars. In the depth of winter he set out again in the company of Melanchthon with the foreboding that he would lay his bones to rest in the place where they had been born. Melanchthon was taken ill and Luther returned with his dear friend, preaching at Halle *en route*. When the Elector pressed for a Wittenberg theologian to represent the evangelical cause at Ratisbon, Luther said that he had not brought back his precious Melanchthon to Wittenberg to risk his death at Ratisbon, indeed to waste his time.

Luther knew his own days were approaching their end. 'Old, spent, worn, weary, cold, and with but one eye to see with,' was how he described himself at this time. On 17 January he preached his last sermon at Wittenberg. He spared Melanchthon the journey to Ratisbon as well as the journey to Mansfeld and set off on his own on 23 January, taking with him his three sons to see their native parts. Owing to heavy floods he was delayed for a few days at Halle where he again preached. The rain, the physical strain in the depth of a cold German winter, were too much for his constitution. He felt ill when he reached Eisleben. The work was difficult and it dragged on. He found the brothers avaricious, the lawyers stubbornly fighting for each side regardless of seeking a just settlement. He found the conduct and the number of Jews in the whole business most vexatious. But he wrote cheerfully to Katie and faithful Melanchthon, full of humour and affection. During his last sermon on 14 February 1546 at Eisleben he had to leave off, too weak to continue.

Finally he succeeded on this same day in effecting a most successful reconciliation. All rejoiced. The young lords and ladies gave a party; the countess sent trout to Katie. Luther made but one request: to be allowed to return to Wittenberg and die there. Even this was not possible, for he had spent himself and could but lie down and die where he was, in the town where he was born and baptised. His friends and his sons thronged his bedside to hear him pray loudly to God and thank Him for his Son. They heard him commend his spirit into God's hands. They heard him murmur three times, 'God so loved the world, that he gave his only begotten Son, that whosoever believeth in him should not perish, but have everlasting life' (John iii, 16), the foundation of his whole life. He then lay still. Jonas and Cölius (the court chaplain) asked him, 'Reverend father, wilt thou stand by Christ and the doctrine thou hast preached?' 'Yes,' the old man breathed. With that he fell asleep, never to awake this side of the tomb.

It was a desolate cry of lamentation that went up throughout the evangelical Church of Germany. When the news came to Wittenberg, Melanchthon was lecturing his students. The messenger interrupted him with the final and fatal message that Luther had died. He could only cry, 'Alas! the chariot of Israel and the horseman thereof.' The Church had lost another Elijah, and Elisha could but cry. He left the students stricken and silent, too full of tears to find room for words.

The Elector insisted that the mortal remains be returned to Wittenberg and buried there. A service was first held at Eisleben attended by all the nobility and all the countryside, and the body was escorted on its way by light cavalry. As the sad procession passed through the wintry villages, every bell tolled, every man stopped to pay his last respects. The coffin was received with great solemnity at Halle and rested there. On the morning of 22 February it loomed up at Wittenberg and was taken in solemn procession through the town to the Castle Church, preceded by the nobility, the Counts of Mansfeld and their horsemen, and followed by the little widow supported by a few ladies. Then followed his sons and his brother James, the university, the Council. The town preacher Bugenhagen preached the sermon, Melanchthon, representing the university, gave a Latin oration. In the Church on whose door he had nailed up the Theses a short twenty-five years earlier Luther was lowered to his long last rest.

CHRONOLOGICAL TABLE

	EVENTS IN LUTHER'S LIFE	OTHER EVENTS
		1455 John Gutenberg prints first Bible
		1471 Albrecht Dürer born
		1475 Michelangelo born
	1483 10 Nov.: Martin Luther born in Eisleben	
	1484 May: Luther family moves to Mansfeld	1484 Zwingli born in Wildhaus, Switzerland
		1492 Columbus discovers America
		1487–1525 Frederick the Wise
		1492–1503 Pope Alexander VI
		1493–1519 Emperor Maximilian
	1497–8 Schooldays in Magdeburg	1497 Melanchthon born
	1498–1501 Latin school in Eisenach	
1500		1500–39 Duke George
	1501–5 Luther at University of Erfurt	
	1502 Bachelor of Arts	1502 University of Wittenberg founded
	1505 Master of Arts	1503–13 Pope Julius II
		1504 Tetzel begins indulgence traffic
	1505 17 July: Luther enters Augustinian cloister at Erfurt	
		1506 Construction of St Peter's at Rome begins

EVENTS IN LUTHER'S LIFE	OTHER EVENTS
1507 May: Ordination, Erfurt Cathedral	
1508 Called to University of Wittenberg to teach Aristotle's *Ethics*	
1509 Called to teach Lombard's *Sentences* at Erfurt	1509–47 Henry VIII King of England
1510 1510 Oct.–1511 Feb.: Journey to Rome	
1511 Return to Erfurt; transferred to Wittenberg	
1512 Doctor of Theology Lectures on Genesis (text lost)	1512 Michelangelo painting Sistine Chapel
1513 Lectures on Psalms begin	1513–21 Pope Leo X
1515 Lectures on Romans	1515 *Letters of Obscure Men*
1516 Lectures on Galatians	1516 Erasmus Greek edition of N.T. Thomas More's *Utopia*
1517 31 Oct.: Ninety-five Theses	
1518 26 April: Disputation at Heidelberg	1518 Melanchthon's Greek Grammar
July: Prierias attacks Luther	Raphael's Sistine Madonna
7 Aug.: Pope cites Luther to Rome	
8 Aug.: Luther appeals to Frederick	
25 Aug.: Melanchthon appointed	
31 Aug.: Luther's reply to Prierias	
12–14 Oct.: Before Cajetan at Augsburg	
1519 4–6 Jan.: Interview with von Miltitz	1519 Death of Leonardo da Vinci

	EVENTS IN LUTHER'S LIFE	OTHER EVENTS
	4–14 July: Leipzig Debate	1519–55 Charles V emperor
1520	1520 May: *Sermon on Good Works*	
	June: *The Papacy at Rome*	
	15 June: *Exsurge Domine* gives Luther 60 days to submit	
	Aug.: *Address to German Nobility*	
	Oct.: *Babylonian Captivity*	
	10 Oct.: Luther receives Pope's bull	
	Nov.: *Freedom of a Christian Man*	
	28 Nov.: Luther invited to Worms	
	10 Dec.: Burning of papal bull	
	1521 3 Jan.: Bull excommunicating Luther goes into effect	
	16 April: Luther in Worms	
	4 May: Luther in Wartburg	1521 Dec.: Death of Leo
		1522 Adrian VI pope
		1523–34 Pope Clement VII
	1522 1 March: Return to Wittenberg	1522 First circumnavigation of world
	Sept.: German N. T. published	1522, Sept.–1523, May: Sickingen's attack on Trier
	Diet of Nürnberg	
	On Civil Government	
	On the Order of Worship	
	1524 Hymn-book	
	To Councilmen about Schools	

EVENTS IN LUTHER'S LIFE	OTHER EVENTS
April: Diet of Nürnberg	
Sept.: Erasmus *On the Freedom of the Will*	
1525 Jan.: *Against the Heavenly Prophets*	
March: Twelve articles of the peasants	
19 April: *Admonition to Peace*	
5 May: *Against the Robbing and Murdering Hordes*	1525 5 May: Death of Frederick
June: Peasants crushed	
Luther's marriage	
The German Mass	1525–32 Elector John the Steadfast
Dec.: *The Bondage of the Will*	
1526 May: League of Torgau	
June: Diet of Speier	
1527 *A Mighty Fortress*	1527 Sack of Rome
1529 Catechisms published	
April: Diet of Speier	
1–4 Oct.: Marburg Colloquy	
1530 Diet of Augsburg	1530 Formation of Schmalkald League
Luther at Coburg	1531 Death of Zwingli at Cappell
	1532–47 Elector John Frederick
1534 Publication of German Bible	1534 Ignatius Loyola founds Jesuits
	1534–49 Pope Paul III
1536 Wittenberg Concord with Swiss	
Outbreak of Anabaptists at Münster	

	EVENTS IN LUTHER'S LIFE	OTHER EVENTS
1540	1537 Schmalkald Articles 1539 Bigamy of Philip of Hesse 1541 *Against Hans Worst* 1543 *Against the Jews* *Commentary on Genesis* 1545 *Against the Papacy* 1546 18 Feb.: Death of Luther	 1541 John Calvin (1509–64) introduces Reformation in Geneva 1543 Deaths of Copernicus and Holbein 1545–63 Council of Trent 1546–7 Schmalkald War

SELECT BIBLIOGRAPHY OF
BOOKS IN ENGLISH

ALTHAUS, PAUL, *The Theology of Martin Luther*, tr. Robert C. Schultz, Philadelphia, 1966. (A weighty, scholarly German work)

ATKINSON, JAMES, *Rome and Reformation*, London, 1966. (Ecumenical discussion)

The Reformation, Vol IV, The Paternoster Church History, Exeter, 1958–68.

BAINTON,[1] ROLAND, *Here I Stand*, London, 1950. (A life of Luther, historical rather than theological; bibliography)

Reformation Essays, Richmond, Virginia, 1962. (Essays in honour of R. H. B.)

Studies on the Reformation, London, 1963

The Reformation of the Sixteenth Century, London, 1953

BOEHMER, HEINRICH, *Luther and the Reformation*, London, 1930

Martin Luther: Road to Reformation, London, 1946. (Excellent; ends 1521)

BORNKAMM, HEINRICH, *Luther's World of Thought*, tr. Martin H. Bertram, St Louis, Missouri, 1958. (Interesting background material)

BOUYER, LOUIS, *The Spirit and Forms of Protestantism*, tr. A. V. Littledale, London, 1956. (Roman convert writing on Protestantism)

CARLSON, EDGAR M., *The Reinterpretation of Luther*, Philadelphia, 1948. (Good readable account of recent Luther research)

CHADWICK, OWEN, *The Reformation* (Pelican History of the Church, Vol. 3), Harmondsworth, 1964

DENIFLE, HEINRICH, *Luther and Lutherdom*, tr. Raymond Volz, Somerset, Ohio, 1917. (Virulent anti-Protestantism from a nineteenth-century author)

EHRENBERG, HANS, ed., *Luther Speaks*, essays by Lutheran ministers, Preface by the Bishop of Oslo, London, 1947

FIFE, ROBERT H., *Young Luther*, New York, 1928

The Revolt of Martin Luther, New York 1957. (Excellent, detailed and documented account to 1521; bibliography)

1. Bainton is a leading authority on the Reformation.

GREEN, VIVIAN H. H., *Luther and the Reformation*, London, 1964. (Reliable historical account; bibliography and advice on Luther literature)

GRIMM, HAROLD J., *The Reformation Era, 1500–1650*, New York, 1954, 1965. (Excellent; good comprehensive bibliographies)

GRISAR, HARTMANN, *Luther*, 6 vols, London 1913–17. (Extremely biased against Luther; unreliable)

HILLERBRAND, HANS J., *The Reformation in Its Own Words*, London, 1964. (Excellent source-book with pictures; bibliographies)

JEDIN, HUBERT, *The Council of Trent*, tr. Ernest Graf, London, 1957. (Definitive)

KERR, HUGH T., ed., *A Compend of Luther's Theology*, Philadelphia, 1943

KIDD, B. J., *Documents Illustrative of the Continental Reformation*, Oxford, 1911. (Old but excellent source-book)

KOESTLIN, JULIUS T., *The Life of Martin Luther*, London, 1883. (Very old but still very good)
The Theology of Luther, tr. Charles E. Hay, 2 vols, Philadelphia, 1897. (Very good)
and KAWERAU, GEORG, *Martin Luther*, 2 vols, Berlin, 1903. (Kawerau's re-editing of Koestlin's work; unsurpassable; known affectionately as 'KK')

KRAMM, H. H., *The Theology of Martin Luther*, London, 1947. (Short, simple and helpful)

LAU, FRANZ, *Luther*, tr. Robert H. Fischer, London, 1963. (Brief but authoritative)

LINDSAY, T. M., *Luther and the German Reformation*, Edinburgh, 1900
A History of the Reformation, 2 vols, Edinburgh, 1910. (Old but still valuable)

LORTZ, JOSEPH, *Reformation*, Westminster, Md, 1964. (A discussion of its meaning for today; Lortz presents a balanced and informed view of Luther among current Roman Catholic writers)

LUTHER, MARTIN, *Luther's Works*, general editors Jarislav Pelikan and Helmuth Lehmann, St Louis, 1955 ff. (A 56-volume translation, generally referred to as the 'American edition', of the essential third of Luther; about one third is completed)
Luther's Early Theological Works, Library of Christian Classics, Vol. 16, tr. and ed. James Atkinson, London, 1962. (Disputations, exposition, theological argument)

The Large Catechism, tr. Robert H. Fischer, Philadelphia, 1959

Lectures on Romans, Library of Christian Classics, Vol. 15, tr. and ed. Wilhelm Pauck, London, 1961

Letters of Spiritual Counsel, Library of Christian Classics, Vol. 18, tr. and ed. Theodore G. Tappert, London, 1955

Luther's Correspondence, ed. Preserved Smith, 2 vols, Philadelphia, 1913–18

Primary Works, ed. Henry Wace and C. A. Buchheim, London, 1896

Reformation Writings, vols. 1, 2, ed. Bertram Lee Woolf, London, 1953, 1956

Table Talk of Martin Luther, tr. William Hazlitt, London, 1868; re-edited Thomas S. Kepler, London, 1952

Three Treatises, preface by John Dillenberger, New York, 1947

The Bondage of the Will, ed. J. I. Packer and O. R. Johnston, London, 1957

Commentary on Galatians, re-edited P. S. Watson, Edinburgh, 1953

MACKINNON, JAMES, *Luther and the Reformation*, 4 vols, London, 1925–30. (Solid and reliable)

The Origins of the Reformation, London, 1939

PAUCK, WILHELM, *The Heritage of the Reformation*, Boston, 1950. (Scholarly and readable)

PFUERTNER, WILHELM, *Luther and Aquinas on Salvation*, tr. Edmund Quinn, London, 1965. (Scholarly monograph)

PINOMAA, LENNART, *Faith Victorious*, tr. Walter J. Kukkonen, Philadelphia, 1963. (Good popular introduction to Luther's theology)

RASHDALL, HASTINGS, *The Universities of Europe in the Middle Ages*, 3 vols, Oxford, 1936. (Standard)

RITTER, GERHARD, *Luther – His Life and Work*, tr. John Riches, London, 1963. (Short but excellent and authoritative)

RUPP,[1] E. GORDON, *Martin Luther: Hitler's Cause or Cure?* London, 1945

Luther's Progress to the Diet of Worms, London, 1951

The Righteousness of God: Luther Studies, London, 1953

SCHWIEBERT, E. G., *Luther and His Times*, St Louis, Missouri, 1950. (Detailed survey with full bibliographies)

SMITH, PRESERVED, *The Life and Letters of Martin Luther*, Boston, 1911. (Good)

1. The leading English authority in the field.

THIEL, RUDOLPH, *Luther*, 2 vols, Berlin, 1936–7. (Good, comprehensive)
  Luther, 1955

TODD, J. M., *Martin Luther*, London, 1964. (Fair, readable Roman Catholic account, dependent on Rupp)

WATSON, PHILIP S., *Let God Be God!*, London, 1947. (Good study of Luther's theology; bibliography)

WHALE, J. S., *The Protestant Tradition*, Cambridge, 1955. (Lively account of Protestantism)

WILLIAMS, GEORGE H., *The Radical Reformation*, London, 1962. (Authoritative)

Erasmus

ERASMUS, *Discourse on Free Will*, tr. and ed. Ernest F. Winter, Ungar, 1961

FROUDE, JAMES A., *Life and Letters of Erasmus* (lectures delivered 1893–4), London, 1927

HUIZINGA, JOHAN, *Erasmus of Rotterdam*, tr. F. Hopman, London, 1924, 1952

SMITH, PRESERVED, *Erasmus*, London, 1923

ZWEIG, STEFAN, *Erasmus of Rotterdam*, tr. Eden and Cedar Paul, New York, 1934, 1956

Melanchthon

MELANCHTHON, *Selected Writings*, tr. Charles Leander Hill, Augsburg, 1962

HILDERBRANDT, FRANZ, *Melanchthon: Alien or Ally?*, London, 1946. (Short, popular)

MANSCHREK, CLYDE L., *Melanchthon: The Quiet Reformer*, 2 vols, New York, 1958. (Good)

STUPPERICH, ROBERT, *Melanchthon*, London, 1965. (Scholarly but popular)

INDEX OF BIBLICAL REFERENCES

INDEX OF REFERENCES TO THE WEIMAR EDITION

(see Abbreviations, page 7)

GENERAL INDEX